2005 Supplement

for

Constitutional Interpretation
Eighth Edition

Constitutional Interpretation
Powers of Government
Volume I
Eighth Edition

Constitutional Interpretation
Rights of the Individual
Volume II
Eighth Edition

Craig R. Ducat
Northern Illinois University

THOMSON
———★———™
WEST

Australia • Brazil • Canada • Mexico • Singapore • Spain • United Kingdom • United States

© 2006 Thomson West, a part of The Thomson Corporation. Thomson, the Star logo, and West are trademarks used herein under license.

ALL RIGHTS RESERVED. No part of this work covered by the copyright hereon may be reproduced or used in any form or by any means—graphic, electronic, or mechanical, including photocopying, recording, taping, Web distribution, information storage and retrieval systems, or in any other manner—without the written permission of the publisher.

Printed in the United States of America

2 3 4 5 6 7 09 08 07 06

Printer: Thomson West

ISBN 0-534-61402-7

Thomson Higher Education
10 Davis Drive
Belmont, CA 94002-3098
USA

For more information about our products, contact us at:
Thomson Learning Academic Resource Center
1-800-423-0563

For permission to use material from this text or product, submit a request online at
http://www.thomsonrights.com.
Any additional questions about permissions can be submitted by email to **thomsonrights@thomson.com**.

PREFACE

This Supplement is intended to accompany the eighth edition of the casebook, CONSTITUTIONAL INTERPRETATION, and its two constituent paperback volumes, *Powers of Government* and *Rights of the Individual*. It includes significant constitutional decisions from the most recent three Terms of the United States Supreme Court. Highlights include recent rulings on government display of the Ten Commandments, enforcement of the federal Controlled Substances Act against users and cultivators of medical marijuana, and deployment of the eminent domain power by local government for purposes of urban redevelopment. Noteworthy state and lower federal court decisions—such as those dealing with the trial of enemy combatants by military tribunals and same-sex marriage—have also been included. Where the Supreme Court already has docketed potentially significant constitutional cases for argument at its upcoming October 2005 Term, it has been noted.

This Supplement follows the style of the casebook and new text, major cases, notes, and charts have been keyed to it by the use of insert statements. Chapter, section, and subsection headings have been retained to help integrate these materials with those in the Text.

CRAIG R. DUCAT
DeKalb, Illinois
July 2005

TABLE OF CONTENTS

Preface iii
Table of Cases ix

CHAPTER 1 JUDICIAL POWER

A. THE SUPREME COURT'S JURISDICTION AND ITS ASSUMPTION OF JUDICIAL REVIEW
   Judicial Review
      Two Motions for Justice Scalia's Recusal 1
   The Structure of the Judicial System
      The House Votes to Split the Ninth Circuit 2
   Writ of Certiorari
      The Supreme Court's October 2002, 2003, and 2004 Terms 3
B. INSTITUTIONAL CONSTRAINTS ON THE EXERCISE OF JUDICIAL POWER
   Case and Controversy
      The Class Action Fairness Act 4
   Ripeness
      Doe v. Bush 4
   Standing
      "Prudential Standing" and the Pledge 8
   Political Questions
      Terminating the ABM Treaty 8

CHAPTER 2 THE MODES OF CONSTITUTIONAL INTERPRETATION

The Court in American History: Judicial Values and Constitutional Interpretation
      Filling Judicial Vacancies in an Era of Divided Government 10

CHAPTER 3 LEGISLATIVE POWER

A. THE SOURCES AND SCOPE OF CONGRESS'S POWER TO LEGISLATE
   Amendment-Enforcing Powers
      Cutter v. Wilkinson 13
      The Family Medical Leave Act 14
   Inherent Powers
      Recent Cases on the Detention and Deportation of Aliens 14
C. THE POWER TO INVESTIGATE
      Mark McGwire and the Hearing on Steroids in Professional Baseball 15
      Subpoenaing Terry Schiavo 15

CHAPTER 4 EXECUTIVE POWER

B. THE SCOPE OF EXECUTIVE POWER
   Theories of Executive Power
      Hamdi v. Rumsfeld 16
      Rasul v. Bush 25
         Rumsfeld v. Padilla 28
         Note—Anti-Terrorism Legislation in Britain 29
      In re Guantanamo Detainees Cases 31
         Conflicting Decisions on the Detainees 38
         The Moussaoui Case 38
   Executive Privilege
      Cheney v. United States District Court for District of Columbia 39
D. EXECUTIVE AUTHORITY IN THE CONDUCT OF FOREIGN AFFAIRS
   Executive Agreements
      American Insurance Association v. Garamendi 41
         Republic of Austria v. Altmann 45
         Trimming the PATRIOT Act 45

CHAPTER 5 POWERS OF THE NATIONAL GOVERNMENT IN THE FEDERAL SYSTEM

C. REKINDLING DUAL FEDERALISM: THE REHNQUIST COURT
   The Rehnquist Court and the Commerce Clause
      Gonzales v. Raich 46

The House Vote on Medical
Marijuana 55
Judicial Voting in Constitutional
Cases: The October 2002, 2003,
and 2004 Terms 55
The Eleventh Amendment
Nevada Department of Human
Resources v. Hibbs 57
Tennessee v. Lane 62
Cert. Granted in United States v.
Georgia 62
D. THE TAXING AND SPENDING POWER
The Decline of Dual Federalism
Sabri v. United States 63

CHAPTER 6 THE REGULATORY POWER OF THE STATES IN THE FEDERAL SYSTEM

Federal Preemption and Federal Dictation
Other Cases on Preemption
—Continued 65
Controversy over the "No Child Left
Behind" Act 66
The Negative or Dormant Commerce Clause
American Trucking Associations, Inc. v.
Michigan Public Service Commission 67
A State Ban on Transporting
Radioactive Material 69
Granholm v. Heald 70

CHAPTER 7 PROPERTY RIGHTS AND ECONOMIC LIBERTIES

C. REGULATION AND THE "TAKING" OF PROPERTY
Kelo v. City of New London 76
The House Disapproves of the *Kelo*
Decision 84
Lingle v. Chevron USA, Inc. 84
D. NON-TRADITIONAL PROPERTY INTERESTS [NEW SECTION]
The "New Property" and Due
Process 85
Town of Castle Rock, Colorado v.
Gonzales 86

CHAPTER 8 DUE PROCESS OF LAW

A. DUE PROCESS AND THE FEDERAL SYSTEM: THE SELECTIVE INCORPORATION OF THE BILL OF RIGHTS INTO THE FOURTEENTH AMENDMENT
The Jury Trial Guarantee: A Case Study of Incorporation
Blakely v. Washington 93
United States v. Booker 94
"Gangbusters" and Other
Mandatory Minimums Legislation 94
B. THE RIGHT TO COUNSEL
The Right to Counsel at Trial
Other Cases on Effective Assistance
to the Defense—Continued 95
Sell v. United States 96
The Pretrial Right to Counsel
Missouri v. Seibert 97
Chavez v. Martinez 97
Yarborough v. Alvarado 98
United States v. Patane 98
D. CONFRONTATION AND CROSS-EXAMINATION
Crawford v. Washington 99
E. CRUEL AND UNUSUAL PUNISHMENT
The Death Penalty
Other Cases on the Imposition of
Capital Punishment—Continued 100
No Bibles in the Jury Room 101
The Illinois Taped Confessions
Law 101
The Justice For All Act 101
DNA Evidence and Federal Habeas
Corpus Relief 102
Mandatory Life Imprisonment
Ewing v. California 102
Prisoners' Rights
Visitation Restrictions 108
Super-Max Confinement 109
Prisoners and the ADA 109
Confining Dangerous Persons Other than Upon Criminal Conviction
Smith v. Doe 110
Megan's Law and Dangerousness 114

The Ex Post Facto Clause
    Stogner v. California 115

CHAPTER 9   OBTAINING EVIDENCE

B. WARRANTLESS SEARCHES AND SEIZURES
Consent
    Kaupp v. Texas 119
Search Incident to Arrest
    Other Cases on Arrests, Searches, and Detentions In and About the Home—Continued 120
    Knock-and-Announce 120
Motor Vehicles
    Other Cases on Automobile Searches—Continued 121
Street Stops
    Other Cases Drawing upon *Terry* v. *Ohio*—Continued 122
Border Searches
    United States v. Flores-Montano 122

C. CURRENT CONTROVERSIES IN SEARCH AND SEIZURE LAW
    Random Drug Testing of Welfare Recipients 123
    Informational Roadblocks 123

D. WIRETAPPING AND EAVESDROPPING
    Judicial Approval of Taps Is Routine 123
    House Votes to Remove Library Provision from the USA PATRIOT Act 124
    The "Terrorist Tipoff Amendment" 124

CHAPTER 10   THE RIGHT OF PRIVACY

Abortion
    The Unborn Victims of Violence Act 125
    Parental Notification and the Absence of a Health Exception 125
    The Congressional Ban on "Partial-Birth" Abortions 126
    Anti-abortion Protest and RICO 126
Privacy and Other Lifestyle Issues
    Lawrence v. Texas 128
    Alabama Outlaws Sex Toys 137
    The Clinton and Bush Administrations and Medical Marijuana 138
The Right to Die
    Note—The Unending Case of Terry Schiavo 139
    Physician-Assisted Suicide and the Federal Government 143

CHAPTER 11   FREEDOM OF SPEECH

B. TIME, PLACE, AND MANNER LIMITATIONS
Speech in a "Public Forum"
    The Prosecution of Begging Continues 144
    Keeping "Druggies" Out of the Neighborhood 144
    Note—If Beef "I[s] What's for Dinner," Who's Paying for It? 145
    Other Cases on Time, Place, and Manner Restrictions Generally—Continued 148

C. SYMBOLIC SPEECH
Compelling the Flag Salute
    Parental Notification and the Flag Salute 148
Flag Burning and Nude Dancing: Whether to Apply the O'Brien Test
    Proposed Flag Desecration Amendment 149
Cross Burning and Hate Speech
    Virginia v. Black 149

D. CAMPAIGN FINANCE REFORM, CORPORATE SPEECH, AND PARTY PATRONAGE
Campaign Finance Reform
    McConnell v. Federal Election Commission 150

E. COMMERCIAL SPEECH
    Illinois ex rel. Madigan v. Telemarketing Associates, Inc. 152
    The Do-Not-Call Registry 152

CHAPTER 12   FREEDOM OF THE PRESS

    Media Acquisitions and the FCC Rules   154

A. CENSORSHIP AND PRIOR RESTRAINT

  The Right to Publish
    Tory v. Cochran   154
    Prompt Judicial Determination   155

  Confidentiality of Sources
    Keeping Your Sources Secret in the Outing of a CIA Operative   155

  The Right of Access
    National Archives and Records Administration v. Favish   157

B. OBSCENITY

    The PROTECT Act and Virtual Child Pornography   158
    United States v. American Library Association   159
    Ashcroft v. American Civil Liberties Union   164

C. LIBEL

    A Case of Cyber-Libel   166

CHAPTER 13   FREEDOM OF RELIGION

A. THE ESTABLISHMENT CLAUSE

  Prayer, Bible-Reading, and Sunday Closing Laws
    The Ten Commandments Monument and the Alabama Chief Justice   168
    McCreary County, Kentucky v. American Civil Liberties Union   169
    Van Orden v. Perry   178
      Cutting Off Funds to Enforce a Court Decision   185
    Elk Grove Unified School District v. Newdow   185

  The Lemon Test and Financial Aid to Religion
    Davey v. Locke   186

B. THE FREE EXERCISE OF RELIGIOUS BELIEF

    The Religious Freedom Restoration Act and the Federal Government   187

CHAPTER 14   EQUAL PROTECTION OF THE LAWS

A. RACIAL DISCRIMINATION

  Proving Discriminatory Intent
    Race and the Use of Peremptories   189

  Affirmative Action or "Reverse Discrimination"
    Grutter v. Bollinger   190
    Gratz v. Bollinger   198

B. "PRIVATE" DISCRIMINATION AND THE CONCEPT OF "STATE ACTION"

  Private Discrimination and First Amendment Issues
    The Validity of the Solomon Amendment   204

C. VOTING RIGHTS AND ELECTORAL DISCRIMINATION

    Clingman v. Beaver   204

D. MALAPPORTIONMENT

    Veith v. Jubelirer   205
    The Colorado, Texas, and Georgia Cases   206

E. ECONOMIC AND SOCIAL DISCRIMINATION

  Gender
    Title IX and Third-Party Damages   207

  Age
    Acting with the Effect (Rather than the Intent) of Age Discrimination   207

  Sexual Preference
    Goodridge v. Department of Public Health   208
      Attempting to Overturn the Massachusetts Ruling   217
      The Proposed Federal Marriage Amendment   218
      Same-Sex Marriage Elsewhere   218

APPENDIX C. BIOGRAPHIES OF THE CURRENT JUSTICES

    Justice O'Connor Announces Her Retirement   221

INDEX   223

TABLE OF CASES

Principal cases are in italic type. Non-principal cases are in roman type. References are to pages. In addition to the principal cases, cases included are those discussed or mentioned in notes, charts, the text, and footnotes to the text. Cases cited within judicial opinions are not included.

A. v. Secretary of State for the Home Department, 30
Abdah v. Rumsfeld, 38
Abraham v. Hodges, 69
Aetna Health, Inc. v. Davila, 66
American Insurance Co. v. Garamendi, 41
American Library Ass'n, United States v., 159
American Trucking Associations, Inc. v. Michigan Public Service Comm'n, 67
Andersen v. King County, 219
Apprendi v. New Jersey, 93
Ashcroft v. American Civil Liberties Union, 164
Ashcroft v. Free Speech Coalition, 158
Ayotte v. Planned Parenthood of Northern New England, 125
Banks, United States v., 120
Blakely v. Washington, 93
Booker, United States v., 94
Bourne, City of v. Flores, 13, 187
Bowers v. Hardwick, 128
Burnett, State v., 144
Burt v. Rumsfeld, 204
Bush v. Schiavo, 139
Castle Rock, Colorado, Town of, v. Gonzales 86
Cathcart v. Ashcroft, 126
Chavez v. Martinez, 97
Cheney v. United States District Court for District of Columbia, 1, 39
Cheney, In re, 40
Church of the Lukumi Babalu Aye, Inc. v. City of Hialeah, 187
Circle School v. Pappert, 148
Citizens for Equal Protection v. Bruning, 219
City of (see name of city)
Clark v. Suarez Martinez, 14
Clingman v. Beaver, 204
Colorado General Assembly v. Salazar, 206
Colorado, People of State of, v. Harlan, 101

Conant v. Walters, 138
Connecticut Dept. of Public Safety v. Doe, 114
Cooper v. United States, 156
Coordination Proceeding ... Marriage Cases, 219
Crawford v. Washington, 99
Crosby v. National Foreign Trade Council, 41
Cutter v. Wilkinson, 13
Davis v. Bandemer, 205
Deck v. Missouri, 100
Demore v. Kim, 14
Doe v. Bush, 4
Elk Grove Unified School Dist. v. Newdow, 1, 185
Employment Division, Dept. of Human Resources of Oregon v. Smith, 188
Evans v. Stephans, 12
Ex parte (see name of party)
Ewing v. California, 102
Flores-Montano, United States v., 122
Florida v. Nixon, 95
Forum for Academic and Institutional Rights v. Rumsfeld, 204
Freedman v. Maryland, 155
Georgia v. Randolph, 119
Georgia, United States v., 63, 109
Glassroth v. Moore, 168
Goldberg v. Kelly, 85
Goldwater v. Carter, 4
Gonzales v. O Centro Espirita Beneficiente Uniao Do Vegetal, 188
Gonzales v. Oregon, 143
Goodridge v. Department of Public Health, 208
Granholm v. Heald, 70
Gratz v. Bollinger, 198
Grutter v. Bollinger, 190
Halpern v. City of Toronto, 219
Hamdan v. Rumsfeld, 38
Hamdi v. Rumsfeld, 16

Hernandez v. Robles, 219
Herrera v. Collins, 102
Hiibel v. Sixth Judicial District Court of Nevada, 122
Hoevenaar v. Lazaroff, 13
House v. Bell, 102
Humanitarian Law Project v. Ashcroft, 45
Illinois v. Caballes, 121
Illinois v. Lidster, 123
Illinois ex rel. Madigan v. Telemarketing Associates, Inc., 152
In re (see name of party)
Indianapolis, City of, v. Edmond, 123
Jackson v. Birmingham Board of Education, 207
Johanns v. Livestock Marketing Ass'n, 145
Johnson v. California, 189
Johnson v. City of Cincinnati, 144
Johnson v. Eisentrager, 25
Kansas v. Hendricks, 114
Kansas v. Marsh, 101
Kaupp v. Texas, 119
Kelo v. City of New London, 76
Kentucky Ass'n of Health Care Plans, Inc. v. Miller, 65
Khalid v. Bush, 38
Kucinich v. Bush, 8
Largess v. Supreme Judicial Court of Massachusetts, 218
Larios v. Cox, 206
Lawrence v. Texas, 128
Lee v. Weisman, 186
Leocal v. Ashcroft, 14
Lingle v. Chrevon USA, Inc., 84
Littleton, Colorado, City of, v. Z.J. Gifts, 155
Locke v. Davey, 187
Mainstream Marketing Services, Inc. v. Federal Trade Comm'n, 153
Marbury v. Madison, 185
Marchwinski v. Howard, 123
Maryland v. Craig, 99
Maryland v. Pringle, 121
Massaoui, United States v., 38
Mathews v. Eldridge, 85
Matlock, United States v., 119
Matter of (see name of party)
McConnell v. Federal Election Comm'n, 150

McCreary County, Kentucky, American Civil Liberties Union, 169
McCulloch v. Maryland, 70
McGinley v. Houston, 168
Miller v. United States, 156
Miller-El v. Dretke, 189
Missouri v. Seibert, 97
Muehler v. Mena, 120
National Abortion Federation v. Ashcroft, 126
National Abortion Rights Federation, 126
National Archives and Records Administration v. Favish, 157
Nevada Dept. of Human Resources v. Hibbs, 40, 57
New York v. United States, 66
Nixon, United States v., 39
Northwestern Memorial Hospital v. Ashcroft, 126
NOW v. Scheidler, 126
O Centro Espirita Beneficiente Uniao Do Vegetal v. Ashcroft, 188
Ohio v. Roberts, 99
Ohio AFL-CIO, State ex rel., v. Ohio Bureau of Workers Compensation, 123
Operation Rescue v. National Organization of Women, 127
Oregon v. Ashcroft, 143
Overton v. Bazzetta, 108
Padilla v. Hanft, 28
Patane, United States v., 98
People v. _____ (see opposing party)
Pharmaceutical Research and Manufacturers of America v. Walsh, 65
Philadelphia, City of v. State of New Jersey, 70
Planned Parenthood Federation of America v. Ashcroft, 126
Planned Parenthood of Northern New England v. Heed, 125
Prometheus v. Federal Communications Comm'n, 154
Rasul v. Bush, 25
Regents of University of California v. Bakke, 190
Republic of Austria v. Altmann, 45
Rochin v. California, 98
Roe v. Wade, 125

Rompilla v. Beard, 96
Roper v. Simmons, 100
Ross v. Hadley, 167
Rumsfeld v. Padilla, 28
Russelburg v. Gibson County, 185
Sabri v. United States, 63
Scheidler v. National Organization of Women, 127
Schiavo ex rel. Schindler v. Schiavo, 140, 141
Sell v. United States, 96
Session v. Perry, 206
Smith v. City of Jackson, 207
Smith v. Doe, 109, *110*, 114
Smith, United States v., 55
Special Counsel Investigation, In re, 156
State v. _____ (see name of state)
Stenberg v. Carhart, 126
Stewart, United States v., 55
Stogner v. California, 115
Strickland v. Washington, 95
Tennessee v. Lane, 62
Thomas v. Collins, 138
Thornton v. United States, 121
Tory v. Cochran, 154
Town of (see name of town)
United States v. _____ (see opposing party)
US Security v. Federal Trade Commission, 153
Van Orden v. Perry, 178
Veith v. Jubelirer, 205
Virginia v. Black, 149
Virginia v. Hicks, 148
Washington v. Harper, 96
Wayne County, Michigan v. Hathcock, 84
West Virginia State Board of Education v. Barnette, 144, 186
Wiggins v. Smith, 95
Wilkinson v. Austin, 109
Williams v. Attorney General of Alabama, 137
Woodley, United States v., 12
Yarborough v. Alvarado, 98
Zadvydas v. Davis, 14
Zelman v. Simmons-Harris, 186

CHAPTER 1

JUDICIAL POWER

A. THE SUPREME COURT'S JURISDICTION AND ITS ASSUMPTION OF JUDICIAL REVIEW

Judicial Review

▶ **Insert at p. 13 at the end of the note**

Twice during the October 2003 Term, the issue of judicial recusal surfaced and with respect to the same member of the Court—Justice Scalia. In the first instance, he disqualified himself from participating in the consideration and decision of *Elk Grove Unified School District v. Newdow* (see p. 185 of this Supplement). Justice Scalia removed himself from sitting in the case because he had expressed a position on the merits of Newdow's Establishment Clause argument in a speech. Newdow contended that compelled recitation of the words "under God" in the Pledge of Allegiance at the beginning of his daughter's school day routine violated the Establishment Clause of the First Amendment. The lower federal courts had ruled in his favor. Although recusal effectively addresses the real or seeming risk of individual bias, it also creates the possibility of a 4-4 vote by the remaining Justices. In the event of a tie, the appeals court's decision stands.

In the second instance, Justice Scalia refused to disqualify himself from participating in the hearing and disposition of *Cheney v. United States District Court for District of Columbia* (see p. 39 of this Supplement). Controversy over his continued participation in the case erupted when it was reported that the Justice was among the dozen guests who had gone on a private duck-hunting trip with Vice President Dick Cheney. The Sierra Club and others had brought suit to force public disclosure of records pertaining to the operation of the Energy Task Force chaired by the Vice President. Critics alleged that the committee was loaded with oil industry contributors to the 2000 Bush-Cheney campaign and that, in turn for their financial support during the presidential race, they had been the at the table crafting the Administration's energy policy. The plaintiffs sought to force the Vice President to turn over a list of who attended the meetings and the minutes of those meetings. Cheney responded by invoking executive privilege. Justice Scalia declined to step-aside. He responded that the Court had voted to grant cert. in the case before the duck-hunting trip had taken place, that he was always in the company of others when he was with the Vice President, and that he had never discussed the case with him. He argued that a policy of requiring a Justice to recuse himself in every instance where he had had social interaction with some member of the Washington community named in a legal proceeding before Court was entirely novel, impractical, and institutionally disabling. That didn't stop late-night television host Jay Leno from getting comedy mileage out of the matter: Leno cracked that when the Vice President passed through the White House metal detector, Justice Scalia fell out of his pocket. The point critics made was that a judge should recuse himself not just when there was a real conflict of interest in deciding a case, but also when the circumstances fostered a plausible inference of favoritism. See "Not Ducking," The Economist, Mar. 27, 2004, p. 30; New York Times, May 27, 2004, p. A30. In a lengthy memorandum opinion denying the motion to recuse, 541 U.S. 913, 124 S.Ct. 1391 (2004), Justice Scalia replied that the relevant standard was whether he could reasonably be expected to remain impartial and to accord the parties a fair hearing. In his view, he could, so there was no problem. He pointed out that members of the Court frequently gave speeches to groups and associations named in pending and future cases, and customarily the Justices' travel and accommodations were paid by the host. Hobnobbing with other Washington influentials had been done by many Justices in the past—some even serving as backdoor presidential advisors—and if that didn't raise doubts about participating in cases before, why should it now?

The Structure of the Judicial System

▶ Insert at p. 27 following the fourth paragraph

There are renewed efforts to expand the number of federal circuits from the current 12 to 14 by splitting the Ninth Circuit in three. The Ninth Circuit currently has 51 appellate judges— twice as many as any other circuit—and hears the most appeals by far, over 14,000—more than eight times as many as the First Circuit. The proposed redrawing would leave only California and Hawaii in the new Ninth Circuit, and add a Twelfth Circuit consisting of Arizona, Idaho, Montana, and Nevada, and a Thirteenth Circuit comprised of Alaska, Oregon, and Washington. While there is surface appeal to dividing up a single circuit that now encompasses 20% of the nation's population, the prospect of a raft of new appellate appointments by a Republican administration also in control of the Senate inspires deep resistance by Democrats. The more so, since this proposal is being reintroduced in the aftermath of a tenuous agreement among Senate centrists over Democrats' use of the filibuster to delay filling appellate vacancies on other circuits (see pp. 11-12 of this Supplement). Critics suspect that the proposal is also motivated by the fact that the Ninth has a reputation of being the most liberal of the federal circuits; it is one of three circuits that does not yet have a majority of Republican judges. But opponents of carving up the Ninth Circuit aren't limited to Democrats; most of the appeals judges in the circuit, even Republicans, are opposed. New York Times, June 19, 2005, p. 12. The proposal, which has been around for years, cleared the House in the last Congress by a vote of 205-194 (overwhelmingly along party lines) but never came to a vote in the Senate. Congressional Quarterly Weekly Report, Oct. 9, 2004, pp. 2375, 2404. The cost of the proposal has been pegged at $131 million and calls for adding 11 new appellate judges and 47 more district judges.

The Writ of Certiorari

▶ Insert at p. 31 after the footnote and at p. 33 following the chart

The following chart of cases decided during the last three Terms of the Court updates and expands material on the size and composition of the Court's docket as well as the level of conflict among the Justices in the disposition of cases. The category "All Cases" includes cases falling under the Court's original jurisdiction, statutory cases, cases interpreting the federal rules of civil and criminal procedure, and others, in addition to cases decided on constitutional grounds. However, only cases decided by signed opinion are counted; this excludes per curiams. The figures of the last three Terms generally confirm trends of the Rehnquist Court noted in the Text: low annual productivity (some 70-odd cases), constitutional cases comprising a minority (around 40%) of the cases given full-dress review by the Court, and a fairly stable dissent rate that shows a substantially higher level of conflict (about 15 points higher) in the decision of constitutional cases as compared with non-constitutional cases.

	All Cases		Constitutional Cases	
October Term	Total Number	Proportion with Dissent	As a Proportion of All Cases	Proportion with Dissent
2002	70	59%	44%	68%
2003	72	60%	44%	72%
2004	74	62%	38%	71%

To see the voting alignment of the Justices in the 64 nonunanimous constitutional cases decided during the last three Terms, see p. 56 of this Supplement.

B. Institutional Constraints on the Exercise of Judicial Power

Case and Controversy

▶ **Insert at p. 40 following the footnote**

Campaigning for reelection in 2004 with tort reform as one of his favored policies, President George W. Bush secured congressional change in jurisdiction over class action suits. Titled the Class Action Fairness Act of 2005, 119 Stat. 4, the new law moves class actions with more than 100 plaintiffs, with at least one of the plaintiffs and one of the defendants domiciled in different states, and with at least $5 million in total damages at stake, to federal district court. The statute aims at furthering the goals of making awards among the plaintiffs more equal, giving the successful plaintiffs more meaningful compensation (money, not coupons), eliminating in-state bias by state courts, reducing the economic destabilization of defendant companies, and scaling down attorney fees. Another motivation behind the law was thought to be that federal courts have much higher standards of evidence and are much less generous in their awards than state courts and thus are preferred venues by defendant corporations. The legislation passed easily: The House vote was 279-149; the Senate vote was 72-26. Congressional Quarterly Weekly Report, Feb. 21, 2005, p. 460; New York Times, Feb. 11, 2005, pp. A1, A16.

Ripeness

▶ **Insert at p. 46 following *NTEU* v. *United States***

In the following case a federal appellate court discusses why adhering to the ripeness doctrine required it not to decide whether Congress's October Resolution (see Text, p. 271) authorized President Bush to conduct a war against Saddam Hussein's regime in Iraq. In its discussion, the appeals court adopts the posture taken by Justice Powell concurring in *Goldwater* v. *Carter* (see Text. p. 75). In the court's view, although disagreement between Congress and the President might materialize in the future, the requisite conflict was not apparent at that time.

DOE V. BUSH
United States Court of Appeals, First Circuit, 2003
323 F.3d 133

BACKGROUND & FACTS Active-duty members of the armed forces, parents of military personnel, and several members of the U.S. House of Representatives sought to enjoin President George W. Bush and Secretary of Defense Donald Rumsfeld from attacking Iraq. Plaintiffs argued that the resolution Congress adopted in October 2002 was constitutionally inadequate for conducting a war. A federal district court dismissed their complaint, and the plaintiffs appealed.

Before LYNCH, Circuit Judge, CYR and STAHL, Senior Circuit Judges.

LYNCH, Circuit Judge.

* * *

[P]laintiffs argue [that] judicial intervention is necessary to preserve the principle of separation of powers which undergirds our constitutional structure. Only the judiciary, they argue, has the constitutionally assigned role and the institutional competence to police the boundaries of the constitutional mandates given to the other branches: Congress alone has the authority to declare war and the President alone has the authority to make war.

The plaintiffs argue that important and increasingly vital interests are served by the requirement that it be Congress which decides whether to declare war. * * * [T]hey argue * * * that Congress, the voice of the people, should make this momentous decision, one which will cost lives; and that congressional support is needed to ensure that the country is behind the war, a key element in any victory. They also argue that, absent an attack on this country or our allies, congressional involvement must come prior to war, because once war has started, Congress is in an uncomfortable default position where the use of its appropriations powers to cut short any war is an inadequate remedy.

The defendants are equally eloquent about the impropriety of judicial intrusion into the "extraordinarily delicate foreign affairs and military calculus, one that could be fatally upset by judicial interference." Such intervention would be all the worse here, defendants say, because Congress and the President are in accord as to the threat to the nation and the legitimacy of a military response to that threat.

* * *

The Constitution reserves the war powers to the legislative and executive branches. This court has declined the invitation to become involved in such matters once before. Over thirty years ago, the First Circuit addressed a war powers case challenging the constitutionality of the Vietnam War on the basis that Congress had not declared war. Massachusetts v. Laird, 451 F.2d 26 (1st Cir. 1971). The court found that other actions by Congress, such as continued appropriations to fund the war over the course of six years * * * provided enough indication of congressional approval to put the question beyond the reach of judicial review:

"The war in Vietnam is a product of the jointly supportive actions of the two branches to whom the congeries of the war powers have been committed. Because the branches are not in opposition, there is no necessity of determining boundaries. Should either branch be opposed to the continuance of hostilities, however, and present the issue in clear terms, a court might well take a different view. This question we do not face."

* * * Applying this precedent to the case at hand today, the district court concluded, "[T]here is a day to day fluidity in the situation that does not amount to resolute conflict between the branches * * *."

The lack of a fully developed dispute between the two elected branches, and the consequent lack of a clearly defined issue, is exactly the type of concern which causes courts to find a case unripe. In his concurring opinion in Goldwater v. Carter, 444 U.S. 996, 100 S.Ct. 533 (1979), Justice Powell stated that courts should decline, on ripeness grounds, to decide "issues affecting the allocation of power between the President and Congress until the political branches reach a constitutional impasse." * * * A number of courts have adopted Justice Powell's ripeness reasoning in cases involving military powers. * * *

Ripeness doctrine involves more than simply the timing of the case. It mixes various mutually reinforcing constitutional and prudential considerations. * * * One such consideration is the need "to prevent the courts, through avoidance of premature adjudication, from entangling themselves in abstract disagreements." * * * Another is to avoid unnecessary constitutional decisions. * * * A third is the recognition that, by waiting until a case is fully developed before deciding it, courts benefit from a focus sharpened by particular facts. * * * The case before us raises all three of these concerns.

* * *

* * * Ripeness is dependent on the circumstances of a particular case. * * * Two factors are used to evaluate ripeness: "the fitness of the issues for judicial decision and the hardship to the parties of withholding court consideration." * * * Ordinarily, both factors must be present. * * *

The hardship prong of this test is most likely satisfied here; the current mobilization already imposes difficulties on the plaintiff soldiers and family members, so that they suffer "present injury from a future contemplated event." * * * Plaintiffs also lack a realistic opportunity to secure comparable relief by bringing the action at a later time. * * *

The fitness inquiry here presents a greater obstacle. Fitness "typically involves subsidiary queries concerning finality, definiteness, and the extent to which resolution of the challenge depends upon facts that may not yet be sufficiently developed." * * * The baseline question is whether allowing more time for development of events would "significantly advance our ability to deal with the legal issues presented [or] aid us in their resolution." * * * These prudential considerations are particularly strong in this case, which presents a politically-charged controversy involving momentous issues, both substantively (war and peace) and constitutionally (the powers of coequal branches). * * *

[Plaintiffs argue that] the October Resolution only permits actions sanctioned by the Security Council. In plaintiffs' view, the Resolution's authorization is so narrow that, even with Security Council approval of military force, Congress would need to pass a new resolution before United States participation in an attack on Iraq would be constitutional. At a minimum, according to plaintiffs, the October Resolution authorizes no military action "outside of a United Nations coalition."

For various reasons, this issue is not fit now for judicial review. * * *

* * * Diplomatic negotiations, in

particular, fluctuate daily. The President has emphasized repeatedly that hostilities still may be averted if Iraq takes certain actions. The Security Council is now debating the possibility of passing a new resolution that sets a final deadline for Iraqi compliance. United Nations weapons inspectors continue their investigations inside Iraq. Other countries ranging from Canada to Cameroon have reportedly pursued their own proposals to broker a compromise. As events unfold, it may become clear that diplomacy has either succeeded or failed decisively. The Security Council, now divided on the issue, may reach a consensus. To evaluate this claim now, the court would need to pile one hypothesis on top of another. We would need to assume that the Security Council will not authorize war, and that the President will proceed nonetheless. * * *

* * *

* * * If courts may ever decide whether military action contravenes congressional authority, they surely cannot do so unless and until the available facts make it possible to define the issues with clarity.

Plaintiffs' collusion theory * * * [argues that] * * * the Constitution deliberately vested power to declare war in the legislative branch as a necessary check on the power of the executive branch, and Congress is not free to upset this careful balance by giving power to the President. * * *

* * *

* * * The Constitution explicitly divides the various war powers between the political branches. To the Congress goes the power to "declare war," * * * to "raise and support armies" through appropriations of up to two years, * * * to "provide and maintain a navy," * * * and to "make rules for the government and regulation of the land and naval forces" * * *. The President's role as commander-in-chief is one of the few executive powers enumerated by the Constitution. * * *

Given this "amalgam of powers," the Constitution overall "envisages the *joint* participation of the Congress and the executive in determining the scale and duration of hostilities." * * *

In this zone of shared congressional and presidential responsibility, courts should intervene only when the dispute is clearly framed. * * * An extreme case might arise, for example, if Congress gave absolute discretion to the President to start a war at his or her will. * * * Plaintiffs' objection to the October Resolution does not, of course, involve any such claim. Nor does it involve a situation where the President acts without any apparent congressional authorization, or against congressional opposition.

The mere fact that the October Resolution grants some discretion to the President fails to raise a sufficiently clear constitutional issue. * * * The plaintiffs argue that Congress is constitutionally forbidden from deciding that certain conditions are necessary to lead to war and then yielding to the President the authority to make the determination of whether those conditions exist. The President, in this view, has power to make such determinations only in the context of repelling sudden attacks on this country or its allies. * * * War powers, in contrast to "*all* legislative power," are shared between the political branches. Furthermore, the Supreme Court has also suggested that the nondelegation doctrine has even less applicability to foreign affairs. See Zemel v. Rusk, 381 U.S. 1, 17, 85 S.Ct. 1271 (1965) (when delegating authority over foreign relations, Congress may leave more details to the President than in domestic affairs, short of granting "totally unrestricted freedom of choice"). The reference to nondelegation is thus of little help to plaintiffs * * *.

Nor is there clear evidence of congressional abandonment of the authority to declare war to the President. To the contrary, Congress has been deeply involved in significant debate, activity, and authorization connected to our relations with Iraq for over a decade, under three different presidents of both major political parties, and during periods when each party has controlled Congress. It has enacted several relevant pieces of legislation expressing support for an aggressive posture toward Iraq, including authorization of the prior war against Iraq and of military assistance for groups that would overthrow Saddam Hussein. It has also accepted continued American participation in military activities in and around Iraq, including flight patrols and missile strikes. Finally, the text of the October Resolution itself spells out justifications for a war and frames itself as an "authorization" of such a war.

[C]ourts are rightly hesitant to second-guess the form or means by which the coequal political branches choose to exercise their textually committed constitutional powers. * * * As the circumstances presented here do not warrant judicial intervention, the appropriate recourse for those who oppose war with Iraq lies with the political branches.

Dismissal of the complaint is affirmed.

Standing

▶ **Insert at p. 56 following note on *City of Los Angeles* v. *Lyons***

The Court recently invoked the notion of "prudential standing" to avoid deciding whether the phrase "under God" in the Pledge of Allegiance violated the Establishment Clause. See p. 185 of this Supplement.

Political Questions

▶ **Insert at p. 77 after the first paragraph**

Consistent with the Supreme Court's posture of judicial self-restraint in *Goldwater* v. *Carter*, a federal district court in Kucinich v. Bush, 236 F.Supp.2d 1 (D.D.C. 2002), held that 32 members of the U.S. House of Representatives lacked standing to challenge President Bush's decision to withdraw from the 1972 Anti-Ballistic Missile Treaty with Russia without the approval of Congress. The court reasoned that the congressmen could not demonstrate a sufficient "personalized or particularized" interest necessary to a real case and controversy as required by Article III. The legislators contended that the President could no more constitutionally terminate a treaty "without congressional consent * * * than he could repeal a statute." The district court also concluded that the dispute presented a "political question," and for the very reason identified in the Supreme Court's plurality opinion. Although not signed by a majority of the Justices and thus not binding as would be an Opinion of the Court, the lower court nonetheless thought the *Goldwater* plurality's position was "instructive and compelling."

CHAPTER 2

THE MODES OF CONSTITUTIONAL INTERPRETATION

The Court in American History: Judicial Values and Constitutional Interpretation

▶ **Insert at p. 101 following the first paragraph**

It is probably still too soon to tell if the results of the 2002 and 2004 elections that brought the Republicans unified control of the national government signify a return to "the sun and moon theory" (see Text, pp. 94-95) that has historically marked American politics. But whether Republican ascendency or divided government is to be the pattern for the foreseeable future, the bitterness of judicial nomination battles has continued apace. Often, the fate of presidential nominations to fill vacancies in the federal judiciary has been—to use Thomas Hobbes' description of the state of nature—"nasty, brutish, and short." This side-effect of divided government (beginning in 1968 with the ill-fated Fortas nomination, see Text, footnote h, p. 525 and p. 221 of this Supplement) has been reflected in long, drawn out confirmation battles, polarizing political rhetoric, burying judicial nominations in the Senate Judiciary Committee, filibustering to prevent votes on confirmation, and more frequent rejection of nominees when they have gotten as far as an up-or-down vote on the Senate floor. The frustration experienced by President George W. Bush is in no sense peculiar. The tactic chosen by Democrats to sandbag several of his nominees has been distinctive—use of the filibuster—only because it was the only option open to them. Republicans achieved precisely the same effect of sidetracking many of Bill Clinton's nominees by letting the nominations languish in the Judiciary Committee, a response made possible by their control of the Senate during six of the eight years of his Presidency. Foot-dragging on filling judicial vacancies has been reciprocal: each party sabotaging the nominees of the other in the hope that the next election will bring electoral success and the spoils that go with victory.

This bipartisan pattern—if it perversely can be called that—has had several notable results. One is more frequent defeat than usual of presidential nominees to fill spots on the Supreme Court. But "more frequent than usual" doesn't seem quite accurate because there have been many fewer vacancies to fill. The ever sharper rough-and-tumble confirmation battles when they have occurred have induced Justices on the bench to stay longer in hopes of being replaced with someone ideologically similar. As reported in footnote t, p. 94 of the Text, the average tenure of a Supreme Court Justice over the span of American history is 16 years; for those Justices now serving on the Court, it is 19 and a half years. Although presidents have generally averaged a Supreme Court appointment every two years, the figure since 1969 has lengthened to about one every three years. This generalization, however, conceals the fact that Republican presidents have made 11 appointments during 24 years in office but Democratic presidents have made only two appointments over 12 years. Before Justice O'Connor's notice of retirement, the current Court had the second longest stretch of American history without any change in its composition (the longest was 1811-1823). Two of the remaining Justices are 80 or over, and three more are very near or over 70. Basic awareness of human mortality suggests the dam may be about to burst.

Little movement at the top and a sharp drop in the rate of granting certiorari have combined to focus attention on the 13 U.S. Courts of Appeals with unusual intensity. The precipitous drop in granting cert. (see Text, pp. 31-32) has meant that increasingly federal appeals judges have the last word. In light of their growing importance, it is not surprising that the sort of controversy that has attended Supreme Court confirmations now colors appellate court nominations. While presidents usually have been more successful filling district court judgeships than appeals court slots (perhaps because the lower court nominations are cleared by senatorial courtesy), the casualty rate for appellate court nominations has skyrocketed. But, again, the nominees of President George W. Bush are not peculiar. Whereas presidential success in appeals court confirmations from Truman to Reagan rarely fell below 90% (five of the nine presidents didn't fall below 95%), neither Bill Clinton nor George W. Bush (as of May 2005) hit 60%. (Bush's father had a batting average of only about three out of four, putting him midway between earlier and more recent presidents.) New York Times, May 19, 2005, p. A35. In other words, as the period of divided government since 1969 has lengthened, acrimony over judicial nominees has deepened and spread.

Throughout George W. Bush's first term, Democrats remained virtually united, opposing approximately 10 of the president's appeals court nominees as "too extreme" and refusing to end debate so that a vote on confirmation could be taken. But the gain of four Republican seats in 2004 altered the Senate's political topography so that conservative Republicans could realistically contemplate changing the rules and proceeding to shut off debate on judicial nominees by a mere majority, instead of the 60 votes generally required to end filibusters. In its simplest terms, the change would be effected by the Republican majority leader raising a point of order during a judicial filibuster that a majority vote is sufficient to end debate. The Vice President would presumably rule in his favor, and Democrats would have to muster 51 votes in the chamber to overturn that ruling. This has been dubbed the "nuclear option" because Democrats have threatened to retaliate by bringing a virtual halt to all Senate business if the ploy succeeds. The Republican strategy, of course, supposes that there are no more than five defections from their side—something that is not at all certain. For the Democrats' part, it is not clear how the public would react to closing down the Senate. Although polls show that public opinion sides with maintaining a check on judicial nominees, in the past it has not supported actions that shut down one of the houses of Congress—as the unpopularity of Republican tactics against President Bill Clinton in 1994 showed.

In late May 2005, as the Senate teetered on the brink of deploying the "nuclear option," seven Republican and seven Democratic "moderates" struck an accord on Bush's judicial nominees. The Democratic senators who signed on agreed to let three of the appeals court nominees come up for a vote and not to filibuster in the future unless a nominee was so extreme as to present an "extraordinary circumstance." The Republican signatories, for their part, agreed not to support the change in Senate rules. As a result, three of the Bush nominees identified in the agreement were confirmed, although very much along party-line votes, and by mid-June, two others as well. Congressional Quarterly Weekly Report, May 23, 2005, pp. 1372-1373; May 30, 2005, pp. 1420-1422, 1440-11443. "Armageddon for the Senate," The Economist, May 21, 2005, pp. 29-30.

But does the agreement really solve the problem? After all, there is no objective definition of what constitutes an "extraordinary circumstance." Democrats are free at any time to resume filibustering and Republicans are likewise free to attempt the rule change. To some critics, it looked as if Democrats retained the judicial filibuster but only if they promised not to use it. And hovering over this drama is the confirmation of a successor to Justice O'Connor, if not other Justices, and the titanic battle for the future of the Supreme Court.

Should the impasse on judicial nominations resume, there is a short-term option open to the President—making recess appointments. It is controversial because it so obviously side-steps the Senate. In relevant part (Article II, sec. 2, para. 3.), the Constitution provides, "The President shall have Power to fill up all Vacancies that may happen during the Recess of the Senate by granting Commissions which shall expire at the End of their next Session." This provision stands in evident tension with the principle of judicial independence that animates Article III (see Text, p. 38) because a recess appointee sits on the bench while his nomination is pending in the Senate, subjecting the nominee to subtle—and perhaps not-so-subtle—coercion from a Senate that is looking over his shoulder as he decides cases. Nevertheless, the constitutionality of recess appointments to the federal bench has been consistently upheld, although not by the Supreme Court. Perhaps the best discussion appears in United States v. Woodley, 751 F.2d 1008 (9th Cir. en banc, 1985), *cert. denied*, 475 U.S. 1048, 106 S.Ct. 1269 (1986). Most recently it was been used by President George W. Bush to advance one of his appeals court nominees, William H. Pryor, Jr., held up in the filibustering described above. The legitimacy of that recess appointment was sustained in Evans v. Stephans, 387 F.3d 1220 (11th Cir. en banc, 2004), *cert. denied*, 544 U.S. —, 125 S.Ct. 1640 (2005). (Justice Stevens said he thought the matter was clearly important enough to warrant a hearing and he inveighed against confusing the Court's denial of cert. with its endorsement of the practice. See 545 U.S. —, 125 S.Ct. 2244 (2005)). Judge Pryor was eventually confirmed as one of three nominees brought up for a vote under the bipartisan agreement among the 14 senators described above.

The last president to make a recess appointment to the Court was Dwight Eisenhower. Three of the five Justices he named got to the Court by recess appointment—Chief Justice Earl Warren and Justices William J. Brennan and Potter Stewart. Eisenhower's motivation was not to out-flank the Senate but to ensure that the Supreme Court was staffed by a full complement of Justices for its October Term which in each instance had just begun. This appears to be precluded by the terms of Justice O'Connor's retirement letter. See p. 221 of this Supplement.

CHAPTER 3

LEGISLATIVE POWER

A. THE SOURCES AND SCOPE OF CONGRESS'S POWER TO LEGISLATE

Amendment-Enforcing Powers

▶ **Insert at p. 122 following *City of Bourne* v. *Flores***

After the Supreme Court's decision in *City of Bourne* v. *Flores*, Congress regrouped and passed the Religious Land Use and Institutionalized Persons Act (RLUIPA), 114 Stat. 804, in 2000. The new law was directed at only two kinds of governmental action: zoning and the rights of inmates at public correctional and mental institutions. Unlike the Religious Freedom Restoration Act struck down in *Flores* which had been based on the amendment-enforcing power, the RLUIPA was anchored in the taxing and spending power and attached conditions to the receipt of federal tax dollars. The law required state and local governments receiving federal funds to apply strict scrutiny to any policy that interfered with religious practices. In Cutter v. Wilkinson, 544 U.S. —, 125 S.Ct. 2113 (2005), a case involving prisoners' rights, the Supreme Court unanimously sustained the law in the face of a claim that it violated the Establishment Clause because it elevated religion above all other reasons for a prisoner seeking special privileges. The legislation was controversial because prison officials said it catered to the demands of non-mainstream beliefs, such as Satanism and white supremacist religions. Among the five Ohio plaintiffs in the cases at hand were adherents to a religion that preached the white race needed to use violence to protect itself from being overtaken by "the mud races." Demands based on the RLUIPA triggered concerns by prison officials about security and gang violence.

Speaking for the Court in *Cutter*, Justice Ginsburg noted that, were the First Amendment claim to be accepted by the Court, "all manner of religious accommodations would fall," including those granted to "traditionally recognized religions." She pointed out that congressional sponsors of the legislation were well aware of the legitimate concerns about prison safety, security, and order. Depending upon the specific manner in which prison regulations advanced them, they certainly constituted "compelling interests." The applicability of the law to instances where religious institutions sought an exemption from local zoning regulations was not before the Court in this case. The Court vacated judgment in, and remanded for further consideration in light of *Cutter*, a second RLUIPA case involving another Ohio inmate, a Native American who wanted to grow his hair long for religious reasons. Hoevenaar v. Lazaroff, 545 U.S. —, 125 S.Ct. 2536 (2005).

Applying the test it announced in *City of Bourne*, the Court sustained constitutionality of the Family Medical Leave Act (FMLA), permitting private damages suits against the states without their consent to redress gender-based discrimination. The law allows employees to take a maximum of 12 weeks of unpaid leave to deal with the health problems of family members. The Court concluded the FMLA was a valid exercise of Congress's power to enforce the equal protection guarantee of the Fourteenth Amendment against gender discrimination. See p. 57 of this Supplement.

Inherent Powers

▶ Insert at p. 124 following the last paragraph

In Demore v. Kim, 538 U.S. 510, 123 S.Ct. 1708 (2004), the Supreme Court subsequently upheld the mandatory detention of aliens awaiting deportation if they had been convicted of certain crimes. The Court, per Chief Justice Rehnquist, reasoned that the relatively short period these aliens spent in custody awaiting deportation (a month and a half to five months) was more than offset by the government's interest in not have them commit additional crimes while free, especially "since congress[ional] investigations showed * * * that the INS could not even identify most deportable aliens, much less locate them and remove them from the country." Indeed, "[c]riminal aliens were the fastest growing segment of the federal prison population, * * * constituting 25% of all federal prisoners, and they formed a rapidly rising share of state prison populations as well." Moreover, "[o]nce released, more than 20% of deportable criminal aliens failed to appear for their removal hearings." *Zadvydas v. Davis* (discussed in the Text, p. 124) was different from this case in two vital respects: (1) the aliens challenging their detention in *Zadvydas* were being detained but their removal was "no longer practically attainable" because the countries of their ethnic origin and former residence would not accept them; and (2) the period of detention at issue in *Zadvydas* was "indefinite" and "potentially permanent" whereas here the period was much shorter.

Justices Stevens, Souter, and Ginsburg dissented. Speaking for the trio, Justice Souter emphasized that "over a century of precedent ackowledg[ed] the rights of permanent residents, including the basic liberty from physical confinement lying at the heart of due process." Congress could not categorically deny a resident alien a hearing on bail in the absence of any national emergency. Kim was therefore entitled to an individual hearing on whether he was eligible to post bail. Justice Breyer dissented separately and only in part.

In Clark v. Suarez Martinez, 543 U.S. —, 125 S.Ct. 716 (2005), the Court reaffirmed the presumption that the detention of aliens pending deportation is limited to six months. This is true whether the alien was admitted to this country or whether the alien is deemed unadmittable. Detention of an alien to be deported is limited to the amount of time reasonably necessary to remove him from this country, otherwise the government bears the burden of showing why his detention should continue. And in a third alien deportation case, Leocal v. Ashcroft, 543 U.S. —, 125 S.Ct. 377 (2004), the Court held that drunk driving is not a "crime of violence" within the meaning of the law that could subject an alien lawfully residing in this country to automatic deportation. (Leocal, who served a two year prison term, injured two people after running a red light.)

C. THE POWER TO INVESTIGATE

▶ **Insert at p. 161 following the note on the *Watkins* and *Barenblatt* cases**

Hearings by the House Government Reform Committee on March 17, 2005 into the use of steroids in professional baseball provided a vivid reminder of just how hot is the seat occupied by a witness summoned before a congressional committee. Among the witnesses subpoenaed to testify were former and current players such as Mark McGwire, Jose Canseco, Rafael Palmeiro, and Curt Schilling. Among other things, they were asked what they knew about the use of performance-enhancing drugs in the sport. One of the things committee members had in mind was whether McGwire had been using steroids in 1998 when he hit a record 70 home runs and shelved the existing single-season home-run record of 61 set by Roger Maris in 1961. Asked whether the use of steroids was cheating, McGwire replied, "That's not for me to say." In response to a couple of other questions about the use of steroids in professional baseball, he answered, "I'm retired." When Rep. Elijah Cummings (D-Md.) inquired, "Are you taking the Fifth?" McGwire replied: "I'm not here to talk about the past. I'm here to be positive about this subject." After "chok[ing] up when he said he hoped the hearings could prevent other families from suffering," he continued: "Asking me, or any other player, to answer questions about who took steroids in front of television cameras will not solve this problem. If a player answers no, he simply will not be believed. If he answers yes, he risks public scorn and endless government investigations." New York Times, Mar. 18, 2005, pp. A1, A19. Undoubtedly, both Watkins and Barenblatt would have agreed.

In a second notable—and even more controversial—use of the subpoena power, the same committee actually ordered Terry Schiavo and her husband to appear at a March 28 hearing. In this instance, the subpoena power was being used tactically—to delay the court-ordered removal of the feeding tube that was keeping alive a Florida woman who been languishing in a vegetative state for some 15 years (see p. 139 of this Supplement). The U.S. Supreme Court denied the committee's application for an injunction that, in effect, would have temporarily countermanded a lower court order removing the feeding tube. Committee on Government Reform of the U.S. House of Representatives v. Schiavo, 544 U.S. —, 125 S.Ct. 1622 (2005). Congressional Quarterly Weekly Report, Mar. 21, 2005, pp. 704-706.

CHAPTER 4

EXECUTIVE POWER

B. THE SCOPE OF EXECUTIVE POWER

Theories of Executive Power

▶ **Insert at p. 199 following footnote d and at p. 200 after the first paragraph**

In two of the three "enemy combatant" cases recently before it, the Supreme Court strongly rebuffed President George W. Bush's view that he could conduct the so-called "war on terrorism" pretty much as he pleased. Fundamentally, the *Hamdi* and *Rasul* cases were about whether detainees being held indefinitely by the American military could secure judicial review of their confinement. In the *Hamdi* case that follows, and the *Rasul* case on p. 25 of this Supplement, the Court deals with habeas corpus petitions by an American citizen and by a foreign national, respectively, challenging the constitutionality of their indefinite and incommunicado detention. The Supreme Court's decision in *Hamdi* vacates the appeals court decision discussed in the footnote.

HAMDI V. RUMSFELD
Supreme Court of the United States, 2004
542 U.S. 507, 124 S.Ct. 2633, 159 L.Ed.2d 578

BACKGROUND & FACTS After Congress passed a resolution, the Authorization for Use of Military Force (AUMF), permitting the Executive to "use all necessary and appropriate force" against "nations, organizations, and persons" he determined had "planned, authorized, committed, or aided" the September 11, 2001 terrorist attacks on the United States, President George W. Bush ordered American armed forces to subdue al Quaeda and to uproot the supporting Taliban regime in Afghanistan. Yasser Hamdi, an American citizen classified by authorities as an "enemy combatant" for taking up arms with the Taliban, was captured in Afghanistan and thereafter detailed in a naval brig in Charleston, South Carolina. Hamdi's father filed a petition for habeas corpus asserting that his son went to Afghanistan to do "relief work" and that he was being held in violation of due process as guaranteed by the Fifth and Fourteenth Amendments. A federal district court agreed, but this judgment was subsequently overturned by a federal appeals court. The appeals panel held that the resolution passed by Congress provided authorization for Hamdi's detention and, since it was undisputed that he had been captured in an active combat zone carrying an assault rifle, a hearing allowing Hamdi to present his side of the story and rebut the government's was neither necessary nor proper. The Supreme Court then granted Hamdi's petition for certiorari.

Justice O'CONNOR announced the judgment of the Court and delivered an opinion, in which THE CHIEF JUSTICE [REHNQUIST], Justice KENNEDY, and Justice BREYER join.

* * * We hold that although Congress authorized the detention of combatants in the narrow circumstances alleged here, due process demands that a citizen held in the United States as an enemy combatant be given a meaningful opportunity to contest the factual basis for that detention before a neutral decisionmaker.

* * *

[T]he "enemy combatant" * * * [the government] is seeking to detain is an individual who, it alleges, was "'part of or supporting forces hostile to the United States or coalition partners'" in Afghanistan and who "'engaged in an armed conflict against the United States'" there. * * *

The Government maintains that no explicit congressional authorization is required, because the Executive possesses plenary authority to detain pursuant to Article II of the Constitution. We do not reach the question whether Article II provides such authority, however, because we agree with the Government's alternative position, that Congress has in fact authorized Hamdi's detention, through the AUMF.

* * * [Hamdi argues] that his detention is forbidden by [The Non-Detention Act,] 18 U.S.C. § 4001(a) [see Text, pp. 207-208] * * * [which] states that "[n]o citizen shall be imprisoned or otherwise detained by the United States except pursuant to an Act of Congress." * * *

* * *

The capture and detention of lawful combatants and the capture, detention, and trial of unlawful combatants, by "universal agreement and practice," are "important incident[s] of war." Ex parte Quirin, 317 U.S., at 28, 63 S.Ct., at 11 (1942). The purpose of detention is to prevent captured individuals from returning to the field of battle and taking up arms once again. * * *

There is no bar to this Nation's holding one of its own citizens as an enemy combatant. In *Quirin,* one of the detainees, Haupt, alleged that he was a naturalized United States citizen. * * * We held that "[c]itizens who associate themselves with the military arm of the enemy government, and with its aid, guidance and direction enter this country bent on hostile acts, are enemy belligerents within the meaning of ... the law of war." * * * A citizen, no less than an alien, can be "part of or supporting forces hostile to the United States or coalition partners" and "engaged in an armed conflict against the United States"[;] * * * such a citizen, if released, would pose the same threat of returning to the front during the ongoing conflict.

[I]t is of no moment that the AUMF does not use specific language of detention. Because detention to prevent a combatant's return to the battlefield is a fundamental incident of waging war, in permitting the use of "necessary and appropriate force," Congress has clearly and unmistakably authorized detention in the narrow circumstances considered here.

Hamdi objects, nevertheless, that Congress has not authorized the *indefinite* detention to which he is now subject. * * *

It is a clearly established principle of the law of war that detention may last no longer than active hostilities. * * *

* * * [I]ndefinite detention for the purpose of interrogation is not authorized. * * * Active combat operations against Taliban fighters apparently are ongoing in Afghanistan. The United States may detain, for the duration of these hostilities, individuals legitimately determined to be Taliban combatants who "engaged in an armed conflict against the United States." If the record establishes that United States troops are still involved in active combat in Afghanistan, those detentions are part of the exercise of "necessary and appropriate force," and therefore are authorized by the AUMF.

Ex parte Milligan, 71 U.S. (4 Wall.) 2, 125, 18 L.Ed. 281 (1866), does not undermine our holding about the Government's authority to seize enemy combatants * * *. Milligan was not a prisoner of war, but a resident of Indiana arrested while at home there. * * * That fact was central to its conclusion. Had Milligan been captured while he was assisting Confederate soldiers by carrying a rifle against Union troops on a Confederate battlefield, the holding of the Court might well have been different. The Court's repeated explanations that Milligan was not a prisoner of war suggest that had these different circumstances been present he could have been detained under military authority for the duration of the conflict, whether or not he was a citizen.

* * *

Even in cases in which the detention of enemy combatants is legally authorized, there remains the question of what process is constitutionally due to a citizen who disputes his enemy-combatant status. * * *

All [of the parties] agree that, absent suspension, the writ of habeas corpus remains available to every individual detained within the United States. U.S. Const., Art. I, § 9, cl. 2. * * *. Only in the rarest of circumstances has Congress seen fit to suspend the writ. * * * At all other times, it has remained a critical check on the Executive, ensuring that it does not detain individuals except in accordance with law. * * * All agree suspension of the writ has not occurred here. Thus, it is undisputed that Hamdi was properly before an Article III court to challenge his detention under 28 U.S.C.A. § 2241. * * *

* * *

* * * Hamdi * * * argues * * * that due process demands that he receive a hearing in which he may challenge the [government's] Declaration [that he is an enemy combatant] and adduce his own counter evidence. The District Court, agreeing with Hamdi, apparently believed that the appropriate process would approach the process that accompanies a criminal trial. It therefore disapproved of the hearsay nature of the [government's] Declaration and anticipated quite extensive discovery of various military affairs. Anything less, it concluded, would not be "meaningful judicial review." * * *

* * * The ordinary mechanism that we use for balancing such serious competing interests, and for determining the procedures that are

necessary to ensure that a citizen is not "deprived of life, liberty, or property, without due process of law," * * * is the test that we articulated in Mathews v. Eldridge, 424 U.S. 319, 96 S.Ct. 893 (1976). * * * *Mathews* dictates that the process due in any given instance is determined by weighing "the private interest that will be affected by the official action" against the Government's asserted interest * * * and the burdens the Government would face in providing greater process. * * *

* * *

[T]he risk of erroneous deprivation of a citizen's liberty in the absence of sufficient process here is very real. * * * Moreover, as critical as the Government's interest may be in detaining those who actually pose an immediate threat to the national security of the United States during ongoing international conflict, history and common sense teach us that an unchecked system of detention carries the potential to become a means for oppression and abuse of others who do not present that sort of threat. * * * Because we live in a society in which "[m]ere public intolerance or animosity cannot constitutionally justify the deprivation of a person's physical liberty," O'Connor v. Donaldson, 422 U.S. 563, 575, 95 S.Ct. 2486 (1975), * * * [w]e reaffirm today the fundamental nature of a citizen's right to be free from involuntary confinement by his own government without due process of law, and we weigh the opposing governmental interests against the curtailment of liberty that such confinement entails.

On the other side of the scale are the weighty and sensitive governmental interests in ensuring that those who have in fact fought with the enemy during a war do not return to battle against the United States. * * * Without doubt, our Constitution recognizes that core strategic matters of warmaking belong in the hands of those who are best positioned and most politically accountable for making them. * * *

The Government also argues at some length that its interests in reducing the process available to alleged enemy combatants are heightened by the practical difficulties that would accompany a system of trial-like process. In its view, military officers who are engaged in the serious work of waging battle would be unnecessarily and dangerously distracted by litigation half a world away, and discovery into military operations would both intrude on the sensitive secrets of national defense and result in a futile search for evidence buried under the rubble of war. * * *

* * *

We * * * hold that a citizen-detainee seeking to challenge his classification as an enemy combatant must receive notice of the factual basis for his classification, and a fair opportunity to rebut the Government's factual assertions before a neutral decisionmaker. * * *

At the same time, the exigencies of the circumstances may demand that, aside from these core elements, enemy combatant proceedings may be tailored to alleviate their uncommon potential to burden the Executive at a time of ongoing military conflict. Hearsay, for example, may need to be accepted as the most reliable available evidence from the Government in such a proceeding. Likewise, the Constitution would not be offended by a presumption in favor of the Government's evidence, so long as that presumption remained a rebuttable one and fair opportunity for rebuttal were provided. Thus, once the Government puts forth credible evidence that the habeas petitioner meets the enemy-combatant criteria, the onus could shift to the petitioner to rebut that evidence with more persuasive evidence that he falls outside the criteria. A burden-shifting scheme of this sort would meet the goal of ensuring that the errant tourist, embedded journalist, or local aid worker has a chance to prove military error while giving due regard to the Executive once it has put forth meaningful support for its conclusion that the detainee is in fact an enemy combatant. * * *

We think it unlikely that this basic process will have the dire impact on the central functions of warmaking that the Government forecasts. The parties agree that initial captures on the battlefield need not receive the process we have discussed here; that process is due only when the determination is made to *continue* to hold those who have been seized. The Government has made clear in its briefing that documentation regarding battlefield detainees already is kept in the ordinary course of military affairs. * * * Any factfinding imposition created by requiring a knowledgeable affiant to summarize these records to an independent tribunal is a minimal one. * * *

In sum, while the full protections that accompany challenges to [criminal] detentions * * * may prove unworkable and inappropriate in the enemy-combatant setting, the threats to military operations posed by a basic system of independent review are not so weighty as to trump a citizen's core rights to challenge meaningfully the Government's case and to be heard by an impartial adjudicator.

* * *

* * * We have long since made clear that a state of war is not a blank check for the President when it comes to the rights of the Nation's citizens. * * * [W]hile we do not question that our due process assessment must pay keen attention to the particular burdens faced by the Executive in the context of military action, it would turn our system of checks and balances on its head to suggest that a citizen could not make his way to court with a challenge to the factual basis for his detention by his government, simply because the Executive opposes making available such a challenge. Absent suspension of the writ by Congress, a citizen detained as an enemy combatant is entitled to this process.

Because we conclude that due process demands some system for a citizen detainee to refute his classification, * * * [a]ny process in which the Executive's factual assertions go wholly unchallenged or are simply presumed correct without any opportunity for the alleged combatant to demonstrate otherwise falls constitutionally short. * * *

* * * An interrogation by one's captor, however effective an intelligence-gathering tool, hardly constitutes a constitutionally adequate factfinding before a neutral decisionmaker. * * * Plainly, the "process" Hamdi has received is not that to which he is entitled under the Due Process Clause.

There remains the possibility that the standards we have articulated could be met by an appropriately authorized and properly constituted military tribunal. * * * [M]ilitary regulations already provide for such process in related instances, dictating that tribunals be made available to determine the status of enemy detainees who assert prisoner-of-war status under the Geneva Convention. * * * In the absence of such process, however, a court that receives a petition for a writ of habeas corpus from an alleged enemy combatant must itself ensure that the minimum requirements of due process are achieved. * * * [A] habeas court in a case such as this may accept affidavit evidence like that contained in the [government's] Declaration, so long as it also permits the alleged combatant to present his own factual case to rebut the Government's return. We anticipate that * * * courts * * * will pay proper heed both to the matters of national security that might arise in an individual case and to the constitutional limitations safeguarding essential liberties that remain vibrant even in times of security concerns.

* * * Since our grant of certiorari in this case, Hamdi has been appointed counsel, with whom he has met for consultation purposes on several occasions, and with whom he is now being granted unmonitored meetings. He unquestionably has the right to access to counsel in connection with the proceedings on remand. * * *

The judgment of the United States Court of Appeals for the Fourth Circuit is vacated, and the case is remanded for further proceedings.

It is so ordered.

Justice SOUTER, with whom Justice GINSBURG joins, concurring in part, dissenting in part, and concurring in the judgment.

* * *

* * * The Government has failed to demonstrate that the Force Resolution authorizes the detention complained of here even on the facts the Government claims. If the Government raises nothing further than the record now shows, the Non-Detention Act entitles Hamdi to be released.

* * *

The threshold issue is how broadly or narrowly to read the Non-Detention Act, the tone of which is severe: "No citizen shall be imprisoned or otherwise detained by the United States except pursuant to an Act of Congress." Should the severity of the Act be relieved when the Government's stated factual justification for incommunicado detention is a war on terrorism, so that the Government may be said to act "pursuant" to congressional terms that fall short of explicit authority to imprison individuals? * * * [Generally,] the answer has to be no. * * *

[T]he circumstances in which the Act was adopted point the way to this interpretation. The provision superseded a cold-war statute, the Emergency Detention Act of 1950 * * * which had authorized the Attorney General, in time of emergency, to detain anyone reasonably thought likely to engage in espionage or sabotage. That statute was repealed in 1971 out of fear that it could authorize a repetition of the World War II internment of citizens of Japanese ancestry; Congress meant to preclude another episode like the one described in Korematsu v. United States, 323 U.S. 214, 65 S.Ct. 193 (1944). * * * While Congress might simply have struck the 1950 statute, in considering the repealer the point was made that the existing statute provided some express procedural protection, without which the Executive would seem to be subject to no statutory limits protecting individual liberty. * * * It was in these circumstances that a proposed limit on Executive action was expanded to the inclusive scope of § 4001(a) as enacted.

The fact that Congress intended to guard against a repetition of the World War II internments when it repealed the 1950 statute and gave us § 4001(a) provides a powerful reason to think that § 4001(a) was meant to require clear congressional authorization before any citizen can be placed in a cell. * * *

* * *

[Moreover,] [i]n a government of separated powers, deciding finally on what is a reasonable degree of guaranteed liberty whether in peace or war (or some condition in between) is not well entrusted to the Executive Branch of Government, whose particular responsibility is to maintain security. [T]he branch of the Government asked to counter a serious threat is not the branch on which to rest the Nation's entire reliance in striking the balance between the will to win and the cost in liberty on the way to victory; the responsibility for security will naturally amplify the claim that security legitimately raises. A reasonable balance is more likely to be reached on the judgment of a different branch * * *. Hence the need for an assessment by Congress before citizens are subject to lockup, and likewise the need for a clearly expressed congressional resolution of the competing claims.

* * *

Justice SCALIA, with whom Justice STEVENS joins, dissenting.

* * *

Where the Government accuses a citizen of waging war against it, our constitutional tradition has been to prosecute him in federal court for treason or some other crime. Where the exigencies of war prevent that, the Constitution's Suspension Clause, Art. I, § 9, cl. 2, allows Congress to relax the usual protections temporarily. Absent suspension [of habeas corpus], however, the Executive's assertion of military exigency has not been thought sufficient to permit detention without charge. No one contends that the congressional Authorization for Use of Military Force, on which the Government relies to justify its actions here, is an implementation of the Suspension Clause. Accordingly, I would reverse the decision below.

* * *

There are times when military exigency renders resort to the traditional criminal process impracticable. English law accommodated such exigencies by allowing legislative suspension of the writ of habeas corpus for brief periods. * * * Where the Executive has not pursued the usual course of charge, committal, and conviction, it has historically secured the Legislature's explicit approval of a suspension. * * *

Our Federal Constitution contains a provision explicitly permitting suspension, but limiting the situations in which it may be invoked: * * * "when in Cases of Rebellion or Invasion the public Safety may require it." Art. I, § 9, cl. 2. Although this provision does not state that suspension must be effected by, or authorized by, a legislative act, it has been so understood, consistent with English practice and the Clause's placement in Article I. * * *

* * *

The proposition that the Executive lacks indefinite wartime detention authority over citizens is consistent with the Founders' general mistrust of military power permanently at the Executive's disposal. * * * Congress's authority "[t]o raise and support Armies" was hedged with the proviso that "no Appropriation of Money to that Use shall be for a longer Term than two Years." U.S. Const., Art. 1, § 8, cl. 12. Except for the actual command of military forces, all authorization for their maintenance and all explicit authorization for their use is placed in the control of Congress under Article I, rather than the President under Article II. * * * A view of the Constitution that gives the Executive authority to use military force rather than the force of law against citizens on American soil flies in the face of the mistrust that engendered these provisions.

* * *

Several limitations give my views in this matter a relatively narrow compass. They apply only to citizens, accused of being enemy combatants, who are detained within the territorial jurisdiction of a federal court. This is not likely to be a numerous group; currently we know of only two, Hamdi and Jose Padilla. Where the citizen is captured outside and held outside the United States, the constitutional requirements may be different. * * * Moreover, even within the United States, the accused citizen-enemy combatant may lawfully be detained once prosecution is in progress or in contemplation. * * *

* * *

Many think it not only inevitable but entirely proper that liberty give way to security in times of national crisis—that, at the extremes of military exigency, *inter arma silent leges.* Whatever the general merits of the view that war silences law or modulates its voice, that view has no place in the interpretation and application of a Constitution designed precisely to confront war and, in a manner that accords with democratic principles, to accommodate it. Because the Court has proceeded to meet the current emergency in a manner the Constitution does not envision, I respectfully dissent.

Justice THOMAS, dissenting.

The Executive Branch, acting pursuant to the powers vested in the President by the Constitution and with explicit congressional approval, has determined that Yaser Hamdi is an enemy combatant and should be detained. This detention falls squarely within the Federal Government's war powers, and we lack the expertise and capacity to second-guess that decision. As such, petitioners' habeas challenge should fail, and there is no reason to remand the case. * * * Arguably, Congress could provide for additional procedural protections, but until it does, we have no right to insist upon them. * * *

* * *

The Founders intended that the President have primary responsibility—along with the necessary power—to protect the national security and to conduct the Nation's foreign relations. They did so principally because the structural advantages of a unitary Executive are essential in these domains. "Energy in the executive is a leading character in the definition of good government. It is essential to the protection of the community against foreign attacks." The Federalist No. 70, p. 471 (A. Hamilton). The principle "ingredien[t]" for "energy in the executive" is "unity." * * * This is because "[d]ecision, activity, secrecy, and dispatch will generally characterise the proceedings of one man, in a much more eminent degree, than the proceedings of any greater number." * * *

These structural advantages are most important in the national-security and foreign-affairs contexts. * * *

This Court has long recognized these features and has accordingly held that the President has *constitutional* authority to protect the national security and that this authority carries with it broad discretion. * * *

Congress, to be sure, has a substantial and essential role in both foreign affairs and national security. But it is crucial to recognize that *judicial* interference in these domains destroys the purpose of vesting primary responsibility in a unitary Executive. * * * First, with respect to certain decisions relating to national security and foreign affairs, the courts simply lack the relevant information and expertise to second-guess determinations made by the President based on information properly withheld. Second, even if the courts could compel the Executive to produce the necessary information, such decisions are simply not amenable to judicial determination because "[t]hey are delicate, complex, and involve large elements of prophecy." Third, the Court * * * elsewhere has correctly recognized the primacy of the political branches in the foreign-affairs and national-security contexts.

[I]n these domains, the fact that Congress has provided the President with broad authorities does not imply—and the Judicial Branch should not infer—that Congress intended to deprive him of particular powers not specifically enumerated. * * *

Finally, * * * where "the President acts pursuant to an express or implied authorization from Congress, he exercises not only his powers but also those delegated by Congress[, and i]n such a case the executive action 'would be supported by the strongest of presumptions and the widest latitude of judicial interpretation, and the burden of persuasion would rest heavily upon any who might attack it.'" Dames & Moore [v. Regan,] 453 U.S., at 668, 101 S.Ct. 2972 (1981) (quoting *Youngstown,* * * * Jackson, J., concurring). * * *

* * *

I * * * cannot agree with Justice SCALIA's conclusion that the Government must choose between using standard criminal processes and suspending the writ. * * *

Accordingly, I conclude that the Government's detention of Hamdi as an enemy combatant does not violate the Constitution. By detaining Hamdi, the President, in the prosecution of a war and authorized by Congress, has acted well within his authority. Hamdi thereby received all the process to which he was due under the circumstances. I therefore believe that this is no occasion to balance the competing interests * * *.

* * *

[Hamdi was subsequently released from custody and was to be flown back to Saudi

Arabia. Although born in Louisiana in 1980, he grew up in Saudi Arabia where his father worked for an oil company. New York Times, September 23, 2004, pp. A1, A19. The agreement between the U.S. and Saudi Arabia, under which he left U.S. custody, called for him to give up his American citizenship.]

RASUL V. BUSH
Supreme Court of the United States, 2004
542 U.S. 466, 124 S.Ct. 2686, 159 L.Ed.2d 548

BACKGROUND & FACTS After Congress passed the resolution authorizing the use of force against nations, organizations, and persons implicated in the September 11, 2001 terrorist attacks on the United States, President George W. Bush sent American troops into Afghanistan to conduct a military campaign against Al Quaeda and the Taliban regime supporting it. Two Australians and 12 Kuwaitis were captured during the hostilities and were subsequently held in military custody at the Guantanamo Naval Base leased indefinitely from Cuba by the United States. Rasul and the others filed suit against the President under the federal habeas corpus statute, 28 U.S.C.A. § 2241, challenging the lawfulness of their detention on grounds they had never engaged in terrorist acts. They also argued that they had not been charged with any offense, had not been permitted to see counsel, and had not been allowed access to any court or other tribunal. A federal district court dismissed the suits on grounds it did not have jurisdiction and cited the Supreme Court's 1950 decision in *Johnson v. Eisentrager*. A federal appellate court affirmed this judgment, and the detainees successfully sought certiorari from the Supreme Court.

Justice STEVENS delivered the opinion of the Court.

* * *

The question * * * before us is whether the habeas statute confers a right to judicial review of the legality of Executive detention of aliens in a territory over which the United States exercises plenary and exclusive control but not "ultimate sovereignty."

* * *

* * * In * * * [Johnson v.] Eisentrager, [339 U.S. 763, 70 S.Ct. 936 (1950)], we held that a Federal District Court lacked authority to issue a writ of habeas corpus to 21 German citizens who had been captured by U. S. forces in China, tried and convicted of war crimes by an American military commission headquartered in Nanking, and incarcerated in the Landsberg Prison in occupied Germany. * * * [Refusing to adopt the lower court's view that] "any person who is deprived of his liberty by officials of the United States, acting under purported authority of that Government, and who can show that his confinement is in violation of a provision of the Constitution, has a right to the writ" of habeas corpus], this Court summarized the six critical facts in the case:

"We [decline to] * * * hold that a prisoner of our military authorities is constitutionally entitled to the writ, even though he (a) is an enemy alien; (b) has never been or resided in the United States; (c) was captured outside of our territory and there held in military custody as a prisoner of war; (d) was tried and convicted by a Military Commission sitting outside the United States; (e) for offenses against laws of war committed outside the United States; (f) and is at all times imprisoned outside the United States." * * *

Petitioners in these cases differ from the *Eisentrager* detainees in important respects: They are not nationals of countries at war with the United States, and they deny that they have engaged in or plotted acts of aggression against the United States; they have never been afforded access to any tribunal, much less charged with and convicted of wrongdoing; and for more than two years they have been imprisoned in territory over which the United States exercises exclusive jurisdiction and control.

* * *

[The government also] contend[s] * * * that congressional legislation [§ 2241] is presumed not to have extraterritorial application unless such intent is clearly manifested. * * * Whatever traction the presumption against extraterritoriality might have in other contexts, it certainly has no application to the operation of the habeas statute with respect to persons detained within "the territorial jurisdiction" of the United States. * * * By the express terms of its agreements with Cuba, the United States exercises "complete jurisdiction and control" over the Guantanamo Bay Naval Base, and may continue to exercise such control permanently if it so chooses. 1903 Lease Agreement, Art. III; 1934 Treaty, Art. III. Respondents themselves concede that the habeas statute would create federal-court jurisdiction over the claims of an American citizen held at the base. * * * Considering that the statute draws no distinction between Americans and aliens held in federal custody, there is little reason to think that Congress intended the geographical coverage of the statute to vary depending on the detainee's citizenship. Aliens held at the base, no less than American citizens, are entitled to invoke the federal courts' authority under § 2241.

Application of the habeas statute to persons detained at the base is consistent with the historical reach of the writ of habeas corpus. At common law, courts exercised habeas jurisdiction over the claims of aliens detained within sovereign territory of the realm * * * and all other dominions under the sovereign's control. * * *

* * *

Whether and what further proceedings may become necessary after respondents make their response to the merits of petitioners' claims are matters that we need not address now. What is presently at stake is only whether the federal courts have jurisdiction to determine the legality of the Executive's potentially indefinite detention of individuals who claim to be wholly innocent of wrongdoing. Answering that question in the affirmative, we reverse the judgment of the Court of Appeals and remand for the District Court to consider in the first instance the merits of petitioners' claims.

It is so ordered.

Justice KENNEDY, concurring in the judgment.

* * *

The facts here are distinguishable from those in *Eisentrager* in two critical ways * * *. First, Guantanamo Bay is in every practical respect a United States territory, and it is one far removed from any hostilities. * * * [T]his lease is no ordinary lease. Its term is indefinite and at the discretion of the United States. What matters is the unchallenged and indefinite control that the United States has long exercised over Guantanamo Bay. From a practical perspective, the indefinite lease of Guantanamo Bay has produced a place that belongs to the United States, extending the "implied protection" of the United States to it. * * *

The second critical set of facts is that the detainees at Guantanamo Bay are being held indefinitely, and without benefit of any legal proceeding to determine their status. In *Eisentrager*, the prisoners were tried and convicted by a military commission of violating the laws of war and were sentenced to prison terms. Having already been subject to procedures establishing their status, they could not justify "a limited opening of our courts" to show that they were "of friendly personal disposition" and not enemy aliens. * * * Indefinite detention without trial or other proceeding presents altogether different considerations. It allows friends and foes alike to remain in detention. It suggests a weaker case of military necessity and much greater alignment with the traditional function of habeas corpus. Perhaps, where detainees are taken from a zone of hostilities, detention without proceedings or trial would be justified by military necessity for a matter of weeks; but as the period of detention stretches from months to years, the case for continued detention to meet military exigencies becomes weaker.

In light of the status of Guantanamo Bay and the indefinite pretrial detention of the detainees, I would hold that federal-court jurisdiction is permitted in these cases. This approach would avoid creating automatic statutory authority to adjudicate the claims of persons located outside the United States, and remains true to the reasoning of *Eisentrager*. For these reasons, I concur in the judgment of the Court.

Justice SCALIA, with whom THE CHIEF JUSTICE [REHNQUIST], and Justice THOMAS join, dissenting.

* * *

* * * Today's opinion * * * extends the habeas statute, for the first time, to aliens held beyond the sovereign territory of the United States and beyond the territorial jurisdiction of its courts. * * * Today, the Court springs a trap on the Executive, subjecting Guantanamo Bay to the oversight of the federal courts even though it has never before been thought to be within their jurisdiction—and thus making it a foolish place to have housed alien wartime detainees.

In abandoning * * * [Johnson v.] *Eisentrager*, the Court boldly extends the scope of the habeas statute to the four corners of the earth. * * *

The consequence of this holding, as applied to aliens outside the country, is breathtaking. It permits an alien captured in a foreign theater of active combat to bring a §

2241 petition against the Secretary of Defense. Over the course of the last century, the United States has held millions of alien prisoners abroad. * * * A great many of these prisoners would no doubt have complained about the circumstances of their capture and the terms of their confinement. The military is currently detaining over 600 prisoners at Guantanamo Bay alone; each detainee undoubtedly has complaints—real or contrived—about those terms and circumstances. * * * From this point forward, federal courts will entertain petitions from these prisoners, and others like them around the world, challenging actions and events far away, and forcing the courts to oversee one aspect of the Executive's conduct of a foreign war.

* * *

* * * The Commander in Chief and his subordinates had every reason to expect that the internment of combatants at Guantanamo Bay would not have the consequence of bringing the cumbersome machinery of our domestic courts into military affairs. Congress is in session. If it wished to change federal judges' habeas jurisdiction from what this Court had previously held that to be, it could have done so. * * *

The Court side-stepped decision in a third habeas case, Rumsfeld v. Padilla, 542 U.S. 426, 124 S.Ct. 2711 (2004), ruling that the detainee improperly named Secretary of Defense Donald Rumsfeld as the defendant. The *Padilla* case raises the question whether an American citizen, arrested on American soil, can be detained indefinitely. Padilla was told to refile his suit naming as defendant the officer in charge of the Navy brig in Charleston, South Carolina, where he is being held. He was alleged to have been involved in a plot to build and detonate a "dirty bomb" that would release radiation within the United States. Dissenting and speaking also for Justices Souter, Ginsburg, and Breyer, Justice Stevens rejected the majority's "slavish" adherence to formalities and would have addressed the legality of Padilla's continued detention, which "raises questions of profound importance to the Nation." He continued: "Executive detention of subversive citizens, like detention of enemy soldiers to keep them off the battlefield, may sometimes be justified to prevent persons from launching or becoming missiles of destruction. It may not, however, be justified by the naked interest in using unlawful procedures to extract information. Incommunicado detention for months on end is such a procedure."

On remand, in Padilla v. Hanft, 2005 WL 465691 (D.S.C. 2005), a federal district court ordered Padilla's release. The court ruled that "[t]he Non-Detention Act [see Text, pp. 207-208] expressly forbids the president from holding [Padilla] as an enemy combatant, and * * * the AUFM does not authorize such detention * * *." The court also rejected the argument that the president's constitutional authority as Commander-in-Chief provided justification. The judge—himself a Bush appointee—wrote that, in sum, "[T]he president has no power, neither express nor implied, neither constitutional nor statutory, to hold petitioner as an enemy combatant." To do otherwise, he added, would "be to engage in judicial activism,"—an ironic touch, since the phrase often is used by the Bush Administration to criticize judicial rulings it disagrees with. The case is scheduled to be argued to the U.S. Court of Appeals for the Fourth Circuit in July 2005. The Supreme Court denied a petition for cert. before that judgment is rendered, 545 U.S. —, 125 S.Ct. 2906 (2005).

The disposition of the detainees' cases by military commissions took a hit, too, and from perhaps a surprising source—Britain, the staunchest coalition member. Under pressure from Prime Minister Tony Blair, the Bush Administration turned over five British citizens being detained at Guantanamo (the remaining six were turned over at a later date). They were quickly freed after British magistrates determined there was no evidence to hold them. British Attorney General, Lord Goldsmith, reportedly "fed up" with the continued detention of other British citizens, made it clear by June 2004 that there would be "no compromise" on the notion of British citizens being tried by U.S. military commissions because the tribunals would not guarantee a fair trial. See http://news.bbc.co.uk/2/hi/uk_news/politics/3841731.stm; and http://news.bbc.co.uk/2/hi/uk_news/politics/3837823.stm.

NOTE—ANTI-TERRORISM LEGISLATION IN BRITAIN

In the wake of the September 11, 2001 attack on the World Trade Center and the Pentagon, the British parliament passed the Anti-Terrorism, Crime and Security Act of 2001 (ATCSA). That law enabled the British government to detain indefinitely and without trial aliens suspected of posing "a risk to national security and ha[ving] links with an international terrorist group" who cannot be deported because they faced persecution in their home countries. Foreigners suspected of terrorist activities could return voluntarily or go to any other country that would accept them. Like the detainees confined by the U.S. at Guantanamo Bay, the terrorism suspects in Britain were not allowed to know the charges against them, to see any of the evidence, or to hire their own lawyers. The British government appointed attorneys with security clearances to represent the detainees, but the lawyers could not discuss any of the evidence with the individuals they represented.

To pass the ATCSA, Britain opted out of Article 5 of the European Convention on Human Rights which guarantees the right to liberty. The European Convention also provides that member states may opt out when "war or public emergency threaten[s] the life of the nation" and if the measures adopted are "strictly required by the exigencies of the situation." Britain is the only European nation to have so acted. Prime Minister Tony Blair's government justified its action on the grounds that it faced an "unprecedented form of terrorism" and that the measures were "necessary and proportionate" to the threat. Between September 11, 2001 and December 31, 2004, there were over 700 arrests under the ATCSA and other laws for related terrorist offenses, but only 17 individuals were detained.

The Law Lords* ruled that the ATCSA was unconstitutional in a decision rendered on

---

* The Law Lords, a body of twenty-some members of the House of Lords (the upper house of Parliament) constitute Britain's Supreme Court. Usually, the Law Lords sit to hear cases in panels of five, drawn at random (just as panels of three judges are drawn to hear cases in the U.S. Courts of Appeals). The Lords'

December 16, 2004 by a vote of 8-1. Voting with the majority, Lord Nicholls concluded, "Indefinite imprisonment without charge or trial is anathema in any country which observes the rule of law" because "[i]t deprives the detained person of the protection a criminal trial is intended to afford." Another member of the panel held that the statute unlawfully discriminated on the basis of nationality and immigration status. A third, Lord Hoffmann, wrote, "The real threat to the life of the nation, in the sense of a people living in accordance with its traditional laws and political values, comes not from terrorism but from laws such as these." At issue was the detention of 11 north African Muslims, evidence of whose involvement in terrorism the government argued was too sketchy and too sensitive to be revealed in court. The Lords' ruling roughly parallels the U.S. Supreme Court decisions in *Hamdi* and *Rasul*. The detainees were not immediately released so as to give the government time to respond. New York Times, December 17, 2004, pp. A1,A13.

But how to respond? The government could either acquiesce in the release of those being unlawfully detained or modify the law to conform with the European Convention. Prime Minister Blair's government reacted by introducing the Prevention of Terrorism bill. Among other things, the legislation provides that suspects could be banned from meeting with certain people, limited in their travel, restricted in their access to telephones and the Internet, monitored by electronic tagging, compelled to surrender their passport, required to produce papers and give information, and placed under house arrest. Blair's government introduced the new legislation just as the detainees were scheduled to be released from London's Belmarsh Prison, known to civil rights supporters as Britain's Guantanamo Bay.

Passing the new legislation proved unusually tricky, despite the fact that Blair's Labour Party enjoyed a 157-vote majority in the House of Commons. The vigorous opposition of both the Conservative Party and the Liberal Democrats, plus votes from the smaller nationalist parties, and defections and abstentions from the Labour side, combined to reduce the margin of victory in the Commons to a scant 14 votes. Nor was that the end of it. When the bill reached the unelected House of Lords, it was substantially amended over the opposition of Blair's government which lacked a majority in the upper house. Among the changes adopted by the Lords were provisions requiring all such control orders to be approved by a judge, not just on the say-so of the Home Secretary (the member of the Cabinet responsible for public safety); raising the standard of proof the government would have to meet from reasonable suspicion to the greater weight of the evidence (before any control orders could be imposed on an individual); prohibiting the use of any evidence obtained by torture; forbidding the imposition of any controls other than those specified in the bill; and imposing a one-year "sunset clause" that would end the law unless Parliament voted to renew it. The Lords adopted all of these by substantial majorities, none by less than 60 votes and some by double that.

The House of Commons subsequently voted down these amendments and returned the bill to the Lords, which again voted to adopt them. Along the way, the government made concessions,

---

decision in A. v. Secretary of State for the Home Department, 2004 WL 2810935 (HL), was remarkable not only for its outcome but also because it was only the second time since the end of World War II that a panel of nine Lords sat to hear a case. The reason was its constitutional importance.

most notably to require judicial approval of all such control orders, but the Prime Minister refused to accede to the "sunset clause." In its third longest continuous sitting on record, 30 hours, the Lords finally secured the Prime Minister's promise that Parliament would revisit the legislation within a year. The bill finally passed, but there was no formal adoption of a "sunset clause" lest, in Prime Minister Blair's view, it send a signal to terrorists that the government was weakened in its resolve to deal with threats. Although the absence of an expiration date was literally true, Michael Howard, the Leader of the Opposition, shot back that the Prime Minister's promise amounted to "a sunset clause in all but name." The parliamentary tug-of-war, which saw the bill make four complete roundtrips between the Commons and the Lords within 48 hours, was undoubtedly fueled by the fact that the Iraq war is a whole lot less popular in Britain than in the United States. The law made the 11 detainees subject to control orders just as they were to leave prison.

After the decisions in *Hamdi* and *Rasul*, the Bush Administration quickly announced that the determination of whether each of the more than 550 Guantanamo inmates was an "enemy combatant" would be made by panels of three commissioned military officers—Combatant Status Review Tribunals (CSRT)—not by a federal judge. Approximately a week and a half after the Supreme Court's decision in *Rasul*, Deputy Secretary of Defense Paul Wolfowitz issued the order creating CSRTs to review the classification of each detainee. As the first formal document to define the term, Wolfowitz's order said "enemy combatant" meant "an individual who was part of or supporting Taliban or al Qaeda forces, or associated forces that are engaged in hostilities against the United States or its coalition partners." The term also included "any person who has committed a belligerent act or has directly supported hostilities in aid of enemy forces." Noting somewhat ambiguously that those detained had been "previously determined" to be enemy combatants, the order set forth procedures by which the Guantanamo detainees could contest their status before a CSRT. In the case that follows, Guantanamo detainees objected to the operation of the CSRTs as violating both the Fifth Amendment's guarantee of due process, other constitutional and statutory provisions, and the Geneva Convention.

IN RE GUANTANAMO DETAINEE CASES
United States District Court, District of Columbia, 2005
355 F.Supp.2d 443

BACKGROUND & FACTS   Under the Defense Department order creating the Combatant Status Review Tribunal (CSRT) to make findings as to whether individuals already held at the Guantanamo Bay naval base were being lawfully detained as "enemy combatants," detainees for the first time had the right to hear the factual bases for their detention, but only if such facts were not classified. Moreover, they had the right to testify about why they should not be considered enemy combatants and to present additional information in their favor, at least to the extent that the tribunal regarded such evidence as relevant and "reasonably available."

An individual being detained had no right to counsel but did have assigned to him a military officer acting as a "Personal Representative" to assist the detainee in understanding the proceedings and in presenting his case. Formal rules of evidence did not apply, and the government's classification of the individual as an "enemy combatant" was presumed to be accurate until proven otherwise. Although the CSRT was free to consider classified evidence supporting the classification of the detainee as an enemy combatant, the individual was not entitled to have access to, or to know about, that classified evidence. Defense Department procedures provided for review of the CSRT's determination but, if such a determination was affirmed, the government argued the enemy combatant could be held in custody until either the President declared the war on terrorism to be over or the detainee was no longer a threat to national security. If the tribunal determined the detainee was not an enemy combatant, the Defense Department was obligated to contact the Secretary of State for transfer of the detainee to his country of citizenship or to another country in accordance with U.S. foreign policy.

In addition to the cases remanded by the Supreme Court in *Rasul*, other detainees filed petitions of habeas corpus arguing that the procedures set out in the Defense Department orders violated the Fifth (due process), Sixth (counsel), and Eighth (cruel and unusual punishment) Amendments, the War Powers Clause (Art. I, § 8, cl. 11), the Suspension Clause (Art. I, § 9, cl. 2), the Alien Tort Claims Act, the Administrative Procedure Act, and the Geneva Convention, among other things. The district court's opinion, which follows, focused on the detainees' claims that they had been denied due process under the Fifth Amendment and on violations of the Geneva Convention and dismissed the others.

GREEN, District Judge.

* * *

* * * [B]y definition, constitutional limitations often, if not always, burden the abilities of government officials to serve their constituencies. Although this nation unquestionably must take strong action under the leadership of the Commander in Chief to protect itself against enormous and unprecedented threats, that necessity cannot negate the existence of the most basic fundamental rights for which the people of this country have fought and died for well over two hundred years. * * *

[T]here can be no question that the Fifth Amendment right asserted by the Guantanamo detainees in this litigation—the right not to be deprived of liberty without due process of law—is one of the most fundamental rights recognized by the U.S. Constitution. In light of the Supreme Court's decision in *Rasul* [v. *Bush*, see p. 25 of this Supplement], it is clear that Guantanamo Bay must be considered the equivalent of a U.S. territory in which fundamental constitutional rights apply. * * * [R]espondents' contention that the Guantanamo detainees have no constitutional rights is rejected, and the Court recognizes the detainees' rights under the Due Process Clause of the Fifth Amendment.

* * *

* * * Due process is an inherently flexible concept, and the specific process due in a particular circumstance depends upon the context in which the right is asserted. * * * Resolution of a due process challenge requires the consideration and weighing of three factors: the private interest of the person asserting the lack of due process; the risk of erroneous deprivation of that interest through use of existing procedures and the probable value of additional or substitute procedural safeguards; and the competing interests of the government, including the financial, administrative, and other burdens that would be incurred were additional safeguards to be provided. Mathews v. Eldridge, 424 U.S. 319, 335, 96 S.Ct. 893, 903 (1976).

The Supreme Court applied a *Mathews v. Eldridge* analysis in *Hamdi v. Rumsfeld*, [see p. 16 of this Supplement], a decision issued the same day as *Rasul* which considered an American citizen's due process challenge to the U.S. military's designation of him as an "enemy combatant." Although none of the detainees in the cases before this Court is an American citizen, the facts under *Hamdi* are otherwise identical in all material respects to those in *Rasul*. Accordingly, *Hamdi* forms both the starting point and core of this Court's consideration of what process is due to the Guantanamo detainees in these cases.

* * *

As was the case in *Hamdi*, the potential length of incarceration is highly relevant to the weighing of the individual interests at stake here. The government asserts the right to detain an "enemy combatant" until the war on terrorism has concluded or until the Executive, in its sole discretion, has determined that the individual no longer poses a threat to national security. The government, however, has been unable to inform the Court how long it believes the war on terrorism will last. * * * Indeed, the government cannot even articulate at this moment how it will determine when the war on terrorism has ended. * * * At a minimum, the government has conceded that the war could last several generations, thereby making it possible, if not likely, that "enemy combatants" will be subject to terms of life imprisonment at Guantanamo Bay. * * * Short of the death penalty, life imprisonment is the ultimate deprivation of liberty, and the uncertainty of whether the war on terror—and thus the period of incarceration—will last a lifetime may be even worse than if the detainees had been tried, convicted, and definitively sentenced to a fixed term.

It must be added that the liberty interests of the detainees cannot be minimized for purposes of applying the *Mathews v. Eldridge* balancing test by the government's allegations that they are in fact terrorists or are affiliated with terrorist organizations. The purpose of imposing a due process requirement is to prevent mistaken characterizations and erroneous detentions, and the government is not entitled to short circuit this inquiry by claiming [at the outset] that the individuals are alleged to have committed bad acts. * * *

On the other side of the *Mathews v. Eldridge* analysis is the government's significant interest in safeguarding national security. * * * . Congress itself expressly recognized this when it enacted the AUMF [Authorization for the Use of Military Force, 115 Stat. 224 (2001)] authorizing the President to use all necessary and appropriate force against those responsible for the September 11 attacks. The Supreme Court also gave significant weight to this governmental concern and responsibility in *Hamdi* * * *. Indeed, a majority of the

Court affirmed the Executive's authority to seize and detain Taliban fighters as long as the conflict in Afghanistan continues, regardless of how indefinite the length of that war may be. * * *

Given the existence of competing, highly significant interests on both sides of the equation[,] * * * the question becomes what procedures will help ensure that innocents are not indefinitely held as "enemy combatants" without imposing undue burdens on the military to ensure the security of this nation and its citizens. * * *

According to the plurality in *Hamdi*, an individual detained by the government on the ground that he is an "enemy combatant" "must receive notice of the factual basis for his classification, and a fair opportunity to rebut the Government's factual assertions before a neutral decisionmaker." * * * Noting the potential burden these requirements might cause the government at a time of ongoing military conflict, the plurality stated that it would not violate due process for the decision maker to consider hearsay as the most reliable available evidence. * * * In addition, the plurality declared it permissible to adopt a presumption in favor of "enemy combatant" status, "so long as that presumption remained a rebuttable one and fair opportunity for rebuttal were provided." * * * For that presumption to apply and for the onus to shift to the detainee, however, the plurality clarified that the government first would have to "put[ ] forth credible evidence that the [detainee] meets the enemy-combatant criteria." * * *

After setting forth these standards, the plurality suggested the "possibility" that constitutional requirements of due process could be met by an "appropriately authorized and properly constituted military tribunal" and referenced the military tribunals used to determine whether an individual is entitled to prisoner of war status under the Geneva Convention. * * * In the absence of a tribunal following constitutionally mandated procedures, however, the plurality declared that it was the District Court's obligation to provide those procedural rights to the detainee in a *habeas* action. * * * The plurality concluded by affirming that the detainee "unquestionably [had] the right to access to counsel in connection with the proceedings on remand." * * *

Hamdi was decided before the creation of the Combatant Status Review Tribunal, and the respondents contend in their motion to dismiss that were this Court to conclude that the detainees are entitled to due process under the Fifth Amendment, the CSRT proceedings would fully comply with all constitutional requirements. * * * [T]he Court[,] [however,] * * * finds that the procedures provided in the CSRT regulations fail to satisfy constitutional due process requirements in several respects.

* * *

[A]ll of the CSRT's decisions substantially relied upon classified evidence. No detainee, however, was ever permitted access to any classified information nor was any detainee permitted to have an advocate review and challenge the classified evidence on his behalf. Accordingly, the CSRT failed to provide any detainee with sufficient notice of the factual basis for which he is being detained and with a fair opportunity to rebut the government's evidence supporting the determination that he is an "enemy combatant."

The inherent lack of fairness of the CSRT's consideration of classified information not disclosed to the detainees is perhaps most vividly illustrated in the following unclassified colloquy, which * * * exemplifies the practical and severe disadvantages faced by all Guantanamo prisoners. In reading a list of allegations forming the basis for the detention of Mustafa Ait Idr, * * * the Recorder of the CSRT asserted, "While living in Bosnia, the Detainee associated with a known Al Qaida operative." In response, the following exchange occurred:

> Detainee: Give me his name.
> Tribunal President: I do not know.
> Detainee: How can I respond to this?
> Tribunal President: Did you know of anybody that was a member of Al Qaida?

* * *

> Detainee: No. This is something the interrogators told me a long while ago. I asked the interrogators to tell me who this person was. Then I could tell you if I might have known this person, but not if this person is a terrorist. Maybe I knew this person as a friend. Maybe it was a person that worked with me. Maybe it was a person that was on my team. But I do not know if this person is Bosnian, Indian or whatever. If you tell me the name, then I can respond and defend myself against this accusation.
> Tribunal President: We are asking you the questions and we need you to respond to what is on the unclassified summary.

Subsequently, after the Recorder read the allegation that the detainee was arrested because of his alleged involvement in a plan to attack the U.S. Embassy in Sarajevo, the detainee expressly asked in the following colloquy to see the evidence upon which the government's assertion relied:

> Detainee: ... The only thing I can tell you is I did not plan or even think of [attacking the Embassy]. Did you find any explosives with me? Any weapons? Did you find me in front of the embassy? Did you find me in contact with the Americans? Did I threaten anyone? I am prepared now to tell you, if you have anything or any evidence, even if it is just very little, that proves I went to the embassy and looked like that [Detainee made a gesture with his head and neck as if he were looking into a building or a window] at the embassy, then I am ready to be punished. I can just tell you that I did not plan anything. * * *

* * *

> * * * These accusations, my answer to all of them is I did not do these things. But I do not have anything to prove this. The only thing is the citizenship. I can tell you where I was and I had the papers to prove so. But to tell me I planned to bomb, I can only tell you that I did not plan.
> Tribunal President: Mustafa, does that conclude your statement?
> Detainee: That is it, but I was hoping you had evidence that you can give me. If I was in your place—and I apologize in advance for these words—but if a supervisor came to me and showed me accusations like these, I would take these accusations and I would hit him in the face with them. Sorry about that.
> [Everyone in the Tribunal room laughs.]
> Tribunal President: We had to laugh, but it is okay.
> Detainee: Why? Because these are accusations that I can't even answer. I am not able to answer them. You tell me I am from Al Qaida, but I am not an Al Qaida. I don't have any proof to give you except to ask you to catch Bin Laden and ask him if I am a part of Al Qaida. To tell me that I thought, I'll just tell you that I did not. I don't have proof regarding this. What should be done is you should give me evidence regarding these

accusations because I am not able to give you any evidence. I can just tell you no, and that is it.

* * * The laughter reflected in the transcript is understandable, and this exchange might have been truly humorous had the consequences of the detainee's "enemy combatant" status not been so terribly serious and had the detainee's criticism of the process not been so piercingly accurate.

* * *

The Court fully appreciates the strong governmental interest in not disclosing classified evidence to individuals believed to be terrorists intent on causing great harm to the United States * * * [and] this Cour[t] prohibits the disclosure of any classified information to any of the petitioners in these *habeas* cases. * * * To compensate for the resulting hardship to the petitioners and to ensure due process in the litigation of these cases, however, * * * all relevant classified information [must be disclosed] to the petitioners' counsel who have the appropriate security clearances. * * * Although counsel are not permitted to share any classified information with their clients, they at least [must] have the opportunity to examine all evidence relied upon by the government in making an "enemy combatant" status determination and to investigate and ensure the accuracy, reliability and relevance of that evidence. * * * [T]he CSRT regulations do not properly balance the detainees' need for access to material evidence considered by the tribunal against the government's interest in protecting classified information.

[I]mplementing regulations create the position of "Personal Representative" for the purpose of "assist[ing] the detainee in reviewing all relevant unclassified information, in preparing and presenting information, and in questioning witnesses at the CSRT." * * * But notwithstanding the fact that the Personal Representative may review classified information considered by the tribunal, that person is neither a lawyer nor an advocate and thus cannot be considered an effective surrogate to compensate for a detainee's inability to personally review and contest classified evidence against him. * * * Additionally, there is no confidential relationship between the detainee and the Personal Representative, and the Personal Representative is obligated to disclose to the tribunal any relevant inculpatory information he obtains from the detainee. * * * Consequently, there is inherent risk and little corresponding benefit should the detainee decide to use the services of the Personal Representative.

* * *

[Moreover,] * * * the [CRST has relied] on statements allegedly obtained through torture or otherwise alleged to have been provided by some detainees involuntarily. The Supreme Court has long held that due process prohibits the government's use of involuntary statements obtained through torture or other mistreatment. In the landmark case of Jackson v. Denno, 378 U.S. 368, 84 S.Ct. 1774 (1964), the Court gave two rationales for this rule: first, "because of the probable unreliability of confessions that are obtained in a manner deemed coercive," and second "because of the 'strongly felt attitude of our society that important human values are sacrificed where an agency of the government, in the course of securing a conviction, wrings a confession out of an accused against his will.'" * * *

* * *

Although the government has been detaining individuals as "enemy combatants" since * * * [Congress's authorization of military force] in 2001, it apparently did not formally define the term until the July 7, 2004 Order creating the CSRT. The lack of a formal definition seemed to have troubled at least the plurality of the Supreme Court in *Hamdi,* * * * [and] [t]he plurality cautioned * * * "that indefinite detention for the purpose of interrogation is not authorized" by the AUMF, and added that a congressional grant of authority to the President to use "necessary and appropriate force" might not be properly interpreted to include the authority to detain individuals for the duration of a particular conflict if that conflict does not take a form that is based on "longstanding law-of-war principles." * * *

The definition of "enemy combatant" contained in the Order creating the CSRT is significantly broader than the definition considered in *Hamdi.* According to the definition currently applied by the government, an "enemy combatant" "shall mean an individual who was part of or supporting Taliban or al Qaeda forces, or associated forces that are engaged in hostilities against the United States or its coalition partners. This *includes* any person who has committed a belligerent act or has directly supported hostilities in aid of enemy armed forces." * * * (emphasis added). Use of the word "includes" indicates that the government interprets the AUMF to permit the indefinite detention of individuals who never committed a belligerent act or who never directly supported hostilities against the U.S. or its allies. * * *

* * *

Whether the detention of each individual petitioner is authorized by the AUMF and satisfies the mandates of due process must ultimately be determined on a detainee by detainee basis. At this stage of the litigation, however, sufficient allegations have been made by at least some of the petitioners and certain evidence exists in some CSRT factual returns to warrant the denial of the respondents' motion to dismiss on the ground that the respondents have employed an overly broad definition of "enemy combatant." * * *

[The court's discussion of claims under the Geneva Convention is omitted. The district court held that the Convention amounted to a self-executing treaty (i.e., no implementing legislation by Congress was necessary), and that detainees therefore possessed certain applicable rights.]

* * *

For the reasons provided above, the Court holds that the petitioners have stated valid claims under the Fifth Amendment and that the CSRT procedures are unconstitutional for failing to comport with the requirements of due process. * * *

* * *

Two weeks before this ruling, another federal district court—also in the District of Columbia—held that the Guantanamo detainees could not receive any judicial relief because they were foreign nationals being detained abroad and, as such, had no constitutional rights. See Khalid v. Bush, 355 F.Supp.2d 311 (D.D.C. 2005). The district court also held that the President's authority under the AUMF was not confined to the capture and detention of individuals near the Afghan battlefields, that the confinement of alleged enemy combatants did not violate any federal statute or treaty with applicable rights, and that the separation of powers doctrine precluded inquiry into conditions of confinement in light of Congress's authorization to detain enemy combatants. In another case, Hamdan v. Rumsfeld, 344 F.Supp.2d 152 (D.D.C. 2004), *reversed*, 2005 WL 1653046 (D.C. Cir. 2005), a federal appeals court rejected a district court ruling that Osama bin Laden's former driver and four other foreign terror suspects were prisoners of war and therefore could only be tried by courts-martial in accordance with the Third Geneva Convention. Instead, the appeals court said that trial of war crimes by military commissions could continue because they did not violate the Constitution, international law, or military law. The military commissions were set up to try war crimes (as distinguished from the CSRTs which decide who is an "enemy combatant") and—unlike customary courts-martial—are configured to permit the introduction of some evidence and testimony out of the presence of the accused. The appeals court in *Hamdan* said that the Geneva conventions "d[id] not create judicially enforceable rights" and that the military commissions were legitimately authorized by Congress in the AUMF. So far, only Hamdan and the four other detainees (of over 500 still being held) have been charged with war crimes. New York Times, July 16, 2005, pp. A1, A9. Finally, in yet another lower court ruling, this time in a suit brought by several Yemeni detainees, a U.S. district judge blocked any attempt by the government to transfer Guantanamo detainees overseas in an attempt to put them beyond federal court jurisdiction. Abdah v. Bush, 2005 WL 589812 (D.D.C. 2005). It is unclear at this point whether further intervention by the Supreme Court will be necessary or whether the Court will simply leave it to the conservative majority on the U.S. Court of Appeals for the D.C. Circuit to sort things out.

▶ Insert at p. 200 at the end of the first paragraph

Zacarias Moussaoui, arrested as the would-be twentieth 9/11 hijacker, had requested that he be allowed to call in his defense individuals being held by the federal government on suspicion of terrorist activities. The government refused to make them available, citing a risk to national security. A federal appellate court subsequently upheld Moussaoui's Sixth Amendment right to confront and cross-examine witnesses but modified the lower court's ruling. With regard to statements made by alleged terrorists held in detention, the appeals panel required the government "to produce an adequate substitute for * * * [any] classified information in the form of a series of statements derived from summaries of reports accurately reflecting the witnesses' statements" and the jury would "be made aware of * * * the substitutions." See United States v. Moussaoui, 365 F.3d 292 (4th Cir. 2004), *amended on rehearing*, 382 F.3d 453 (4th Cir. 2004), *cert. denied*, 544 U.S. —, 125 S.Ct. 1670 (2005). But, in a bizarre twist, Moussaoui then pleaded guilty, leaving himself open to four counts potentially carrying the death penalty. He said he would rather focus his resources on fighting the government's efforts to impose the death penalty. He asserted he was part of a different criminal conspiracy—one to hijack a Boeing 747 and fly it "into the White House if he could not negotiate the release of another militant imprisoned for the 1993 bombing of the World Trade Center * * *." Chicago Tribune, Apr. 23, 2005, pp. 1, 13.

Executive Privilege

▶ Insert at p. 228 following the third paragraph

On review by the Supreme Court in Cheney v. United States District Court for District of Columbia, 542 U.S. 367, 124 S.Ct. 2576 (2004), seven Justices voted to vacate the lower court judgment and to remand the case with instructions. In the spirit of the Freedom of Information Act, which was enacted to open up governmental decisionmaking so that people who are affected by policies could understand what factors were considered in their adoption, Congress also passed the Federal Advisory Committee Act (FACA) which imposes several open-meeting and disclosure requirements on the operation of consultative bodies that are not, technically speaking, federal agencies. The Court held that the lower court's imposition of discovery orders for attendance records and minutes of the meetings of the National Energy Policy Development Group (NEPDG, the Bush Administration's Energy Task Force), chaired by Vice President Cheney, needed to be reconsidered in light of certain principles governing the assertion of executive privilege. Cheney offered the customary rationale for invoking the privilege—that confidentiality of the advice the President received was essential to the operation of the executive branch—but the courts below held this was limited by the Supreme Court's decision in *United States* v. *Nixon*. Speaking for the Court, Justice Kennedy explained:

> *Nixon* cannot bear the weight the Court of Appeals puts upon it. First, unlike this case, which concerns respondents' requests for information for use in a civil suit, *Nixon* involves the proper balance between the Executive's interest in the confidentiality of its communications and the "constitutional need for production of relevant evidence in a criminal proceeding." * * *
>
> * * * The need for information for use in civil cases * * * does not share the urgency or significance of the criminal subpoena requests in *Nixon*. * * *
>
> The Court * * * observed in *Nixon* that a "primary constitutional duty of the Judicial Branch [is] to do justice in criminal prosecutions." * * * Withholding materials from a tribunal in an ongoing criminal case when the information is necessary to the court in carrying out its tasks "conflict[s] with the function of the courts under Art. III." * * * Such an impairment of the "essential functions of [another] branch" * * * is impermissible. Withholding the information in this case, however, does not hamper another branch's ability to perform its "essential functions" in quite the same way. * * * The District Court ordered discovery here, not to remedy known statutory violations, but to ascertain whether FACA's disclosure requirements even apply to the NEPDG in the first place. Even if FACA embodies important congressional objectives, the only consequence from respondents' inability to obtain the discovery they seek is that it would be more difficult for private complainants to vindicate Congress' policy objectives under FACA. * * *

*** This is not a routine discovery dispute. The discovery requests are directed to the Vice President and other senior Government officials who served on the NEPDG to give advice and make recommendations to the President. The Executive Branch, at its highest level, is seeking the aid of the courts to protect its constitutional prerogatives. *** [S]pecial considerations control when the Executive Branch's interests in maintaining the autonomy of its office and safeguarding the confidentiality of its communications are implicated. ***

*** The observation in *Nixon* that production of confidential information would not disrupt the functioning of the Executive Branch cannot be applied in a mechanistic fashion to civil litigation. In the criminal justice system, there are various constraints *** to filter out insubstantial legal claims. The decision to prosecute a criminal case, for example, is made by a publicly accountable prosecutor subject to budgetary considerations and under an ethical obligation, not only to win and zealously to advocate for his client but also to serve the cause of justice. *** In contrast, there are no analogous checks in the civil discovery process here. ***

Finally, *** [t]he criminal subpoenas in *Nixon* were required to satisfy exacting standards of "(1) relevancy; (2) admissibility; [and] (3) specificity." *** They were "not intended to provide a means of discovery." *** The burden of showing these standards were met, moreover, fell on the party requesting the information. ***

In contrast to *Nixon*'s subpoena orders that "precisely identified" and "specific[ally] ... enumerated" the relevant materials, *** the discovery requests here *** ask for everything under the sky ***.

Justices Souter and Ginsburg dissented.

But any politically damaging revelations about what influence energy producers and drillers—such as Haliburton—had with the Energy Task Force never emerged because, on remand, the federal appeals court held that the FACA, under which suit had been brought, did not apply to the Energy Task Force. The FACA exempts from its day-light provisions meetings of committees comprised entirely of federal employees whose decisions are not subject to approval or veto by any outside individuals or entities. Neither of the plaintiffs in the case—the right-wing group Judicial Watch or the liberal Sierra Club—had explicitly claimed that any non-federal official had a vote on the NEPDG or had a veto over its decisions. "[E]ven influential participation" by energy producers, campaign contributors, or lobbyists did not somehow make them federal policymakers and create a legal right of access to Energy Task Force meeting information under the FACA. In re Cheney, 406 F.3d 723, (D.C. Cir. en banc, 2005).

D. Executive Authority in the Conduct of Foreign Affairs

Executive Agreements

▶ **Insert at p. 253 following *United States* v. *Belmont***

Despite the clarity of the Court's opinion in *Belmont*, states still attempt to exert what leverage they can to effect change in the policies pursued by foreign governments and multi-national corporations. One such example is the controversy in *Crosby* v. *National Foreign Trade Council* (see Text, p. 258). In that case, Massachusetts tried to withhold its state purchasing power as a way of inducing greater respect for human rights in Myanmar. In another case, which follows, California sought to leverage insurance companies doing business in the state to disclose whether they were derelict in making good on the insurance claims of Holocaust victims and their survivors. In both instances, the states were unsuccessful because their exercise of power was held to conflict with the President's direction of foreign policy.

AMERICAN INSURANCE ASSOCIATION V. GARAMENDI
Supreme Court of the United States, 2003
539 U.S. 396, 123 S.Ct. 2374, 156 L.Ed.2d 376

BACKGROUND & FACTS As part of its program of seizing the wealth of Jews, the Nazi government of Germany also confiscated the value or proceeds of Jewish life insurance policies. In the years following World War II, insurance companies frequently denied that such life insurance policies existed or asserted that they had lapsed because premiums had not been paid. In addition, the West German government often failed to provide the heirs with documentation certifying the deaths of policyholders. War reparations arrangements, however, required the German government to provide restitution to victims of Nazi persecution and there were agreements to provide compensation to citizens in other countries. The response of insurance companies and the German government fell well short of what was required and, following German reunification, class action lawsuits flooded American courts to recover the money due. Protests by the insurance companies and several governments prompted President Clinton to act. What emerged in July 2000 was the German Foundation Agreement in which Germany agreed to establish a foundation with 10 billion deutsch marks, contributed equally by the companies and the German government, to compensate victims and set up procedures to deal with the claims. Similar agreements were negotiated with the Austrian and French governments. It was agreed all would work with the International Commission on Holocaust Era Insurance Claims, a voluntary organization to provide information about and settle unpaid insurance policies.

In the meantime, California began its own investigation of the problem and passed legislation to compel payment from defaulting insurance companies. The Holocaust Victim Insurance Relief Act (HVIRA), passed by the state in 1999, required any insurer (or any agent "related" to it) doing business in the state to disclose information about all policies it sold in Europe between 1920 and 1945. Failure to comply was punishable by loss of the company's state business license. Insurance companies brought suit against the state insurance commissioner attacking the constitutionality of the statute. A federal district court permanently enjoined enforcement of the statute but the U.S. Court of Appeals for the Ninth Circuit reversed, and the insurance companies successfully petitioned the U.S. Supreme Court for certiorari.

Justice SOUTER delivered the opinion of the Court.

* * *

* * * There is * * * no question that at some point an exercise of state power that touches on foreign relations must yield to the National Government's policy, given the "concern for uniformity in this country's dealings with foreign nations" that animated the Constitution's allocation of the foreign relations power to the National Government in the first place. * * *

Nor is there any question generally that there is executive authority to decide what that policy should be. Although the source of the President's power to act in foreign affairs does not enjoy any textual detail, the historical gloss on the "executive Power" vested in Article II of the Constitution has recognized the President's "vast share of responsibility for the conduct of our foreign relations." Youngstown Sheet & Tube Co. v. Sawyer, 343 U.S. 579, 610-611, 72 S.Ct. 863 (1952) (Frankfurter, J., concurring). While Congress holds express authority to regulate public and private dealings with other nations in its war and foreign commerce powers, in foreign affairs the President has a degree of independent authority to act. * * *

[O]ur cases have recognized that the President has authority to make "executive agreements" with other countries, requiring no ratification by the Senate or approval by Congress, this power having been exercised since the early years of the Republic. * * *

The executive agreements at issue here do differ in one respect from * * * [others] insofar as they address claims * * * against corporations, not the foreign governments. But the distinction does not matter. Historically, wartime claims against even nominally private entities have become issues in international diplomacy, and three of the postwar settlements dealing with reparations implicating private parties were made by the Executive alone. Acceptance of this historical practice is supported by a good pragmatic reason for depending on executive agreements to settle claims against foreign corporations associated with wartime experience. As shown by the history of insurance confiscation[,] * * * untangling government policy from private initiative during war time is often so hard that diplomatic action settling claims against private parties may well be just as essential in the aftermath of hostilities as diplomacy to settle claims against foreign governments. While a sharp line between public and private acts works for many purposes in the domestic law, insisting on the same line in defining the legitimate scope of the Executive's international negotiations would hamstring the President in settling international controversies. * * *

Generally, * * * valid executive agreements are fit to preempt state law, just as treaties are, * * * and if the agreements here had expressly preempted laws like HVIRA, the issue would be straightforward. * * * But * * * the[se] agreements include no preemption clause, and so leave their claim of preemption to rest on asserted interference with the foreign policy those agreements embody. * * *

* * *

[Nevertheless,] we think petitioners and the Government have demonstrated a sufficiently clear conflict to require finding preemption here.

* * *

To begin with, resolving Holocaust-era insurance claims that may be held by residents of this country is a matter well within the Executive's responsibility for foreign affairs. Since claims remaining in the aftermath of hostilities may be "sources of friction" acting as an "impediment to resumption of friendly relations" between the countries involved, * * * there is a "longstanding practice" of the national Executive to settle them in discharging its responsibility to maintain the Nation's relationships with other countries * * *. The issue of restitution for Nazi crimes has in fact been addressed in Executive Branch diplomacy and formalized in treaties and executive agreements over the last half century, and although resolution of private claims was postponed by the Cold War, securing private interests is an express object of diplomacy today, just as it was addressed in agreements soon after the Second World War. * * *

* * * [T]he consistent Presidential foreign policy has been to encourage European governments and companies to volunteer settlement funds in preference to litigation or coercive sanctions. * * * As for insurance claims in particular, the national position, expressed unmistakably in the executive agreements signed by the President with Germany and Austria, has been to encourage European insurers to work with the International Commission on Holocaust Era Insurance Claims (ICHEIC) to develop acceptable claim procedures, including procedures governing disclosure of policy information. * * * The approach taken serves to resolve the several competing matters of national concern[:] * * * the national interest in maintaining amicable relationships with current European allies; survivors' interests in a "fair and prompt" but nonadversarial resolution of their claims so as to "bring some measure of justice ... in their lifetimes"; and the companies' interest in securing "legal peace" when they settle claims in this fashion. * * *

* * * HVIRA's economic compulsion to make public disclosure, of far more information about far more policies than the ICHEIC's rules require, employs "a different, state system of economic pressure," and in doing so undercuts the President's diplomatic discretion and the choice he has made exercising it. * * * Whereas the President's authority to provide for settling claims in winding up international hostilities requires flexibility in wielding "the coercive power of the national economy" as a tool of diplomacy, * * * HVIRA denies this, by making exclusion from a large sector of the American insurance market the automatic sanction for noncompliance with the State's own policies on disclosure." * * * The law thus "compromise[s] the very capacity of the

President to speak for the Nation with one voice in dealing with other governments" to resolve claims against European companies arising out of World War II. * * *

* * *

The basic fact is that California seeks to use an iron fist where the President has consistently chosen kid gloves. We have heard powerful arguments that the iron fist would work better, and it may be that if the matter of compensation were considered in isolation from all other issues involving the European allies, the iron fist would be the preferable policy. But our thoughts on the efficacy of the one approach versus the other are beside the point, since our business is not to judge the wisdom of the National Government's policy; dissatisfaction should be addressed to the President or, perhaps, Congress. * * *

* * *

* * * Congress has not acted on the matter addressed here. Given the President's independent authority "in the areas of foreign policy and national security, ... congressional silence is not to be equated with congressional disapproval." Haig v. Agee, 453 U.S. 280, 291, 101 S.Ct. 2766 (1981).

The judgment of the Court of Appeals for the Ninth Circuit is reversed.

* * *

Justice GINSBURG, with whom Justice STEVENS, Justice SCALIA, and Justice THOMAS join, dissenting.

* * * Although the federal approach differs from California's, no executive agreement or other formal expression of foreign policy disapproves state disclosure laws like the HVIRA. Absent a clear statement aimed at disclosure requirements by the "one voice" to which courts properly defer in matters of foreign affairs, I would leave intact California's enactment.

* * *

* * * The HVIRA entails no * * * state action or policy. It takes no position on any contemporary foreign government and requires no assessment of any existing foreign regime. It is directed solely at private insurers doing business in California, and it requires them solely to disclose information in their or their affiliates' possession or control. * * *

I [would not] stretch * * * [previous Court decisions] to support implied preemption by executive agreement. * * *

* * *

Sustaining the HVIRA would not compromise the President's ability to speak with one voice for the Nation. * * * To the contrary, by declining to invalidate the HVIRA in this case, we would reserve foreign affairs preemption for circumstances where the President, acting under statutory or constitutional authority, has spoken clearly to the issue at hand. * * * And judges should not be the expositors of the Nation's foreign policy, which is the role they play by acting when the President himself has not taken a clear stand. As I see it, courts step out of their proper role when they rely on no legislative or even executive text, but only on inference and implication, to preempt state laws on foreign affairs grounds.

* * * Accordingly, I would leave California's enactment in place, and affirm the judgment of the Court of Appeals.

———

A year later, the Supreme Court dealt with another issue of direct interest to Jewish victims of Nazi lawlessness—the theft of art treasures. Since World War II, owners and rightful heirs to works of art seized by the Nazis have brought suit against foreign governments to recover private paintings that are housed abroad in public museums and galleries. In Republic of Austria v. Altmann, 541 U.S. 677, 124 S.Ct. 2240 (2004), the Court, speaking through Justice Stevens, held that plaintiffs could sue in American courts to get the paintings back. The majority ruled that the Foreign Sovereign Immunities Act of 1976 permitted legal actions to be brought against foreign governments even if the claim pre-dated the enactment of the law. The Court did not address the merits of the plaintiff's claim (that is, whether she was entitled to have the paintings returned) but only allowed her suit to be heard by a federal district court. This meant that she was not left to the vagaries of pursuing the suit abroad where the costs of legal action are astronomical and the odds of winning very low. There is little prospect the federal courts will be hit by a flood of similar suits because the process of litigation takes so long and the number of plaintiffs still alive to press the fight is quickly growing shorter and because establishing proof of ownership in any event is usually very difficult since the necessary records were not kept or have been destroyed. The dissenters (Chief Justice Rehnquist and Justices Kennedy and Thomas) disagreed with the retroactive application of the statute. Following remand, Mrs. Altmann, now 89, received the paintings as part of a $21.8 million award to the surviving members of two families victimized in the Holocaust. New York Times, April 14, 2005, pp. A1, 25.

▶ Insert at p. 270 at the end of footnote z

Although the House earlier had adopted an amendment by Rep. Bernard Sanders (I-Vt.) to end the library record and bookstore sales slip provision entirely, in the end this action was reversed when the House voted 257-171 on July 23, 2005 to extend the USA PATRIOT Act, including that provision. As with the Senate bill, 14 of the 16 parts of the Act would become permanent, but the library and bookstore provision would extend only for 10 years and the FBI director would be required to authorize such requests *personally*. The House rejected an effort to set a 10-year limit on *all* provisions of the PATRIOT Act by a vote of 209-218. Congressional Quarterly Weekly Report, June 20, 2005, pp. 1649, 1664; July 25, 2005, pp. 2044-2045.

▶ Insert at p. 271 following the first paragraph

The provision of the USA PATRIOT Act that prohibits giving "expert advice or assistance" to terrorists has been found impermissibly vague. See Humanitarian Law Project v. Ashcroft, 309 F.Supp.2d 1185 (C.D.Cal. 2004).

Chapter 5

Powers of the National Government in the Federal System

C. Rekindling Dual Federalism: The Rehnquist Court

The Rehnquist Court and the Commerce Clause

♦Insert at p. 339 following the first paragraph

In light of the Supreme Court's recent decision in *Gonzales v. Raich*, which follows, *Lopez* (Text, p. 328) and *Morrison* (Text, p. 332) may seem more like mere flickers instead of a rekindling of dual federalism. The coalition that decided those two cases now appears deeply split, since Justices Scalia and Kennedy have now made common cause with the former dissenters. Add to this the retirement of Justice O'Connor—possibly Chief Justice Rehnquist, too—and the future of the one-time dual federalist coalition may seriously be in doubt.

Gonzales v. Raich
Supreme Court of the United States, 2005
545 U.S. —, 125 S.Ct. 2195, — L.Ed.2d —

BACKGROUND AND FACTS After California voters in 1996 approved an initiative legalizing the use of marijuana for medical purposes, the California legislature codified its provisions as the Compassionate Use Act. The law permitted medical patients to possess and use small amounts of marijuana on the recommendation of a certified physician to alleviate pain resulting from illness and the side-effects of medical treatment. Before the end of the next decade, 10 states authorized medical marijuana. Federal law, on the other hand, prohibits the possession and use of marijuana for any reason.

Angel Raich and Diane Monson, California residents who suffered from severe medical conditions sought legal refuge under the state medical marijuana law for themselves and others similarly situated. Raich, for example, suffered from multiple illnesses, among them a form of wasting disease that caused excruciating pain. Use of marijuana alleviated the pain so that she could eat. Other patients used marijuana to relieve the nausea that accompanies chemotherapy. While Raich obtained the marijuana she used from two care-givers at no cost, Monson grew her own and ingested it by smoking and using a vaporizer. Monson's home was raided by county and federal law enforcement officers who seized and destroyed her marijuana plants. Raich and Monson brought suit to enjoin the U.S. attorney general from enforcing the federal Controlled Substances Act. They argued that the federal law, as applied to users of medical marijuana, violated the Commerce Clause, denied due process under the Fifth Amendment by depriving them of medical treatment, and infringed the doctrine of medical necessity. Addressing only the Commerce Clause contention, a federal appeals court sustained the state law and invalidated the federal statute as applied. The attorney general then successfully petitioned for certiorari.

Justice STEVENS delivered the opinion of the Court.

* * *

* * * The case is made difficult by respondents' strong arguments that they will suffer irreparable harm * * *. The question before us, however, is not whether it is wise to enforce the statute in these circumstances; rather, it is whether Congress' power to regulate interstate markets for medicinal substances encompasses the portions of those markets that are supplied with drugs produced and consumed locally. * * *

* * *

[The Controlled Substances Act of 1970 (CSA)] repealed most of the earlier antidrug laws in favor of a comprehensive regime to combat the international and interstate traffic in illicit drugs. The main objectives of the CSA were to conquer drug abuse and to control the legitimate and illegitimate traffic in controlled substances. Congress was particularly concerned with the need to prevent the diversion of drugs from legitimate to illicit channels. * * *

* * *

Respondents in this case do not dispute that passage of the CSA * * * was well within Congress' commerce power. * * * [They] argue [only] that the CSA's categorical prohibition of the manufacture and possession of marijuana as applied to the intrastate manufacture and possession of marijuana for medical purposes pursuant to California law exceeds Congress' authority under the Commerce Clause.

* * *

Our case law firmly establishes Congress' power to regulate purely local activities that are part of an economic "class of activities" that have a substantial effect on interstate commerce. See * * * Wickard v. Filburn, 317 U.S. 111, 128-129, 63 S.Ct. 82 (1942). As we stated in *Wickard,* "even if appellee's activity be local and though it may not be regarded as commerce, it may still, whatever its nature, be reached by Congress if it exerts a substantial economic effect on interstate commerce." * * * We have never required Congress to legislate with scientific exactitude. When Congress decides that the '"total incidence"' of a practice poses a threat to a national market, it may regulate the entire class. * * * [W]hen '"a general regulatory statute bears a substantial relation to commerce, the *de minimis* character of individual instances arising under that statute is of no consequence.'" * * *

* * *

* * * Like the farmer in *Wickard*, respondents are cultivating, for home consumption, a fungible commodity for which there is an established, albeit illegal, interstate market. Just as the Agricultural Adjustment Act [of 1938 (AAA)] was designed "to control the volume [of wheat] moving in interstate and foreign commerce in order to avoid surpluses ..." and consequently control the market price, * * * a primary purpose of the CSA is to control the supply and demand of controlled substances in both lawful and unlawful drug markets. * * * In *Wickard,* we had no difficulty concluding that Congress had a rational basis for believing that, when viewed in the aggregate, leaving home-consumed wheat outside the regulatory scheme would have a substantial influence on price and market conditions. Here too, Congress had a rational basis for concluding that leaving home-consumed marijuana outside federal control would similarly affect price and market conditions.

[O]ne concern prompting inclusion of wheat grown for home consumption in the [AAA] was that rising market prices could draw such wheat into the interstate market, resulting in lower market prices. * * * The parallel concern * * * [here] is the likelihood that the high demand in the interstate market will draw * * * [home-grown] marijuana into that market. * * * In both cases, the regulation is squarely within Congress' commerce power because production of the commodity meant for home consumption, be it wheat or marijuana, has a substantial effect on supply and demand in the national market for that commodity.

Nonetheless, respondents suggest that *Wickard* differs from this case in three respects: (1) the Agricultural Adjustment Act, unlike the CSA, exempted small farming operations; (2) *Wickard* involved a "quintessential economic activity"—a commercial farm—whereas respondents do not sell marijuana; and (3) the *Wickard* record made it clear that the aggregate production of wheat for use on farms had a significant impact on market prices. Those differences, though factually accurate, do not diminish the precedential force of this Court's reasoning.

* * *

In assessing the scope of Congress' authority under the Commerce Clause, * * * [w]e need not determine whether respondents' activities, taken in the aggregate, substantially affect interstate commerce in fact, but only whether a "rational basis" exists for so concluding. * * * Given the enforcement difficulties * * * [of] distinguishing between marijuana cultivated locally and marijuana grown elsewhere, * * * and concerns about diversion into illicit channels, * * * we have no difficulty concluding that Congress had a rational basis for believing that failure to regulate the intrastate manufacture and possession of marijuana would leave a gaping hole in the CSA. * * * That the regulation ensnares some purely intrastate activity is of no moment. * * *

To support their contrary submission, respondents rely heavily on * * * *Lopez,* 514 U.S. 549, 115 S.Ct. 1624 and *Morrison,* 529 U.S. 598, 120 S.Ct. 1740. * * * Here, respondents ask us to excise individual applications of a concededly valid statutory scheme. In contrast, in both *Lopez* and

Morrison, the parties asserted that a particular statute or provision fell outside Congress' commerce power in its entirety. * * *

* * *

Unlike those at issue in *Lopez* and *Morrison,* the activities regulated by the CSA are quintessentially economic. "Economics" refers to "the production, distribution, and consumption of commodities." Webster's Third New International Dictionary 720 (1966). The CSA is a statute that regulates the production, distribution, and consumption of commodities for which there is an established, and lucrative, interstate market. Prohibiting the intrastate possession or manufacture of an article of commerce is a rational (and commonly utilized) means of regulating commerce in that product. Such prohibitions include specific decisions requiring that a drug be withdrawn from the market as a result of the failure to comply with regulatory requirements as well as decisions excluding Schedule I drugs entirely from the market. Because the CSA is a statute that directly regulates economic, commercial activity, our opinion in *Morrison* casts no doubt on its constitutionality.

* * *

First, the fact that marijuana is used "for personal medical purposes on the advice of a physician" cannot itself serve as a distinguishing factor. * * * The CSA designates marijuana as contraband for *any* purpose * * *. Moreover, the CSA is a comprehensive regulatory regime specifically designed to regulate which controlled substances can be utilized for medicinal purposes, and in what manner. * * * Thus, even if respondents are correct that marijuana does have accepted medical uses and thus should be redesignated as a lesser schedule drug, the CSA would still impose controls beyond what is required by California law. The CSA requires manufacturers, physicians, pharmacies, and other handlers of controlled substances to comply with statutory and regulatory provisions mandating registration with the [Drug Enforcement Administration], compliance with specific production quotas, security controls to guard against diversion, recordkeeping and reporting obligations, and prescription requirements. * * * Furthermore, the dispensing of new drugs, even when doctors approve their use, must await federal approval. * * * [T]he mere fact that marijuana—like virtually every other controlled substance regulated by the CSA—is used for medicinal purposes cannot possibly serve to distinguish it from the core activities regulated by the CSA.

* * *

Second, limiting the activity to marijuana possession and cultivation "in accordance with state law" cannot serve to place respondents' activities beyond congressional reach. The Supremacy Clause unambiguously provides that if there is any conflict between federal and state law, federal law shall prevail. * * * [The] federal power over commerce is "'superior to that of the States to provide for the welfare or necessities of their inhabitants,'" however legitimate or dire those necessities may be. * * *

Respondents * * * contend that their activities were not "an essential part of a larger regulatory scheme" because they had been "isolated by the State of California, and [are] policed by the State of California," and thus remain "entirely separated from the market." * * * Th[is] notion * * * is a dubious proposition, and * * * one that Congress could have rationally rejected.

[T]hat the California exemptions will have a significant impact on both the supply and demand sides of the market for marijuana is not just "plausible"[,] * * * it is readily apparent. The exemption for physicians provides them with an economic incentive to grant their patients permission to use the drug. In contrast to most prescriptions for legal drugs, which limit the dosage and duration of the usage, under California law the doctor's permission to recommend marijuana use is open-ended. The authority to grant permission whenever the doctor determines that a patient is afflicted with "any other illness for which marijuana provides relief" * * * is broad enough to allow even the most scrupulous doctor to conclude that some recreational uses would be therapeutic. And our cases have taught us that there are some unscrupulous physicians who overprescribe when it is sufficiently profitable to do so.

The exemption for cultivation by patients and caregivers can only increase the supply of marijuana in the California market. The likelihood that all such production will promptly terminate when patients recover or will precisely match the patients' medical needs during their convalescence seems remote; whereas the danger that excesses will satisfy some of the admittedly enormous demand for recreational use seems obvious. Moreover, that the national and international narcotics trade has thrived in the face of vigorous criminal enforcement efforts suggests that no small number of unscrupulous people will make use of the California exemptions to serve their commercial ends whenever it is feasible to do so. * * * Congress could have rationally concluded that the aggregate impact on the national market of all the transactions exempted from federal supervision is unquestionably substantial.

[T]he case for the exemption comes down to the claim that a locally cultivated product that is used domestically rather than sold on the open market is not subject to federal regulation. Given the findings in the CSA and the undisputed magnitude of the commercial market for marijuana, our decisions in *Wickard* v. *Filburn* and * * * later cases endorsing its reasoning foreclose that claim.

Respondents also raise a substantive due process claim and seek to avail themselves of the medical necessity defense. These theories of relief were * * * not reached by the Court of Appeals. We therefore do not address the question whether judicial relief is available to respondents on these alternative bases. * * * But perhaps even more important than these legal avenues is the democratic process, in which the voices of voters allied with these respondents may one day be heard in the halls of Congress. Under the present state of the law, however, the judgment of the Court of Appeals must be vacated. The case is remanded for further proceedings consistent with this opinion.

It is so ordered.

Justice SCALIA, concurring in the judgment.

* * *

* * * Congress's authority to enact * * * prohibitions of intrastate controlled-substance activities depends only upon whether they are appropriate means of achieving the legitimate end of eradicating Schedule I substances from interstate commerce.

* * * Not only is it impossible to distinguish "controlled substances manufactured and distributed intrastate" from "controlled substances manufactured and distributed interstate," but it hardly makes sense to speak in such terms. Drugs like marijuana are fungible commodities. [M]arijuana that is grown at home and possessed for personal use is never more than an instant from the interstate market—and this is so whether or not the possession is for medicinal use or lawful use under the laws of a particular State. * * * Congress need not accept on faith that state law will be effective in maintaining a strict division between a lawful market for "medical" marijuana and the more general marijuana market. * * * "To impose on [Congress] the necessity of resorting to means which it cannot control, which another government may furnish or withhold, would render its course precarious, the result of its measures uncertain, and create a dependence on other governments, which might disappoint its most important designs, and is incompatible with the language of the constitution." McCulloch [v. Maryland], 17 U.S. (4 Wheat.), at 424, 4 L.Ed., at 606.

* * *

Justice O'CONNOR, with whom THE CHIEF JUSTICE [REHNQUIST] and Justice THOMAS join as to * * * [part], dissenting.

* * * One of federalism's chief virtues * * * is that it promotes innovation by allowing for the possibility that "a single courageous State may, if its citizens choose, serve as a laboratory; and try novel social and economic experiments without risk to the rest of the country." New State Ice Co. v. Liebmann, 285 U.S. 262, 311, 52 S.Ct. 371 (1932) (Brandeis, J., dissenting).

This case exemplifies the role of States as laboratories. The States' core police powers have always included authority to define criminal law and to protect the health, safety, and welfare of their citizens. * * * Today the Court sanctions an application of the federal Controlled Substances Act that extinguishes that experiment, without any proof that the personal cultivation, possession, and use of marijuana for medicinal purposes * * * has a substantial effect on interstate commerce and is therefore an appropriate subject of federal regulation. * * * [It is] irreconcilable with our decisions in *Lopez* * * * and *Morrison* * * *.

* * *

Today's decision allows Congress to regulate intrastate activity without check, so long as there is some implication by legislative design that regulating intrastate activity is essential * * * to the interstate regulatory scheme. Seizing upon our language in *Lopez* that the statute prohibiting gun possession in school zones was "not an essential part of a larger regulation of economic activity, in which the regulatory scheme could be undercut unless the intrastate activity were regulated," * * * the Court appears to reason that the placement of local activity in a comprehensive scheme confirms that it is essential to that scheme. * * * If the Court is right, then *Lopez* stands for nothing more than a drafting guide: Congress should have described the relevant crime as "transfer or possession of a firearm anywhere in the nation"—thus including commercial and noncommercial activity, and clearly encompassing some activity with assuredly substantial effect on interstate commerce. Had it done so, the majority hints, we would have sustained its authority to regulate possession of firearms in school zones. * * *

* * *

The hard work for courts * * * is to identify objective markers for confining the analysis in Commerce Clause cases. Here, respondents challenge the constitutionality of the CSA as applied to them and those similarly situated. I agree with the Court that we must look beyond respondents' own activities. Otherwise, individual litigants could always exempt themselves from Commerce Clause regulation merely by pointing to the obvious—that their personal activities do not have a substantial effect on interstate commerce. * * * The task is to identify a mode of analysis that allows Congress to regulate more than nothing * * * and less than everything * * *.

A number of objective markers are available to confine the scope of constitutional review here. Both federal and state legislation * * * recognize that medical and nonmedical (*i.e.*, recreational) uses of drugs are realistically distinct and can be segregated, and regulate them differently. * *

* Respondents challenge only the application of the CSA to medicinal use of marijuana. * * * California, like other States, has drawn on its reserved powers to distinguish the regulation of medicinal marijuana. To ascertain whether Congress' encroachment is constitutionally justified in this case, then, I would focus here on the personal cultivation, possession, and use of marijuana for medicinal purposes.

[E]ven if intrastate cultivation and possession of marijuana for one's own medicinal use can properly be characterized as economic, and I question whether it can, it has not been shown that such activity substantially affects interstate commerce. * * *

* * *

The Court uses a dictionary definition of economics to skirt the real problem of drawing a meaningful line between "what is national and what is local" * * *. It will not do to say that Congress may regulate noncommercial activity simply because it may have an effect on the demand for commercial goods, or because the noncommercial endeavor can, in some sense, substitute for commercial activity. Most commercial goods or services have some sort of privately producible analogue. Home care substitutes for daycare. Charades games substitute for movie tickets. Backyard or windowsill gardening substitutes for going to the supermarket. To draw the line wherever private activity affects the demand for market goods is to draw no line at all, and to declare everything economic. We have already rejected the result that would follow—a federal police power. * * *

In *Lopez* and *Morrison,* we suggested that economic activity usually relates directly to commercial activity. * * * The homegrown cultivation and personal possession and use of marijuana for medicinal purposes has no apparent commercial character. Everyone agrees that the marijuana at issue in this case was never in the stream of commerce, and neither were the supplies for growing it. (Marijuana is highly unusual among the substances subject to the CSA in that it can be cultivated without any materials that have traveled in interstate commerce.) *Lopez* makes clear that possession is not itself commercial activity. And respondents have not come into possession by means of any commercial transaction; they have simply grown, in their own homes, marijuana for their own use, without acquiring, buying, selling, or bartering a thing of value. * * *

The Court suggests that *Wickard* * * * established federal regulatory power over any home consumption of a commodity for which a national market exists. * * * [T]he Agricultural Adjustment Act of 1938 (AAA), [challenged there,] * * * provided an exemption * * * [from production quotas and penalties] for small producers. When Filburn * * * [harvested the wheat at issue in *Wickard,*] the statute exempted * * * plantings less than six acres. [Filburn had planted 23 acres.] * * * *Wickard,* then, did not extend Commerce Clause authority to something as modest as the home cook's herb garden. This is not to say that Congress may never regulate small quantities of commodities possessed or produced for personal use, or to deny that it sometimes needs to enact a zero tolerance regime for such commodities. It is merely to say that *Wickard* did not hold or imply that small-scale production of commodities is always economic, and automatically within Congress' reach.

Even assuming that economic activity is at issue in this case, the Government has made no showing in fact that the possession and use of homegrown marijuana for medical purposes, in California or elsewhere, has a substantial effect on interstate commerce. * * * [Nor has] the Government * * * shown that regulating such activity is necessary to an interstate regulatory scheme. * * *

[S]omething more than mere assertion is required when Congress purports to have power over local activity whose connection to an intrastate market is not self-evident. * * * Indeed, if it were enough in "substantial effects" cases for the Court to supply conceivable justifications for intrastate regulation related to an interstate market, then we could have surmised in *Lopez* that guns in school zones are "never more than an instant from the interstate market" in guns already subject to extensive federal regulation, * * * and thereby upheld the Gun-Free School Zones Act of 1990. * * *

There is simply no evidence that homegrown medicinal marijuana users constitute, in the aggregate, a sizable enough class to have a discernable, let alone substantial, impact on the national illicit drug market—or otherwise to threaten the CSA regime. * * *

* * *

[In this case, the] Court refers to a series of declarations in the introduction to the CSA saying that (1) local distribution and possession of controlled substances causes "swelling" in interstate traffic; (2) local production and distribution cannot be distinguished from interstate production and distribution; (3) federal control over intrastate incidents "is essential to effective control" over interstate drug trafficking. * * *

[These bare declarations] amount to nothing more than a legislative insistence that the regulation of controlled substances must be absolute. They are asserted without any supporting evidence—descriptive, statistical, or otherwise. "[S]imply because Congress may conclude a particular activity substantially affects interstate commerce does not necessarily make it so." * * *

* * *

Relying on Congress' abstract assertions, the Court has endorsed making it a federal crime to grow small amounts of marijuana in one's own home for one's own medicinal use. This overreaching stifles an express choice by some States, concerned for the lives and liberties of their people, to regulate medical marijuana differently. * * * [W]hatever the wisdom of California's experiment with medical marijuana, the federalism principles that have driven our Commerce Clause cases require that room for experiment be protected in this case. * * *

Justice THOMAS, dissenting.

* * *

On its face, a ban on the intrastate cultivation, possession and distribution of marijuana may be plainly adapted to stopping the interstate flow of marijuana. * * * But respondents do not challenge the CSA on its face. Instead, they challenge it as applied to their conduct. The question is thus whether the intrastate ban is "necessary and proper" as applied to medical marijuana users like respondents.

* * *

[N]either in enacting the CSA nor in defending its application to respondents has the Government offered any obvious reason why banning medical marijuana use is necessary to stem the tide of interstate drug trafficking. Congress' goal of curtailing the interstate drug trade would not plainly be thwarted if it could not apply the CSA to patients like Monson and Raich. That is, unless Congress' aim is really to exercise police power of the sort reserved to the States in order to eliminate even the intrastate possession and use of marijuana.

* * *

* * * Congress is authorized to regulate "Commerce," and respondents' conduct does not qualify under any definition of that term. The majority's opinion only illustrates the steady drift away from the text of the Commerce Clause. There is an inexorable expansion from "commerce, " * * * to "commercial" and "economic" activity, * * * and finally to all "production, distribution, and consumption" of goods or services for which there is an "established ... interstate market" * * *. Federal power expands * * * with each new locution. The majority is not interpreting the Commerce Clause, but rewriting it.

* * *

One searches the Court's opinion in vain for any hint of what aspect of American life is reserved to the States. * * * Congress may regulate interstate commerce—not things that affect it, even when summed together, unless truly "necessary and proper" to regulating interstate commerce.

* * *

The decision in *Raich* did not declare the California statute unconstitutional, so it and the medical marijuana laws of nine other states remain on the books. What it did was uphold federal authority to prosecute those who cultivate, possess, and use marijuana. But the week after Justice Stevens said in *Raich* that only Congress could make medical marijuana legal, the House voted not to. The vote was on an amendment that would have denied funding to the U.S. Justice Department to enforce the Controlled Substances Act in a manner that would interfere with medical marijuana in any of the states that voted to make it legal. The amendment was defeated in the House by a vote of 161-264. Congressional Quarterly Weekly Report, June 20, 2005, pp. 1649, 1664. The vote in favor of the bill was 13 more than proponents of medical marijuana had been able to muster in the attempt a year earlier.

On the heels of its decision in *Raich*, the Supreme Court granted cert., vacated judgment, and remanded for lower court reconsideration, decisions in two cases: United States v. Stewart, 348 F.3d 1132 (9th Cir. 2003), in which defendant's federal conviction for possession of a home-made machine gun had been overturned on grounds regulating mere possession did not have a commercial purpose and therefore did not fall within the reach of the Commerce Clause; and United States v. Smith, 402 F.3d 1303 (11th Cir. 2005), in which the appeals court reversed a federal criminal conviction for producing and possessing child pornography on grounds the defendant's noncommercial and intrastate activities did not substantially affect interstate commerce (notwithstanding the fact that the film, photographic paper, and film processor had once moved in interstate commerce).

The chart on the following page shows voting alignments among the Justices in all of the nonunanimous constitutional cases decided by the Court during the three Terms that began October 7, 2002 and ran through June 27, 2005. Judging by the inter-agreement scores in the chart and compared with Exhibit 5.4 in the Text (p. 338), Justices O'Connor, Kennedy, and Breyer occupy a more centrist position on the Court and Chief Justice Rehnquist has moved over a bit. Consequently, although Justices Scalia and Thomas agree more with each other than any other pair on the Court, they appear to have grown more isolated on the Court's far right. As the chart shows, a majority of the Justices leaned to the political right decidedly more than half the time in the 64 nonunanimous constitutional cases.

Among the centrist Justices who hold the balance of power on the Court, Justice O'Connor was the most influential, if that is measured by how often a Justice voted with the majority. She voted with the majority 83% of the time in the 64 nonunanimous cases. Justice Kennedy came in second at 78%, and Justice Breyer at 72% was third. In the really close cases—

AGREEMENT BETWEEN PAIRS OF JUSTICES IN NONUNANIMOUS CONSTITUTIONAL CASES DECIDED DURING THE OCTOBER 2002, 2003, AND 2004 TERMS

PERCENTAGE OF THE TIME EACH PAIR OF JUSTICES VOTED THE SAME WAY
IN THE 64 NONUNANIMOUS CONSTITUTIONAL CASES
(Justices are designated by the first two letters of their last name)

Justice	ST	GI	SO	BR	OC	KE	RE	SC	TH
ST									
GI	88								
SO	86	86							
BR	77	77	75						
OC	50	45	47	63					
KE	41	41	45	58	70				
RE	24	26	27	45	74	79			
SC	16	19	20	36	52	59	71		
TH	16	16	14	14	47	56	69	91	

PERCENTAGE OF EACH JUSTICE'S 64 VOTES THAT WERE CONSERVATIVE
(As defined in the Text, pp. 338-339)

Justice	ST	GI	SO	BR	OC	KE	RE	SC	TH
% Con	9	13	14	33	58	69	81	84	84

those decided by a 5-4 vote—of which there were 31, the ranking still remains the same: Justice O'Connor 77%, Justice Kennedy 58%, and Justice Breyer 48%.

But if the Court's most recent Term is considered separately, it reveals a striking shift in the center of the Court's political gravity. In the 20 nonunanimous cases decided in the October 2004 Term, Justice Breyer was the most influential. He joined the majority 90% of the time (as compared with Kennedy's 75% and O'Connor's 70%); and in the 5-4 decisions, of which there were seven, he voted with the majority in five, compared with only three each for Kennedy and O'Connor. And if *all* of the Court's nonunanimous cases are considered—not just its constitutional decisions—the influence of Justice Breyer this past Term was possibly greater. See New York Times, July 4, 2005, pp. A1, A10.

The Eleventh Amendment

▸ **Insert at p. 341 following the second full paragraph**

Startling many observers accustomed to the vice-like grip dual federalism has acquired over the Rehnquist Court's thinking about the federal relationship, the Justices upheld the Family Medical Leave Act (FMLA) in the teeth of an Eleventh Amendment challenge—and by a decisive majority. The following 6-3 decision in *Nevada Department of Human Resources v. Hibbs*, was a stunning departure from a spate of rulings that have rendered the states' immunity from private damage suits virtually bullet-proof. In *Hibbs* the Court, speaking through Chief Justice Rehnquist (another surprise), distinguished Congress's effort to tackle gender discrimination from its efforts to authorize private suits against the states to redress age and disability discrimination. Critical to understanding why the Court sustained the FMLA in *Hibbs*, but scuttled damage suits authorized by the legislation challenged in *Kimel* and *Garrett* (discussed in the Text), is the different level of constitutional scrutiny triggered by different kinds of discrimination.

NEVADA DEPARTMENT OF HUMAN RESOURCES V. HIBBS
Supreme Court of the United States, 2003
538 U.S. 721, 123 S.Ct. 1972, 155 L.Ed.2d 953

BACKGROUND & FACTS The Family and Medical Leave Act of 1993 (FMLA) entitles employees of both private businesses and state and local agencies to 12 weeks of unpaid leave annually to deal with a "serious health condition" of a child, parent, or spouse. The law also creates a right to sue for money damages if this right is infringed by the employer. William Hibbs, who worked for the Nevada Department of Human Resources, sued the state for damages after state officials cut short his leave to deal with the effects of his wife's neck surgery and injuries she sustained in an automobile accident. After having been given some time off, he was then told to report for work or be fired. In his suit for damages against Nevada following the termination of his employment, the state argued that the Eleventh Amendment made it immune from suit without its consent. A federal district court agreed and awarded the state summary judgment, which was later reversed on appeal. The state then successfully sought certiorari from the Supreme Court.

Chief Justice REHNQUIST delivered the opinion of the Court.

* * *

[W]e have made clear that the Constitution does not provide for federal jurisdiction over suits against nonconsenting States. Board of Trustees of Univ. of Ala. v. Garrett, 531 U. S. 356, 121 S.Ct. 955, (2001); Kimel v. Florida Bd. of Regents, 528 U. S. 62, 120 S.Ct. 631 (2000) * * *.

Congress may, however, abrogate such immunity in federal court if it makes its intention to abrogate unmistakably clear in the language of the statute and acts pursuant to a valid exercise of its power under §5 of the Fourteenth Amendment. * * * The clarity of Congress' intent here is not fairly debatable. * * * This case turns, then, on whether Congress acted within its constitutional authority when it sought to abrogate the States' immunity for purposes of the FMLA's family-leave provision.

In enacting the FMLA, Congress relied on two of the powers vested in it by the Constitution: its Article I commerce power and its power under §5 of the Fourteenth Amendment to enforce that Amendment's guarantees. Congress may not abrogate the States' sovereign immunity pursuant to its Article I power over commerce. * * * Congress may, however, abrogate States' sovereign immunity through a valid exercise of its §5 power, for "the Eleventh Amendment, and the principle of state sovereignty which it embodies, are necessarily limited by the enforcement provisions of §5 of the Fourteenth Amendment." * * * See * * * Garrett * * * [and] Kimel * * *.

* * * Section 5 grants Congress the power "to enforce" the substantive guarantees of §1—among them, equal protection of the laws—by enacting "appropriate legislation." Congress may, in the exercise of its §5 power, do more than simply proscribe conduct that we have held unconstitutional. * * * Congress may enact so-called prophylactic legislation that proscribes facially constitutional conduct in order to prevent and deter unconstitutional conduct.

City of Boerne [v. Flores, 521 U.S. 507, 117 S.Ct. 2157 (1997)] * * * confirmed * * * that it falls to this Court, not Congress, to define the substance of constitutional guarantees. * * * Section 5 legislation reaching beyond the scope of §1's actual guarantees must be an appropriate remedy for identified constitutional violations, not "an attempt to substantively redefine * * *" [what the Fourteenth Amendment guarantees]. [T]he [applicable] test [is] set forth in City of Boerne: Valid §5 legislation must exhibit "congruence and proportionality between the injury to be prevented or remedied and the means adopted to that end." * * *

The FMLA aims to protect the right to be free from gender-based discrimination in the workplace. * * * We now inquire whether Congress had evidence of a pattern of constitutional violations on the part of the States in this area.

[M]any state laws limiting women's employment opportunities * * * w[ere] sanctioned by this Court's own opinions. For example, in Bradwell v. State, 83 U.S. (16 Wall.) 130, 21 L.Ed. 442 (1873), * * * and Goesaert v. Cleary, 335 U.S. 464, 69 S.Ct. 198 (1948), * * * the Court upheld state laws prohibiting women from practicing law and tending bar, respectively. State laws frequently subjected women to distinctive restrictions, terms, conditions, and benefits for those jobs they could take. * * *

Congress responded to this history of discrimination by abrogating States' sovereign immunity in Title VII of the Civil Rights Act of 1964 * * * and we sustained this abrogation * * *. But state gender discrimination did not cease. * * * According to evidence that was before Congress when it enacted the FMLA, States continue to rely on invalid gender stereotypes in the employment context, specifically in the administration of leave benefits. * * *

As the FMLA's legislative record reflects, a 1990 Bureau of Labor Statistics (BLS) survey stated that 37 percent of surveyed private-sector employees were covered by maternity leave policies, while only 18 percent were covered by paternity leave policies. * * * [S]tereotype-based beliefs about the allocation of family duties remained firmly rooted, and employers' reliance on them in establishing discriminatory leave policies remained widespread.

Congress also heard testimony that "[p]arental leave for fathers ... is rare. Even ... [w]here child-care leave policies do exist, men, *both in the public and private sectors*, receive notoriously discriminatory treatment in their requests for such leave." * * *

Finally, Congress had evidence that, even where state laws and policies were not facially discriminatory, they were applied in discriminatory ways. * * * Testimony supported that conclusion, explaining that "[t]he lack of uniform parental and medical leave policies in the work place has created an environment where [sex] discrimination is rampant." * * *

* * *

[T]he States' record of unconstitutional participation in, and fostering of, gender-based discrimination in the administration of leave benefits is weighty enough to justify the enactment of prophylactic §5 legislation.

We reached the opposite conclusion in *Garrett* and *Kimel*. In those cases, the §5 legislation under review responded to a purported tendency of state officials to make age- or disability-based distinctions. Under our equal protection case law, discrimination on the basis of such characteristics is not judged under a heightened review standard, and passes muster if there is "a rational basis for doing so at a class-based level * * *. Thus, in order to impugn the constitutionality of state discrimination against the disabled or the elderly, Congress must identify, not just the existence of age- or disability-based state decisions, but a "widespread pattern" of irrational reliance on such criteria. * * * We found no such showing [in *Garrett* and *Kimel*].

Here, however, Congress directed its attention to state gender discrimination, which triggers a heightened level of scrutiny. * * * Because the standard for demonstrating the constitutionality of a gender-based classification is more difficult to meet than our rational-basis test * * * it was easier for Congress to show a pattern of state constitutional violations. Congress was similarly successful in South Carolina v. Katzenbach, 383 U. S. 301, 86 S.Ct. 803 (1966), where we upheld the Voting Rights Act of 1965: Because racial classifications are presumptively invalid, most of the States' acts of race discrimination violated the Fourteenth Amendment.

The impact of the discrimination targeted by the FMLA is significant. Congress determined: "Historically, denial or curtailment of women's employment opportunities has been traceable directly to the pervasive presumption that women are mothers first, and workers second. This prevailing ideology about women's roles has in turn justified discrimination against women when they are mothers or mothers-to-be." * * *

Stereotypes about women's domestic roles are reinforced by parallel stereotypes presuming a lack of domestic responsibilities for men. Because employers continued to regard the family as the woman's domain, they often denied men similar accommodations or discouraged them from taking leave. These mutually reinforcing stereotypes created a self-fulfilling cycle of discrimination that forced women to continue to assume the role of primary family caregiver, and fostered employers' stereotypical views about women's commitment to work and their value as employees. Those perceptions, in turn, Congress reasoned, lead to subtle discrimination that may be difficult to detect on a case-by-case basis.

We believe that Congress' chosen remedy, the family-care leave provision of the FMLA, is "congruent and proportional to the targeted violation" * * *. Congress had already tried unsuccessfully to address this problem through Title VII and the amendment of Title VII by the Pregnancy Discrimination Act * * *. Here, as in *Katzenbach*, Congress again confronted a "difficult and intractable proble[m]," * * * where previous legislative attempts had failed. * * * Such problems may justify added prophylactic measures in response. * * *

By creating an across-the-board, routine employment benefit for all eligible employees, Congress sought to ensure that family-care leave would no longer be stigmatized as an inordinate drain on the workplace caused by female employees, and that employers could not evade leave obligations simply by hiring men. By setting a minimum standard of family leave for *all* eligible employees, irrespective of gender, the FMLA attacks the formerly state-sanctioned stereotype * * *.

The dissent characterizes the FMLA as a "substantive entitlement program" rather than a remedial statute because it establishes a floor of 12 weeks' leave. * * * In the dissent's view, in the face of evidence of gender-based discrimination by the States in the provision of leave benefits, Congress could do no more in exercising its §5 power than simply proscribe such discrimination. But this position cannot be squared with our recognition that Congress "is not confined to the enactment of legislation that merely parrots the precise wording of the Fourteenth Amendment," but may prohibit "a somewhat broader swath of conduct, including that which is not itself forbidden by the Amendment's text." *Kimel*, 528 U.S., at 81, 120 S.Ct., at 644. * * *

* * *

Unlike the statutes at issue in *City of Boerne*, *Kimel*, and *Garrett*, which applied broadly to every aspect of state employers' operations, the FMLA is narrowly targeted at the fault line between work and family—precisely where sex-based over-generalization has been and remains strongest—and affects only one aspect of the employment relationship. * * *

* * *

[W]e conclude that * * * [the FMLA] is congruent and proportional to its remedial object, and can "be understood as responsive to, or designed to prevent, unconstitutional behavior." * * *

The judgment of the Court of Appeals is therefore

Affirmed.

Justice KENNEDY, with whom Justice SCALIA and Justice THOMAS join, dissenting.

* * *

[T]he Eleventh Amendment * * * protects a State's fiscal integrity from federal intrusion by vesting the States with immunity from private actions for damages pursuant to federal laws. The Commerce Clause likely would permit the National Government to enact an entitlement program such as this one; but when Congress couples the entitlement with the authorization to sue the States for monetary damages, it blurs the line of accountability the State has to its own citizens. * * *

* * *

The relevant question * * * is whether, notwithstanding the passage of Title VII and similar state legislation, the States continued to engage in widespread discrimination on the basis of gender in the provision of family leave benefits. * * * If such a pattern were shown, the Eleventh Amendment would not bar Congress from devising a congruent and proportional remedy. The evidence to substantiate this charge must be far more specific, however, than a simple recitation of a general history of employment discrimination against women. * * *

Persisting overall effects of gender-based discrimination at the workplace must not be ignored; but simply noting the problem is not a substitute for evidence which identifies some real discrimination the family leave rules are designed to prevent.

* * *

[T]he evidence considered by Congress concerned discriminatory practices of the private sector, not those of state employers. * * * The statistical information compiled by the Bureau of Labor Statistics * * *, which are the only factual findings the Court cites, surveyed only private employers. * * * While the evidence of discrimination by private entities may be relevant, it does not, by itself, justify the abrogation of States' sovereign immunity. * * *

* * *

* * * The application of heightened scrutiny * * * to ensure gender-based classifications are not based on the entrenched and pervasive stereotypes which inhibit women's progress in the workplace * * * does not divest respondents of their burden to show that "Congress identified a history and pattern of unconstitutional employment discrimination by the States." * * * Given the insufficiency of the evidence that States discriminated in the provision of family leave, the unfortunate fact that stereotypes about women continue to be a serious and pervasive social problem would not alone support the charge that a State has engaged in a practice designed to deny its citizens the equal protection of the laws. * * *

* * * [Here,] Congress was not

responding with a congruent and proportional remedy to a perceived course of unconstitutional conduct. Instead, it enacted a substantive entitlement program of its own. If Congress had been concerned about different treatment of men and women with respect to family leave, a congruent remedy would have sought to ensure the benefits of any leave program enacted by a State are available to men and women on an equal basis. Instead, the Act imposes, across the board, a requirement that States grant a minimum of 12 weeks of leave per year. * * * This requirement may represent Congress' considered judgment as to the optimal balance between the family obligations of workers and the interests of employers, and the States may decide to follow these guidelines in designing their own family leave benefits. It does not follow, however, that if the States choose to enact a different benefit scheme, they should be deemed to engage in unconstitutional conduct and forced to open their treasuries to private suits for damages.

* * *

[I]ndividuals whose rights under the Act were violated would not be without recourse. The Act is likely a valid exercise of Congress' power under the Commerce Clause * * * and so the standards it prescribes will be binding upon the States. * * * [P]rivate individuals may bring actions against state officials for *injunctive* relief * * *. [Emphasis supplied.] What is at issue is only whether the States can be subjected, without consent, to suits brought by private persons seeking to collect moneys from the state treasury. Their immunity cannot be abrogated without documentation of a pattern of unconstitutional acts by the States, and only then by a congruent and proportional remedy. * * *

In a second surprising, but more limited, decision departing from the pro-states' rights tack of its many recent Eleventh Amendment decisions, the Court upheld state liability for discriminating against the disabled when inaction by a state or any of its subdivisions impeded access to the judicial process. George Lane, a paraplegic, filed suit for damages against Tennessee and several of its counties for violating Title II of the Americans with Disabilities Act. The law prohibits discrimination against handicapped persons when it comes to participating in public programs and receiving government benefits. Lane argued that he had been denied access to the courts when he was cited for not appearing to answer a criminal traffic complaint. The courthouse contained no elevator, and he refused to drag himself, or be carried, up two flights of stairs to the courtroom. Focusing only on the statute as it applied to participation in the judicial process, Justice Stevens, speaking for a 5-4 majority in Tennessee v. Lane, 541 U.S. 509, 124 S.Ct. 1978 (2004), reasoned that access to the courts was implicit in the right to due process guaranteed by the Fourteenth Amendment. Enforcing that right under §5 of the Amendment, Congress could legitimately override the states' immunity from suit, otherwise protected by the Eleventh Amendment. Chief Justice Rehnquist and Justices Scalia, Kennedy, and Thomas dissented and voted to uphold the states' sovereign immunity.

In an upcoming Eleventh Amendment case, the Supreme Court will consider at its October 2005 Term whether state prisoners with disabilities can sue for damages under the Americans With Disabilities Act. The inmate, a paraplegic, argued that he could not maneuver his wheelchair in his small cell and was deprived of access to a toilet, a shower, and his bed. United States v. Georgia, 545 U.S. —, 125 S.Ct. 2256 (2005).

D. THE TAXING AND SPENDING POWER

The Decline of Dual Federalism

▶ **Insert at p. 363 at the end of the chapter**

Notwithstanding the Rehnquist Court's predisposition toward a rather vigorous application of dual federalism in its reading of the Commerce Clause, the Justices have reaffirmed the long-standing broad view of Congress's spending power in their recent ruling in Sabri v. United States, 541 U.S. 600, 124 S.Ct. 1941 (2004). Sabri, a real estate developer, was indicted under a federal criminal statute, 18 U.S.C.A. § 666(a)(2), which punishes bribery that is intended top influence any organization that receives more than $10,000 in federal funds in a one-year period. A federal district court dismissed the charges against Sabri because, among other contentions, that law amounted to an unconstitutional exercise of Congress's spending power. A federal appellate court reversed, and the Supreme Court affirmed and remanded the case for trial. Speaking for the Court, Justice Souter gave short shrift to this notion:

> Congress has authority under the Spending Clause to appropriate federal monies to promote the general welfare, * * * and it has corresponding authority under the Necessary and Proper Clause * * * to see to it that taxpayer dollars appropriated under that power are in fact spent for the general welfare, and not frittered away in graft or on projects undermined when funds are siphoned off or corrupt public officers are derelict about demanding value for dollars. See generally McCulloch v. Maryland, 17 U.S. (4 Wheat.) 316, 4 L.Ed. 579 (1819) * * *. Congress does not have to sit by and accept the risk of operations thwarted by local and state improbity. * * * Section 666(a)(2) addresses the problem at the sources of bribes, by rational means, to safeguard the integrity of the state, local, and tribal recipients of federal dollars.

> It is true * * * that not every bribe or kickback offered or paid to agents of governments covered by § 666(b) will be traceably skimmed from specific federal payments, or show up in the guise of a *quid pro quo* for some dereliction in spending a federal grant. * * * But * * * corruption does not have to be that limited to affect the federal interest. * * * [O]fficials are not any the less threatening to the objects behind federal spending just because they may accept general retainers. * * * It is certainly enough that the statutes condition the offense on a threshold amount of federal dollars defining the federal interest, such as that provided here,

and on a bribe that goes well beyond liquor and cigars.

> * * * Congress's decision to enact § 666 only after other legislation had failed to protect federal interests is further indication that it was acting within the ambit of the Necessary and Proper Clause.

The dual federalist spirit, however, was alive and well in Justice Thomas's opinion concurring only in the Court's judgment. Chiding Justice Souter for "a not-wholly-convincing job of tying the broad scope of [the statute] to a federal interest in federal funds and programs[,]" he argued that the law "appears to be no more plainly adapted to protecting federal funds or federally funded programs than a hypothetical federal statute criminalizing fraud of any kind perpetrated on any individual who happens to receive federal welfare benefits." Such an interest was, in Justice Thomas's view, too "attenuated" to be covered by the reach of the Necessary and Proper Clause. He nonetheless went on to sustain the statute as a valid exercise of Congress's power under the Commerce Clause.

Chapter 6

The Regulatory Power of the States in the Federal System

Federal Preemption and Federal Dictation

▶ **Insert at p. 375 at the end of the chart**

OTHER CASES ON PREEMPTION--CONTINUED		
CASE	RULING	VOTE
Kentucky Association of Health Care Plans, Inc. v. Miller, 538 U.S. 329, 123 S.Ct. 1471 (2003)	If state law requires it, HMOs must open their networks to any doctor who agrees to their conditions and rates. State "any willing provider" laws are not preempted by the federal Employee Retirement Income Security Act of 1974. If a doctor is willing to function under the HMO's conditions and rates, the managed care organization cannot bar a patient from a doctor of his choice.	9-0.
Pharmaceutical Research and Manufacturers of America v. Walsh, 538 U.S. 644, 123 S.Ct. 1855 (2003)	State prescription drug program to reduce the price of drugs for all needy state residents as well as Medicaid recipients does not violate the Commerce Clause where the state required drug manufacturers who did not sign a price rebate agreement with it to then obtain prior approval from a state agency to qualify a doctor's prescription for reimbursement. Whether it is in conflict with, and pre-empted by, federal Medicaid law is premature to say, since program had not yet been submitted to the Secretary of Health and Human Services for his approval.	6-3; Chief Justice Rehnquist and Justices O'Connor and Kennedy dissented.

OTHER CASES ON PREEMPTION--CONTINUED		
CASE	RULING	VOTE
Aetna Health, Inc. v. Davila, 542 U.S. 200, 124 S.Ct. 2488 (2004)	Patients bringing legal action because their HMOs allegedly would not pay for necessary medical services cannot sue for damages in state court under state law because the Employee Retirement Income Security Act of 1974 (ERISA) completely preempts the field. ERISA requires that such malpractice suits be brought only in federal court.	9-0.

▶ **Insert at p. 382 following *New York* v. *United States***

The fault identified in Part C of Justice O'Connor's opinion for the Court in *New York v. United States* (see Text, p. 375) is essentially what we have come to call "an unfunded federal mandate." By this we mean that Congress orders the states to do something within their jurisdiction but doesn't provide the money. In other words, rather than conditioning action upon the receipt of federal funds, policy is simply imposed. As we saw in Chapter 5, section D, Congress may attach strings to its exercise of the taxing and spending power, but just telling the states what to do in areas of their own jurisdiction is unconstitutional.

There is much of the ring of an "unfunded federal mandate" in Utah's recent characterization of the "No Child Left Behind" Law (NCLB). That statute has been heralded as a significant education achievement of President George W. Bush's Administration. The state's decision to defy the federal government over the statute is the more remarkable because Utah is arguably the most Republican state in the Nation: It voted to re-elect President Bush with 72% of the vote in 2004 and has two Republican senators, a Republican governor, and a solidly Republican state legislature. So why the fuss?

In an attempt to raise the quality of public education, NCLB requires that every racial and ethnic ground—most notably disabled students—in every school score increasingly higher on standardized tests every year. A lesser performance can trigger sanctions, such as the transfer of students or closing schools. The inflexibility with which the law has been applied and burgeoning cost to the states has set off a rebellion, especially in the Republican heartland. Although NCLB itself specifically provides that states cannot be forced to spend their own money to meet federal requirements, the states argue that is what has happened. The country's largest teachers' union and eight school districts in Michigan, Texas, and Vermont have sued the U.S. Department of Education to vindicate this provision, but Utah has gone the furthest. It passed legislation that gives Utah's educational standards priority over NCLB requirements and authorizes state education officials to ignore federal testing requirements that conflict with the state's program. Other states are considering similar legislation. New York Times, Apr. 21, 2005, pp. A1, A19; New York Times, May 11, 2005, p. A15.

Critics argue that, although the federal government pays only about 8 cents of every education dollar spent, NCLB has given it almost total control. Connecticut's attorney general has announced he intends to sue the federal government for forcing that state to conduct more testing without paying for it. He argues that NCLB requires Connecticut to spend $112.2 million to expand its testing program and otherwise assist local school districts but that Congress has only appropriated $70.6 million, leaving the state to come up with the balance. New York Times, Apr. 6, 2005, p. A21. The U.S. Department of Education has not relented, although it has announced greater flexibility on the states' testing of disabled students. Seen in this light, the problem may not be so much an "unfunded federal mandate" as an "inadequately funded" one. Where this sits on the spectrum of constitutionality is anybody's guess.

The Negative or Dormant Commerce Clause

▶ **Insert at p. 404 following *Kassel* v. *Consolidated Freightways Corp.***

AMERICAN TRUCKING ASSOCIATIONS, INC. V. MICHIGAN PUBLIC SERVICE COMMISSION
Supreme Court of the United States, 2005
545 U.S. —, 125 S.Ct. 2419, — L.Ed.2d —

BACKGROUND & FACTS   A trucking company and an industry trade group whose members engaged in both interstate and intrastate hauling sued in state court challenging Michigan's $100 annual fee imposed on all trucks that did commercial hauling within the state. The plaintiffs argued that the flat fee discriminated against interstate carriers and imposed an unconstitutional burden on interstate commerce because trucks carrying both interstate and intrastate loads engaged in less within-state business than trucks carrying only loads to and from points within Michigan. A state trial court rejected this argument, as did the Michigan Court of Appeals. After the Michigan Supreme Court denied review, the plaintiffs successfully petitioned the U.S. Supreme Court for certiorari.

Justice BREYER delivered the opinion of the Court.

* * *

* * * [T]his Court has consistently held

that the Constitution's express grant to Congress of the power to "regulate Commerce ... among the several States" * * * contains "a further, negative command, known as the dormant Commerce Clause" * * * that "create[s] an area of trade free from interference by the States" * * *. This negative command prevents a State from "jeopardizing the welfare of the Nation as a whole" by "plac[ing] burdens on the flow of commerce across its borders that commerce wholly within those borders would not bear." * * *

Thus, we have found unconstitutional state regulations that unjustifiably discriminate on their face against out-of-state entities, * * * or that impose burdens on interstate trade that are "clearly excessive in relation to the putative local benefits" * * *. We have held that States may not impose taxes that facially discriminate against interstate business and offer commercial advantage to local enterprises, * * * that improperly apportion state assessments on transactions with out-of-state components, * * * or that have the "inevitable effect [of] threaten[ing] the free movement of commerce by placing a financial barrier around the State" * * *.

Applying these principles[,] * * * we find nothing in [the law] that offends the Commerce Clause. To begin with, Michigan imposes the flat $100 fee only upon intrastate transactions—that is, upon activities taking place exclusively within the State's borders. [The law] does not facially discriminate against interstate or out-of-state activities or enterprises. * * * [It] applies evenhandedly to all carriers that make domestic journeys. It does not reflect an effort to tax activity that takes place, in whole or in part, outside the State. Nothing in our case law suggests that such a neutral, locally focused fee or tax is inconsistent with the dormant Commerce Clause.

* * * States impose numerous flat fees upon local businesses and service providers, including, for example, upon insurers, auctioneers, ambulance operators, and hosts of others. * * * [T]he Constitution neither displaces States' authority "to shelter [their] people from menaces to their health or safety," * * * nor "unduly curtail[s]" States' power "to lay taxes for the support of state government" * * *.

The record * * * shows no special circumstance suggesting that Michigan's fee operates in practice as anything other than an unobjectionable exercise of the State's police power. To the contrary, * * * the record contains little, if any, evidence that the $100 fee imposes any significant practical burden upon interstate trade. * * * The record does show, for example, that some interstate trucks "top off" some interstate hauls with intrastate pickups and deliveries. * * * But it does not tell us the answers to such questions as: How often does "topping off" occur across the industry? Does the $100 charge make a difference by significantly discouraging interstate carriers from engaging in "topping off"? Does the possibility of obtaining a 72-hour intrastate permit for $10 alleviate the alleged problem? * * * If the fees ($100 and $10) discourage "topping off," does that *local* commercial effect make a significant *interstate* difference? * * *

Neither does the record show that the flat assessment unfairly discriminates against interstate truckers. The fee seeks to defray costs such as those of regulating "vehicular size and weight," of administering "insurance requirements," and of applying "safety standards." * * * The bulk of such costs would seem more likely to vary per truck or per carrier than to vary per-mile traveled. * * * And that fact means that a per-truck, rather than a per-mile, assessment is likely fair. * * * Nothing in the record suggests the contrary.

Nor would an effort to switch the manner of fee assessment—from lump sum to, for example, miles traveled—be burden free. * * * [T]o obtain the same revenue (about $3.5 million) through a per-mile fee would require the State to create a "data accumulation system" capable of separating out intrastate hauls and determining their length, and to develop related liability, billing, and auditing mechanisms. * * * This * * * suggests that the game is unlikely to be worth the candle. While petitioners argue the contrary, they do not provide the details of their preferred alternative administrative system nor point to record evidence showing its practicality. * * *

* * *

The present fee * * * taxes purely local activity; it does not tax an interstate truck's entry into the State nor does it tax transactions spanning multiple States. * * * We lack convincing evidence showing that the tax deters, or for that matter discriminates against, interstate activities. * * * Consequently, we lack any reason to infer that Michigan's lump-sum levy erects * * * an impermissible discriminatory road block * * * or violates the Commerce Clause in any other relevant way. * * *

For these reasons, the judgment of the Michigan Court of Appeals is affirmed.

* * *

Justice THOMAS, concurring in the judgment.

I would affirm the judgment of the Michigan Court of Appeals because[,] [as I have said before] "'[t]he negative Commerce Clause has no basis in the text of the Constitution, makes little sense, and has proved virtually unworkable in application,' * * * and, consequently, cannot serve as a basis for striking down a state statute." * * *

▎ **Insert at p. 408 following *City of Philadelphia* v. *State of New Jersey***

The NIMBY (not-in-my-back-yard) syndrome, so well illustrated by New Jersey's anti-dumping statute, was equally evident when the governor of South Carolina issued an executive order declaring a state of emergency and prohibiting any transportation of weapons-grade plutonium on the state's roads. The governor's action was designed to prevent the federal transfer of weapons-grade plutonium from a Colorado site to South Carolina for long-term storage.

In Abraham v. Hodges, 255 F.Supp.2d 539 (D.S.C. 2002), a federal district court granted summary judgment to the federal Department of Energy and held (1) that the Atomic Energy Act of 1954 preempted state action in the field of nuclear materials safety; (2) that state policy contradicting exercise of the federal government's plenary authority flatly violated the Supremacy Clause; and (3) that state prohibition on the transportation of radioactive material expressly discriminated against interstate commerce and therefore violated the Commerce Clause. The district judge was plainly exasperated at having to discuss the supremacy issue at all and the obvious applicability of *McCulloch v. Maryland*, which he characterized as so "well known" the decision "is one of the first two cases * * * usually taught in the basic constitutional law course at most law schools." As for the Commerce Clause matter, the court found the governor's executive order clearly doomed by the Supreme Court's decision in *City of Philadelphia v. State of New Jersey*. A more patient federal appeals court simply affirmed the district court's judgment on preemption grounds, and the Supreme Court subsequently denied cert. See Abraham v. Hodges, 300 F.3d 432 (4th Cir. 2002), *cert. denied*, 537 U.S. 1105, 123 S.Ct. 871 (2003).

Another line of controversial state regulation has been restricting out-of-state wineries from shipping their product directly to in-state consumers, even though in-state wineries may do so. The stakes are high: Revenue short-falls have spurred states to close tax loopholes and wine producers have sought to maximize their profits by cutting out wholesalers. Viewed narrowly, the validity of out-of-state wine purchasing bans could be seen as turning on the states' power to regulate alcoholic beverages retained by them under the terms of the Twenty-first Amendment. But, if framed in the larger picture of a collision between the police power of the states and the Commerce Clause of Article I, the dispute could invite examination of state power to regulate Internet purchases generally. So, does a ban on direct shipping by out-of-state wineries unconstitutioinally burden interstate commerce? The Supreme Court delivered its answer in the following decision which consolidated for argument cases from Michigan and New York.

GRANHOLM V. HEALD
Supreme Court of the United States, 2005
544 U.S. —, 125 S.Ct. 1885, 161 L.Ed.2d 796

BACKGROUND & FACTS   Heald and others, wine enthusiasts, wine journalists, and one small California winery that ships to customers in other states, brought suit against Governor Jennifer Granholm of Michigan, challenging the constitutionality of that state's law which forbids direct shipments to Michigan customers from out-of-state wineries. Other plaintiffs challenged New York's regulatory scheme which, while not directly forbidding such shipments, heavily burdened such sales by effectively requiring some in-state presence by the seller and imposing a complex licensing scheme. Plaintiffs argued that the state regulations were a flat violation of the Commerce Clause. The states argued that their regulatory schemes were saved by the Twenty-first Amendment and by legitimate concerns about alcohol purchasing by minors and tax collection. A federal appeals court struck down the Michigan statute but another federal appellate court sustained the New York law. The Supreme Court granted certiorari to resolve the conflict between the circuits.

Justice KENNEDY delivered the opinion of the Court.

* * *

Time and again this Court has held that, in all but the narrowest circumstances, state laws violate the Commerce Clause if they mandate "differential treatment of in-state and out-of-state economic interests that benefits the former and burdens the latter." Oregon Waste Systems, Inc. v. Department of Environmental Quality of Ore., 511 U.S. 93, 99, 114 S.Ct. 1345 (1994). * * * States may not enact laws that burden out-of-state producers or shippers simply to give a competitive advantage to in-state businesses. This mandate "reflect[s] a central concern of the Framers that was an immediate reason for calling the Constitutional Convention: the conviction that in order to succeed, the new Union would have to avoid the tendencies toward economic Balkanization that had plagued relations among the Colonies and later among the States under the Articles of Confederation." Hughes v. Oklahoma, 441 U.S. 322, 325-326, 99 S.Ct. 1727 (1979).

The rule prohibiting state discrimination against interstate commerce follows also from the principle that States should not be compelled to negotiate with each other regarding favored or disfavored status for their own citizens. States do not need, and may not attempt, to negotiate with other States regarding their mutual economic interests. * * * Rivalries among the States are thus kept to a minimum, and a proliferation of trade zones is prevented. * * *

Laws of the type at issue in the instant cases * * * deprive citizens of their right to have access to the markets of other States on equal terms. The perceived necessity for reciprocal sale privileges risks generating the trade rivalries and animosities, the alliances and exclusivity, that the Constitution and, in particular, the Commerce Clause were designed to avoid. State laws that protect local wineries have led to the enactment of statutes under which some States condition the right of out-of-state wineries to make direct wine sales to in-state consumers on a reciprocal right in the shipping State. * * * The current patchwork of laws—with some States banning direct shipments altogether, others doing so only for out-of-state wines, and still others requiring reciprocity—is essentially the product of an ongoing, low-level trade war. * * *

The discriminatory character of the Michigan system is obvious. Michigan allows in-state wineries to ship directly to consumers, subject only to a licensing requirement. Out-of-state wineries, whether licensed or not, face a complete ban on direct shipment. The differential treatment requires all out-of-state wine, but not all in-state wine, to pass through an in-state wholesaler and retailer before reaching consumers. These two extra layers of overhead increase the cost of out-of-state wines to Michigan consumers. The cost differential, and in some cases the inability to secure a wholesaler for small shipments, can effectively bar small wineries from the Michigan market.

The New York regulatory scheme differs from Michigan's in that it does not ban direct shipments altogether. Out-of-state wineries are instead required to establish a distribution operation in New York in order to gain the privilege of direct shipment. * * * This, though, is just an indirect way of subjecting out-of-state wineries, but not local ones, to the three-tier system. New York and those allied with its interests defend the scheme by arguing that an out-of-state winery has the same access to the State's consumers as in-state wineries: All wine must be sold through a licensee fully accountable to New York; it just so happens that in order to become a licensee, a winery must have a physical presence in the State. There is some confusion over the precise steps out-of-state wineries must take to gain access to the New York market, in part because no winery has run the State's regulatory gauntlet. * * *

* * * Out-of-state wineries must open a branch office and warehouse in New York, additional steps that drive up the cost of their wine. * * * For most wineries, the expense of establishing a bricks-and-mortar distribution operation in 1 State, let alone all 50, is prohibitive. * * * New York's in-state presence requirement runs contrary to our admonition that States cannot require an out-of-state firm "to become a resident in order to compete on equal terms." Halliburton Oil Well Cementing Co. v. Reily, 373 U.S. 64, 72, 83 S.Ct. 1201 (1963). * * *

* * *

* * * The Michigan and New York laws by their own terms [discriminate against interstate commerce] * * *. The two States, however, contend their statutes are saved by § 2 of the Twenty-first Amendment, which provides: "The transportation or importation into any State, Territory, or possession of the United States for delivery or use therein of intoxicating liquors, in violation of the laws thereof, is hereby prohibited." * * *

* * *

The ratification of the Eighteenth Amendment in 1919 provided a brief respite from the legal battles over the validity of state liquor regulations. With the ratification of the Twenty-first Amendment 14 years later, however, nationwide Prohibition came to an end. Section 1 of the Twenty-first Amendment repealed the Eighteenth Amendment. * * *

Michigan and New York say [§ 2 of the Twenty-first Amendment] grants to the States the authority to discriminate against out-of-state goods. * * *

The aim of the * * * Amendment was to allow States to maintain an effective and uniform system for controlling liquor by regulating its transportation, importation, and use. The Amendment did not give States the authority to pass nonuniform laws in order to discriminate against out-of-state goods, a privilege they had not enjoyed at any earlier time.

* * *

We still must consider whether either State regime "advances a legitimate local purpose that cannot be adequately served by reasonable nondiscriminatory alternatives." * * * The States offer two primary justifications for restricting direct shipments from out-of-state wineries: keeping alcohol out of the hands of minors and facilitating tax collection. * * *

The States, aided by several *amici*, claim that allowing direct shipment from out-of-state wineries undermines their ability to police underage drinking. Minors, the States argue, have easy access to credit cards and the Internet and are likely to take advantage of direct wine shipments as a means of obtaining alcohol illegally.

The States provide little evidence that the purchase of wine over the Internet by minors is a problem. Indeed, there is some evidence to the contrary. A recent study by the staff of the FTC found that the 26 States currently allowing direct shipments report no problems with minors' increased access to wine. * * * This is not surprising for several reasons. First, minors are less likely to consume wine, as opposed to beer, wine coolers, and hard liquor. * * * Second, minors who decide to disobey the law have more direct means of doing so. Third, direct shipping is an imperfect avenue of obtaining alcohol for minors who, in the words of the past president of the National Conference of State Liquor Administrators, "'want instant gratification.'" * * * Without concrete evidence that direct shipping of wine is likely to increase alcohol consumption by minors, we are left with the States' unsupported assertions. * * *

Even were we to credit the States' largely unsupported claim that direct shipping of wine increases the risk of underage drinking, this would not justify regulations limiting only out-of-state direct shipments. As the wineries point out, minors are just as likely to order wine from in-state producers as from out-of-state ones. * * * [Moreover,] [o]ut-of-state wineries face the loss of state and federal licenses if they fail to comply with state law. This provides strong incentives not to sell alcohol to minors. In addition, the States can take less restrictive steps to minimize the risk that minors will order wine by mail. For example, the Model Direct Shipping Bill developed by the National Conference of State Legislatures requires an adult signature on delivery and a label so instructing on each package.

The States' tax-collection justification is also insufficient. Increased direct shipping, whether originating in state or out of state, brings with it the potential for tax evasion. With regard to Michigan, however, the tax-collection argument is a diversion. That is because Michigan, unlike many other States, does not rely on wholesalers to collect taxes on wines imported from out-of-state. Instead, Michigan collects taxes directly from out-of-state wineries on all wine shipped to in-state wholesalers. * * * If licensing and self-reporting provide adequate safeguards for wine distributed through the three-tier system, there is no reason to believe they will not suffice for direct shipments.

New York['s] * * * regulatory objectives [also] can be achieved without discriminating against interstate commerce. In particular, New York could protect itself against lost tax revenue by requiring a permit as a condition of direct shipping. This is the approach taken by New York for in-state wineries. The State offers no reason to believe the system would prove ineffective for out-of-state wineries. * * *

* * *

Michigan and New York offer a handful of other rationales, such as facilitating orderly market conditions, protecting public health and safety, and ensuring regulatory accountability. These objectives can also be achieved through the alternative of an evenhanded licensing requirement. * * * Finally, it should be noted that improvements in technology have eased the burden of monitoring out-of-state wineries. Background checks can be done electronically. Financial records and sales data can be mailed, faxed, or submitted via e-mail.

* * *

* * * If a State chooses to allow direct shipment of wine, it must do so on evenhanded terms. Without demonstrating the need for discrimination, New York and Michigan have enacted regulations that disadvantage out-of-state wine producers. Under our Commerce Clause jurisprudence, these regulations cannot stand.

We affirm the judgment of the Court of Appeals for the Sixth Circuit; and we reverse the judgment of the Court of Appeals for the Second Circuit and remand the case for further proceedings consistent with our opinion.

It is so ordered.

Justice STEVENS, with whom Justice O'CONNOR joins, dissenting.

* * *

The New York and Michigan laws challenged in these cases would be patently invalid under well settled dormant Commerce Clause principles if they regulated sales of an ordinary article of commerce rather than wine. But ever since the adoption of the Eighteenth Amendment and the Twenty-first Amendment, our Constitution has placed commerce in alcoholic beverages in a special category. * * *

Today many Americans * * * regard alcohol as an ordinary article of commerce, subject to substantially the same market and legal controls as other consumer products. That was definitely not the view of the generations that made policy in 1919 when the Eighteenth Amendment was ratified or in 1933 when it was repealed by the Twenty-first Amendment. On the contrary, the moral condemnation of the use of alcohol as a beverage represented not merely the convictions of our religious leaders, but the views of a sufficiently large majority of the population to warrant the rare exercise of the power to amend the Constitution on two occasions. * * *

* * *

In the years following the ratification of the Twenty-first Amendment, States adopted manifold laws regulating commerce in alcohol, and many of these laws were discriminatory. So-called "dry states" entirely prohibited such commerce; others prohibited the sale of alcohol on Sundays; others permitted the sale of beer and wine but not hard liquor; most created either state monopolies or distribution systems that gave discriminatory preferences to local retailers and distributors. The notion that discriminatory state laws violated the unwritten prohibition against balkanizing the American economy * * * would have seemed strange indeed to the millions of Americans who condemned the use of the "demon rum" in the 1920's and 1930's. Indeed, they expressly authorized the "balkanization" that today's decision condemns. Today's decision may represent sound economic policy and may be consistent with the policy choices of the contemporaries of Adam Smith who drafted our original Constitution; it is not, however, consistent with the policy choices made by those who amended our Constitution in 1919 and 1933.

* * *

Justice THOMAS, with whom THE CHIEF JUSTICE [REHNQUIST], Justice STEVENS, and Justice O'CONNOR join, dissenting.

A century ago, this Court repeatedly invalidated, as inconsistent with the negative Commerce Clause, state liquor legislation that prevented out-of-state businesses from shipping liquor directly to a State's residents. The Webb-Kenyon Act and the Twenty-first Amendment cut off this intrusive review, as their text and history make clear and as this Court's early cases on the Twenty-first Amendment recognized. The Court today seizes back this power * * *. Because I would follow * * * the language of both the statute that Congress enacted and the Amendment that the Nation ratified, rather than the Court's questionable reading of history and the "negative implications" of the Commerce Clause, I respectfully dissent.

* * *

Section 2 of the Twenty-first Amendment * * * tracked the Webb-Kenyon Act by authorizing state regulation that would otherwise conflict with the negative Commerce Clause. * * * Though the Twenty-first Amendment mirrors the basic terminology of the Webb-Kenyon Act, its language is broader, authorizing States to regulate all "transportation or importation" that runs afoul of state law. The broader language even more naturally encompasses discriminatory state laws. Its terms suggest, for example, that a State may ban imports entirely while leaving in-state liquor unregulated, for they do not condition the State's ability to prohibit imports on the manner in which state law treats domestic products.

The state laws at issue in these cases * * * prohibit wine manufacturers from "transport[ing] or import[ing]" wine directly to consumers in New York and Michigan "for delivery or use therein." Michigan law does so by requiring all out-of-state wine manufacturers to distribute wine through licensed in-state wholesalers. * * * New York law does so by prohibiting out-of-state wineries from shipping wine directly to consumers unless they establish an in-state physical presence, something that in-state wineries naturally have. * * * The Twenty-first Amendment prohibits out-of-state wineries from shipping wine into Michigan and New York in violation of these laws. In holding that the Constitution prohibits Michigan's and New York's laws, the majority turns the Amendment's text on its head.

* * *

The Court * * * detail[s] the evils of state laws that restrict the direct shipment of wine[,] * * * stresses that allowing the direct shipment of wine would enhance consumer welfare[,] * * * [and] suggests that it believes that its decision serves this Nation well. * * * The Twenty-first Amendment and the Webb-Kenyon Act took those policy choices away from judges and returned them to the States. Whatever the wisdom of that choice, the Court does this Nation no service by ignoring the textual commands of the Constitution and Acts of Congress. * * * They require sustaining the constitutionality of Michigan's and New York's direct-shipment laws. * * *

CHAPTER 7

PROPERTY RIGHTS AND ECONOMIC LIBERTIES

C. THE REGULATION AND "TAKING" OF PROPERTY

▶ **Insert at p. 466 following *Dolan* v. *City of Tigard***

Whatever harbingers of economic judicial activism an observer might have discerned by reading the tea leaves in the *Nollan, Lucas,* and *Dolan* decisions, the Court's most recent Takings Clause decisions hue much more strongly to judicial self-restraint. In the *Kelo* decision that follows—arguably the most important Takings Clause decision of the Rehnquist Court—Justice Kennedy supplied the critical fifth vote that allowed the dissenters in *Dolan* to carry the day.

KELO V. CITY OF NEW LONDON
Supreme Court of the United States, 2005
545 U.S. —, 125 S.Ct. 2655, — L.Ed.2d —

BACKGROUND & FACTS Designated a "distressed municipality" by a state agency a decade earlier, New London approved an urban development plan in 2000 that was projected to create more than 1,000 jobs, substantially increase tax revenues, and revitalize its downtown and waterfront areas. The city's population had dropped to 24,000, the lowest since the 1920s, its unemployment rate was double the state average, and the recent closure of a federal facility had idled 1,500 workers. Some of the land for the urban renewal project was purchased from willing sellers, but other parcels were to be obtained by the city's exercise of eminent domain from residents who did not want to give up their homes, even though they would receive just compensation. The centerpiece of the city's plan was a waterfront conference center surrounded by a "small urban village" with restaurants, shopping, and recreational areas. There would be a pedestrian riverwalk, a state park, a museum, marinas, and some 80 new residences. Adjacent to part of the area, which was to contain 92,000 square feet of research and office space, was to be a facility of the Pfizer drug company. The plan was intended to capitalize on the arrival of Pfizer and to create commercial opportunities.

The city instituted condemnation proceedings to obtain properties from landowners unwilling to sell. Among those was Susette Kelo, who bought her house three years before the city approved the redevelopment plan, and who made extensive improvements to the property which she prized for its waterfront view. Wilhelmina Dery was another property owner unwilling to sell. She had been born in the house she owned and had lived there for 87 years. Kelo and Dery sued to halt the city's acquisition of their properties on grounds the city's use of eminent domain violated the Takings Clause of the Fifth Amendment which states, "[N]or shall private property be taken for public use, without just compensation." They argued that their properties would, in turn, be leased by the city to other private entities—whether businesses or residents—not necessarily with public access, and therefore not constituting a "public use." A state trial court found for the plaintiffs and entered a permanent restraining order against the city. On appeal, the Connecticut Supreme Court, on a 4-3 vote, reversed that judgment and held for the city. Kelo and Dery then successfully petitioned the U.S. Supreme Court for certiorari.

Justice STEVENS delivered the opinion of the Court.

* * * The question presented is whether the city's proposed disposition of this property qualifies as a "public use" within the meaning of the Takings Clause of the Fifth Amendment to the Constitution.

* * *

On the one hand, it has long been accepted that the sovereign may not take the property of A for the sole purpose of transferring it to another private party B, even though A is paid just compensation. On the other hand, it is equally clear that a State may transfer property from one private party to another if future "use by the public" is the purpose of the taking; the condemnation of land for a railroad with common-carrier duties is a familiar example. Neither of these propositions, however, determines the disposition of this case.

As for the first proposition, the City would no doubt be forbidden from taking petitioners' land for the purpose of conferring a private benefit on a particular private party. * * * Nor would the City be allowed to take property under the mere pretext of a public purpose, when its actual purpose was to bestow a private benefit. The takings before us, however, would be executed pursuant to a "carefully considered" development plan. * * * The trial judge and all the members of the Supreme Court of Connecticut agreed that there was no evidence of an illegitimate purpose in this case. Therefore, * * * the City's development plan was not adopted "to benefit a particular class of identifiable individuals."

On the other hand, this is not a case in which the City is planning to open the condemned land—at least not in its entirety—to use by the general public. Nor will the private lessees of the land in any sense be required to operate like common carriers, making their services available to all comers. But although such a projected use would be sufficient to satisfy the public use requirement, this "Court long ago rejected any literal requirement that condemned property be put into use for the general public." * * * Indeed, while many state courts in the mid-19th century endorsed "use by the public" as the proper definition of public use, that narrow view steadily eroded over time. Not only was the "use by the public" test difficult to administer (*e.g.*, what proportion of the public need have access to the property? at what price?), but it proved to be impractical given the diverse and always evolving needs of society. Accordingly, when this Court began applying the Fifth Amendment to the States at the close of the 19th century, it embraced the broader and more natural interpretation of public use as "public purpose." * * *

* * * Without exception, our cases have defined that concept broadly, reflecting our longstanding policy of deference to legislative judgments in this field.

In Berman v. Parker, 348 U.S. 26, 75 S.Ct. 98 (1954), this Court upheld a redevelopment plan targeting a blighted area of Washington, D. C., in which most of the housing for the area's 5,000 inhabitants was beyond repair. Under the plan, the area would be condemned and part of it utilized for the construction of streets, schools, and other public facilities. The remainder of the land would be leased or sold to private parties for the purpose of redevelopment, including the construction of low-cost housing.

The owner of a department store located in the area challenged the condemnation, pointing out that his store was not itself blighted and arguing that the creation of a "better balanced, more attractive community" was not a valid public use. * * * Writing for a unanimous Court, Justice Douglas refused to evaluate this claim in isolation, deferring instead to the legislative and agency judgment that the area "must be planned as a whole" for the plan to be successful. * * * The Court explained that "community redevelopment programs need not, by force of the Constitution, be on a piecemeal basis—lot by lot, building by building." * * * The public use underlying the taking was unequivocally affirmed:

"We do not sit to determine whether a particular housing project is or is not desirable. The concept of the public welfare is broad and inclusive .... The values it represents are spiritual as well as physical, aesthetic as well as monetary. It is within the power of the legislature to determine that the community should be beautiful as well as healthy, spacious as well as clean, well-balanced as well as carefully patrolled. In the present case, the Congress and its authorized agencies have made determinations that take into account a wide variety of values. It is not for us to reappraise them. If those who govern the District of Columbia decide that the Nation's Capital should be beautiful as well as sanitary, there is nothing in the Fifth Amendment that stands in the way." * * *

In Hawaii Housing Authority v. Midkiff, 467 U.S. 229, 104 S.Ct. 2321 (1984), the Court considered a Hawaii statute whereby fee title was taken from lessors and transferred to lessees (for just compensation) in order to reduce the concentration of land ownership. We unanimously upheld the statute and rejected the Ninth Circuit's view that it was "a naked attempt on the part of the state of Hawaii to take the property of A and transfer it to B solely for B's private use and benefit." * * * Reaffirming Berman's deferential approach to legislative judgments in this field, we concluded that the State's purpose of eliminating the "social and economic evils of a land oligopoly" qualified as a valid public use. * * * Our opinion also rejected the contention that the mere fact that the State immediately transferred the properties to private individuals upon condemnation somehow diminished the public character of the taking. "[I]t is only the taking's purpose, and not its mechanics," we explained, that matters in determining public use." * * *

* * *

Viewed as a whole, our jurisprudence has recognized that the needs of society have varied between different parts of the Nation, just as they have evolved over time in response to changed circumstances. Our earliest cases in particular embodied a strong theme of federalism, emphasizing the "great respect" that we owe to state legislatures and state courts in discerning local public needs. * * * For more than a century, our public use jurisprudence has wisely eschewed rigid formulas and intrusive scrutiny in favor of affording legislatures broad latitude in determining what public needs justify the use of the takings power.

[The] determination [of those who govern the City] * * * that the area was sufficiently distressed to justify a program of economic rejuvenation is entitled to our deference. The City has carefully formulated an economic development plan that it believes will provide appreciable benefits to the community, including—but by no means limited to—new jobs and increased tax revenue. As with other exercises in urban planning and development, the City is endeavoring to coordinate a variety of commercial, residential, and recreational uses of land, with the hope that they will form a whole greater than the sum of its parts. To effectuate this plan, the City has invoked a state statute that specifically authorizes the use of eminent domain to promote economic development. Given the comprehensive character of the plan, the thorough deliberation that preceded its adoption, and the limited scope of our review, it is appropriate for us, as it was in *Berman*, to resolve the challenges of the individual owners, not on a piecemeal basis, but rather in light of the entire plan. Because that plan unquestionably serves a public purpose, the takings challenged here satisfy the public use requirement of the Fifth Amendment.

[P]etitioners urge us to adopt a new bright-line rule that economic development does not qualify as a public use. * * * Promoting economic development is a traditional and long accepted function of government. There is, moreover, no principled way of distinguishing economic development from the other public purposes that we have recognized. * * * [I]n *Berman*, we endorsed the purpose of transforming a blighted area into a "well-balanced" community through redevelopment * * *; in *Midkiff*, we upheld the interest in breaking up a land oligopoly that "created artificial deterrents to the normal functioning of the State's residential land market" * * *. It would be incongruous to hold that the City's interest in the economic benefits to be derived from the development of the * * * [designated] area has less of a public character than any of those other interests. Clearly, there is no basis for exempting economic development from our traditionally broad understanding of public purpose.

Petitioners contend that using eminent domain for economic development impermissibly blurs the boundary between public and private takings. * * * [T]he government's pursuit of a public purpose will often benefit individual private parties. For example, in *Midkiff*, the forced transfer of property conferred a direct and significant benefit on those lessees who were previously unable to purchase their homes. * * * The owner of the department store in *Berman* objected to "taking from one businessman for the benefit of another businessman," * * * referring to the fact that under the redevelopment plan land would be leased or sold to private developers for redevelopment. * * * Our rejection of that contention has particular relevance to the instant case: "The public end may be as well or better served through an agency of private enterprise than through a department of government—or so the Congress might conclude. We cannot say that public ownership is the sole method of promoting the public purposes of community redevelopment projects." * * *

It is further argued that without a bright-line rule nothing would stop a city from transferring citizen A's property to citizen B for the sole reason that citizen B will put the property to a more productive use and thus pay more taxes. Such a one-to-one transfer of property, executed outside the confines of an integrated development plan, is not presented in this case. While such an unusual exercise of government power would certainly raise a suspicion that a private purpose was afoot, the hypothetical cases posited by petitioners can be confronted if and when they arise. They do not warrant the crafting of an artificial restriction on the concept of public use.

Alternatively, petitioners maintain that for takings of this kind we should require a "reasonable certainty" that the expected public benefits will actually accrue. Such a rule, however, would represent an even greater departure from our precedent. "When the legislature's purpose is legitimate and its means are not irrational, our cases make clear that empirical debates over the wisdom of takings--no less than debates over the wisdom of other kinds of socioeconomic legislation--are not to be carried out in the federal courts." *Midkiff*, 467 U.S., at 242, 104 S.Ct., at 2330. * * * The disadvantages of a heightened form of review are especially pronounced in this type of case. Orderly implementation of a comprehensive redevelopment plan obviously requires that the legal rights of all interested parties be established before new construction can be commenced. A constitutional rule that required postponement of the judicial approval of every condemnation until the likelihood of success of the plan had been assured would unquestionably impose a significant impediment to the successful consummation of many such plans.

Just as we decline to second-guess the City's considered judgments about the efficacy of its development plan, we also decline to second-guess the City's determinations as to what lands it needs to acquire in order to effectuate the project. "It is not for the courts to oversee the choice of the boundary line nor to sit in review on the size of a particular project area. Once the question of the public purpose has been decided, the amount and character of land to be taken for the project and the need for a particular tract to complete the integrated plan rests in the discretion of the legislative branch." *Berman*, 348 U.S., at 35-36, 75 S.Ct., at 104.

In affirming the City's authority to take petitioners' properties, we do not minimize the hardship that condemnations may entail, notwithstanding the payment of just compensation. We emphasize that nothing in our opinion precludes any State from placing further restrictions on its exercise of the takings power. Indeed, many States already impose "public use" requirements that are stricter than the federal baseline. Some of these requirements have been established as a matter of state constitutional law, while others are expressed in state eminent domain statutes that carefully limit the grounds upon which takings may be exercised. * * * [T]he necessity and wisdom of using eminent domain to promote economic development are certainly matters of legitimate public debate. This Court's authority, however, extends only to determining whether the City's proposed condemnations are for a "public use" within the meaning of the Fifth Amendment to the Federal Constitution. Because over a century of our case law interpreting that provision dictates an affirmative answer to that question, we may not grant petitioners the relief that they seek.

The judgment of the Supreme Court of Connecticut is affirmed.

* * *

Justice KENNEDY, concurring.

* * *

* * * The determination that a rational-basis standard of review is appropriate does not * * * alter the fact that transfers intended to confer benefits on particular, favored private entities, and with only incidental or pretextual public benefits, are forbidden by the Public Use Clause.

* * *

This is not the occasion for conjecture as to what sort of cases might justify a more demanding standard, but it is appropriate to underscore aspects of the instant case that convince me no departure from *Berman* and *Midkiff* is appropriate here. This taking occurred in the context of a comprehensive development plan meant to address a serious city-wide depression, and the projected economic benefits of the project cannot be characterized as [minimal]. The identity of most of the private beneficiaries were unknown at the time the city formulated its plans. The city complied with elaborate procedural requirements that facilitate review of the record and inquiry into the city's purposes. In sum, while there may be categories of cases in which the transfers are so suspicious, or the procedures employed so prone to abuse, or the purported benefits are so trivial or implausible, that courts should presume an impermissible private purpose, no such circumstances are present in this case.

* * *

Justice O'CONNOR, with whom THE CHIEF JUSTICE [REHNQUIST], Justice SCALIA, and Justice THOMAS join, dissenting.

* * *

Under the banner of economic development, all private property is now vulnerable to being taken and transferred to another private owner, so long as it might be upgraded—*i.e.*, given to an owner who will use it in a way that the legislature deems more beneficial to the public—in the process. To reason, as the Court does, that the incidental public benefits resulting from the subsequent ordinary use of private property render economic development takings "for public use" is to wash out any distinction between private and public use of property—and thereby effectively to delete the words "for public use" from the Takings Clause of the Fifth Amendment. * * *

* * *

Where is the line between "public" and "private" property use? We give considerable deference to legislatures' determinations about what governmental activities will advantage the public. But were the political branches the sole arbiters of the public-private distinction, the Public Use Clause would amount to little more than hortatory fluff. An external, judicial check on how the public use requirement is interpreted, however limited, is necessary if this constraint on government power is to retain any meaning. * * *

Our cases have generally identified three categories of takings that comply with the public use requirement, though it is in the nature of things that the boundaries between these categories are not always firm. Two are relatively straightforward and uncontroversial. First, the sovereign may transfer private property to public ownership—such as for a road, a hospital, or a military base. * * * Second, the sovereign may transfer private property to private parties, often common carriers, who make the property available for the public's use—such as with a railroad, a public utility, or a stadium. * * * But "public ownership" and "use-by-the-public" are sometimes too constricting and impractical ways to define the scope of the Public Use Clause. Thus we have allowed that, in certain circumstances and to meet certain exigencies, takings that serve a public purpose also satisfy the Constitution even if the property is destined for subsequent private use. * * *

This case * * * presents an issue of first impression: Are economic development takings constitutional? I would hold that they are not. We are guided by two precedents about the taking of real property by eminent domain * * *.

* * *

* * * [I]n *Berman* and *Midkiff* * * * the extraordinary, precondemnation use of the targeted property inflicted affirmative harm on society—in *Berman* through blight resulting from extreme poverty and in *Midkiff* through oligopoly resulting from extreme wealth. And in both cases, the relevant legislative body had found that eliminating the existing property use was necessary to remedy the harm. * * * Thus a public purpose was realized when the harmful use was eliminated. Because each taking *directly* achieved a public benefit, it did not matter that the property was turned over to private use. Here, in contrast, New London does not claim that Susette Kelo's and Wilhelmina Dery's well-maintained homes are the source of any social harm. Indeed, it could not so claim without adopting the absurd argument that any single-family home that might be razed to make way for an apartment building, or any church that might be replaced with a retail store, or any small business that might be more lucrative if it were instead part of a national franchise, is inherently harmful to society and thus within the government's power to condemn.

In moving away from our decisions sanctioning the condemnation of harmful property use, the Court today significantly expands the meaning of public use. It holds that the sovereign may take private property currently put to ordinary private use, and give it over for new, ordinary private use, so long as the new use is predicted to generate some secondary benefit for the public—such as increased tax revenue, more jobs, maybe even aesthetic pleasure. But nearly any lawful use of real private property can be said to generate some incidental benefit to the public. Thus, if predicted (or even guaranteed) positive side-effects are enough to render transfer from one private party to another constitutional, then the words "for public use" do not realistically exclude *any* takings, and thus do not exert any constraint on the eminent domain power.

* * *

[W]ho among us can say she already makes the most productive or attractive possible use of her property? The specter of condemnation hangs over all property. Nothing is to prevent the State from replacing any Motel 6 with a Ritz-Carlton, any home with a shopping mall, or any farm with a factory. * * *

* * *

It was possible after *Berman* and *Midkiff* to imagine unconstitutional transfers from A to B. Those decisions endorsed government intervention when private property use had veered to such an extreme that the public was suffering as a consequence. Today nearly all real property is susceptible to condemnation on the Court's theory. * * *

[B]ut the fallout from [today's] decision will not be random. The beneficiaries are likely to be those citizens with disproportionate influence and power in the political process, including large corporations and development firms. As for the victims, the government now has license to transfer property from those with fewer resources to those with more. * * *

I would hold that the takings * * * are unconstitutional, reverse the judgment of the Supreme Court of Connecticut, and remand for further proceedings.

Justice THOMAS, dissenting.

[T]he Constitution allow[s] the government to take property not for "public necessity," but instead for "public use." * * * Defying this understanding, the Court replaces the Public Use Clause with a "'[P]ublic [P]urpose'" Clause, * * * a restriction that is satisfied, the Court instructs, so long as the purpose is "legitimate" and the means "not irrational" * * *. This deferential shift in phraseology enables the Court to hold, against all common sense, that a costly urban-renewal project whose stated purpose is a vague promise of new jobs and increased tax revenue, but which is also suspiciously agreeable to the Pfizer Corporation, is for a "public use."

* * * If such "economic development" takings are for a "public use," any taking is, and the Court has erased the Public Use Clause from our Constitution * * *. I do not believe that this Court can eliminate liberties expressly enumerated in the Constitution * * *.

* * *

* * * I would revisit our Public Use Clause cases and consider returning to the original meaning of the Public Use Clause: that the government may take property only if it actually uses or gives the public a legal right to use the property.

* * *

In a session of Congress remarkable for the number of shots taken at the federal courts, the House, in a salvo aimed at the Supreme Court's decision in *Kelo*, voted 231-189 to bar federal transportation funds from being used to make improvements on land seized by eminent domain for private development. The same day the House voted 365-33 in favor of a "sense of the House resolution" that put that body on record as agreeing with the dissenters in *Kelo*. And legislation is in the works to ban the use of any federal money for property development getting the go-ahead using the *Kelo* decision. Congressional Quarterly Weekly Report, July 4, 2005, p. 1818.

A good illustration of the point made by Justice Stevens in the next to the last paragraph of his opinion for the Court is the recent decision by the Michigan Supreme Court in Wayne County v. Hathcock, 471 Mich. 445, 684 N.W.2d 765 (2004), that, *as a matter of state constitutional law*, governmental entities in that state are barred from using their power of eminent domain to take private property and turn it over to a private developer, even if the project would benefit the community. And in November 2004, Oregon voters adopted by 60% to 40% a ballot measure that property owners, who can prove their investments have been hurt by environmental or zoning rules, can force government to compensate them for their losses. New York Times, Nov. 26, 2004, pp. A1, A26.

In another takings case, decided by the Court during its October 2004 Term, Lingle v. Chevron, USA, Inc., 544 U.S. —, 125 S.Ct. 2074 (2005), the Justices reversed summary judgment by lower federal courts invalidating a Hawaii law that capped the rent oil companies could charge gas station operators leasing company-owned service stations. The lower courts had found the Hawaii statute unconstitutional because it effected a taking of Chevron's property without "substantially advancing" the state's asserted interest in keeping a lid on retail gas prices. The Supreme Court held that such a judicial approach was rudderless and revealed nothing about the magnitude or character of the regulatory burden or how that burden was distributed among property owners. On remand, the Justices directed the lower courts to address the alleged taking of the oil company's property in terms of one of the approaches established by the Court's previous decisions: (1) where government requires an owner to suffer a permanent physical invasion of the property, however minor [see the *Loretto* case, Text p. 460]; (2) where government regulates the property in such a way that the owner is completely deprived of *all* economically beneficial use [see the *Nollan* and *Lucas* cases, Text p. 460]; or (3) where government acts so negatively with respect to each of the following factors: (a) the severity of the economic impact, (b) the degree of interference with distinct investment-backed expectations, and (c) the nature of governmental action—whether it amounts to a physical invasion of the property or is "some public program adjusting the benefits and burdens of economic life to promote the common good," that it effectively ousts the owner and appropriates the property [see the *Penn Central* case, Text, p. 453]. (A fourth possibility—inapplicable in this case—is "the special context of land-use exactions" illustrated by the *Dolan* case, see Text, p. 461)). The "substantially advances" formula adopted by the lower courts in *Chevron*, the Justices concluded, was so open-ended in its appraisal of the means-ends relationship as to permit judges to substitute their policy judgment for that of the legislators.

CHAPTER 7   PROPERTY RIGHTS AND ECONOMIC LIBERTIES

▶ **Insert on p. 466 at the end of the chapter**

D. NON-TRADITIONAL PROPERTY INTERESTS

The property and liberty interests covered in the three sections of this chapter in the Text deal with traditional financial interests: money, wages, real estate, and contracts. But since the 1960s, the Court's decisions have recognized new forms of property. Forty years ago, a seminal article by Charles Reich, "The New Property," 73 Yale Law Journal 733 (1964), took notice of government as a major source of wealth. It argued that various forms of government largess—licenses, franchises, public employment, services, benefits, contracts, and grants—were supplementing, or even supplanting, traditional private forms of wealth. For much of our legal history, valuables dispensed by government were classified as *privileges* (as opposed to traditional "property" in which one had *rights*) and thus could be denied, even arbitrarily, without the possibility of violating due process or any other constitutional rights. But as Reich's view took hold, and the courts expanded upon the sorts of interests which qualified as protected property interests, two thorny questions emerged: (1) What interests qualified as property within the protection of the due process clauses of the Fifth and Fourteenth Amendments (or other constitutional guarantees, such as freedom of speech)? and (2) Exactly what amount of process was due before someone could be deprived of these valuables by government? If trial-type hearings were not required before someone could be deprived of his driver's license, social security benefits, worker's compensation, medicare, passport, or defense contract, what less than that would suffice? Would the same amount of due process be required in each instance, or might the degree of due process vary from one situation to another?

In Goldberg v. Kelly, 397 U.S. 254, 90 S.Ct. 1011 (1970), for example, the Court held that procedural due process required that an evidentiary hearing be held before public assistance payments could be discontinued to a welfare recipient. This in-person opportunity to present his or her side of the case required: (1) "timely and adequate notice detailing the reasons for a proposed termination"; (2) "an effective opportunity to defend by confronting any adverse witnesses and by presenting his own arguments and evidence orally"; (3) retained counsel, if desired; (4) an neutral decisionmaker; (5) a decision resting "solely on the legal rules and evidence adduced at the hearing"; and (6) a statement of reasons for the decision and the evidence supporting it. How much process is due, the Court made clear, six years later, in Mathews v. Eldridge, 424 U.S. 319, 96 S.Ct. 893 (1976), depended upon a balancing of such factors as: (1) the importance of the interest at stake, (2) the risk of erroneous deprivation, (3) the fairness and reliability of existing procedures; and (4) the financial costs and administrative burden to the government of implementing more extensive procedural steps. So, revocation of a driver's license might call for less due process than, say, suspending a student from school.

In the case that follows, the Supreme Court was confronted with a novel argument: that a restraining order directed at an abusive spouse was the sort of government action entitling the wife to its enforcement. When government failed to take steps to enforce the restraining order—with tragic consequences—she argued that such dereliction of duty violated the property interest she had in the order, and she sued the police and the town for damages. The Court did not address what steps the government should have taken because it was not persuaded any property interest of hers was violated.

TOWN OF CASTLE ROCK, COLORADO V. GONZALES
Supreme Court of the United States, 2005
455 U.S. —, 125 S.Ct. 2796, — L.Ed.2d —

BACKGROUND & FACTS In connection with divorce procedings, Jessica Gonzales obtained a court order which restrained her husband from disturbing her or their three children (ages 10, 9, and 7) or coming within 100 yards of the family home. Pre-printed on the reverse side of the order was the following text: "WARNING: KNOWING VIOLATION OF A RESTRAINING ORDER IS A CRIME. YOU MAY BE ARRESTED WITHOUT NOTICE IF A LAW ENFORCEMENT OFFICER HAS PROBABLE CAUSE TO BELIEVE YOU HAVE KNOWINGLY VIOLATED THIS ORDER." The pre-printed text on the back of the order also contained a "NOTICE TO LAW ENFORCEMENT OFFICIALS" which, in part, read as follows: "YOU SHALL USE EVERY REASONABLE MEANS TO ENFORCE THIS RESTRAINING ORDER. YOU SHALL ARREST, OR, IF AN ARREST WOULD BE IMPRACTICAL UNDER THE CIRCUMSTANCES, SEEK A WARRANT FOR THE ARREST OF THE RESTRAINED PERSON WHEN YOU HAVE INFORMATION AMOUNTING TO PROBABLE CAUSE THAT THE RESTRAINED PERSON HAS VIOLATED OR ATTEMPTED TO VIOLATE ANY PROVISION OF THIS ORDER AND THE RESTRAINED PERSON HAS BEEN PROPERLY SERVED WITH A COPY OF THIS ORDER OR HAS RECEIVED ACTUAL NOTICE OF THE EXISTENCE OF THIS ORDER." Two weeks after the restraining order was originally issued, it was made permanent and modified so as to give the husband the right to spend time with the three children on alternate weekends, for two weeks in the summer, and "upon reasonable notice" for a mid-week dinner visit arranged by the parties. The modified order allowed him to visit the home to pick up the children on these occasions. He was served with a copy of the modified order on June 4, 1999.

On June 22 about 5 p.m., the husband took the three children who were playing outside the family home without any notice or advance arrangements. When Mrs. Gonzales noticed the children were missing, she suspected he had taken them. At about 7:30 p.m., she called the Castle Rock Police Department which dispatched two officers. When the officers arrived at the home, she showed them a copy of the restraining order and asked them to arrest her husband and return the children. The officers said there was nothing they could do and suggested she call the department again in three hours if the children had not returned. When she called the police department at 10 p.m., she was told to wait until midnight. After calling yet again, she went to her husband's apartment but found no one there. She called the department a fourth time, at 12:10, and was told to wait for an officer to arrive. None did. Forty minutes later, Mrs. Gonzales went to the police department and filed an incident report. But instead of attempting to enforce the restraining order, the officer who took the report went to dinner. At 3:20 a.m., the husband arrived at the police station and opened fire with a semi-automatic handgun. Police returned fire and killed him. Inside the cab of his pickup truck, they discovered the bodies of the three children.

Mrs. Gonzales sued the police and the town under 42 U.S.C.A. § 1983 for violating the Due Process Clause of the Fourteenth Amendment. Her complaint alleged that the department had an official policy or custom of failing to enforce restraining orders and tolerated non-enforcement by its police officers. She characterized the town's inaction as wantonly indifferent to her civil rights. A federal district court dismissed the suit, but was reversed on appeal by a 6-5 vote of the U.S. Court of Appeals for the Tenth Circuit sitting en banc. The town then petitioned the Supreme Court for review.

Justice SCALIA delivered the opinion of the Court.

We decide in this case whether an individual who has obtained a state-law restraining order has a constitutionally protected property interest in having the police enforce the restraining order when they have probable cause to believe it has been violated.

* * *

The procedural component of the Due Process Clause does not protect everything that might be described as a "benefit": "To have a property interest in a benefit, a person clearly must have more than an abstract need or desire" and "more than a unilateral expectation of it. He must, instead, have a legitimate claim of entitlement to it." Board of Regents of State Colleges v. Roth, 408 U.S. 564, 577, 92 S.Ct. 2701 (1972). Such entitlements are "'of course, ... not created by the Constitution. Rather, they are created and their dimensions are defined by existing rules or understandings that stem from an independent source such as state law.'" Paul v. Davis, 424 U.S. 693, 709, 96 S.Ct. 1155 (1976) * * *.

Our cases recognize that a benefit is not a protected entitlement if government officials may grant or deny it in their discretion. * * * The Court of Appeals in this case determined that Colorado law created an entitlement to enforcement of the restraining order because the "court-issued restraining order ... specifically dictated that its terms must be enforced" and a "state statute command[ed]" enforcement of the order when certain objective conditions were met (probable cause to believe that the order had been violated and that the object of the order had received notice of its existence). * * * Respondent contends that we are obliged "to give deference to the Tenth Circuit's analysis of Colorado law on" whether she had an entitlement to enforcement of the restraining order. * * *

We will not, of course, defer to the Tenth Circuit on the ultimate issue: whether what Colorado law has given respondent constitutes a property interest for purposes of the Fourteenth Amendment. That determination, despite its state-law underpinnings, is ultimately one of federal constitutional law. * * * Resolution of the federal issue begins, however, with a determination of what it is that state law provides. In the context of the present case, the central state-law question is whether Colorado law gave respondent a right to police enforcement of the restraining order. It is on this point that respondent's call for deference to the Tenth Circuit is relevant.

* * *

The critical language in the restraining order came not from any part of the order itself * * * but from the preprinted notice to law-enforcement personnel that appeared on the back of the order. * * * That notice effectively restated the statutory provision describing "peace officers' duties" related to the crime of violation of a restraining order. * * *

* * *

We do not believe that these provisions of Colorado law truly made enforcement of restraining orders *mandatory*. A well established tradition of police discretion has long coexisted with apparently mandatory arrest statutes. * * *

The deep-rooted nature of law-enforcement discretion, even in the presence of seemingly mandatory legislative commands, is illustrated by Chicago v. Morales, 527 U.S. 41, 119 S.Ct. 1849 (1999), which involved an ordinance that said a police officer "'shall order'" persons to disperse in certain circumstances * * *. This Court rejected out of hand the possibility that "the mandatory language of the ordinance ... afford[ed] the police *no* discretion." * * * It is, the Court proclaimed, simply "common sense that *all* police officers must use some discretion in deciding when and where to enforce city ordinances." * * * (emphasis added).

Against that backdrop, a true mandate of police action would require some stronger indication from the Colorado Legislature than "shall use every reasonable means to enforce a restraining order" * * *. That language is not perceptibly more mandatory than the Colorado statute which has long told municipal chiefs of police that they "shall pursue and arrest any person fleeing from justice in any part of the state" and that they "shall apprehend any person in the act of committing any offense ... and, forthwith and without any warrant, bring such person before a ... competent authority for examination and trial." * * * It is hard to imagine that a Colorado peace officer would not have some discretion to determine that—despite probable cause to believe a restraining order has been violated—the circumstances of the violation or the competing duties of that officer or his agency counsel decisively against enforcement in a particular instance. The practical necessity for discretion is particularly apparent in a case such as this one, where the suspected violator is not actually present and his whereabouts are unknown. * * *

* * *

Respondent does not specify the precise means of enforcement that the Colorado restraining-order statute assertedly mandated —whether her interest lay in having police arrest her husband, having them seek a warrant for his arrest, or having them "use every reasonable means, up to and including arrest, to enforce the order's terms" * * *. Such indeterminacy is not the hallmark of a duty that is mandatory. Nor can someone be safely deemed "entitled" to something when the identity of the alleged entitlement is vague. * * * After the warrant is sought, it remains within the discretion of a judge whether to grant it, and after it is granted, it remains within the discretion of the police whether and when to execute it. Respondent would have been assured nothing but the seeking of a warrant. This is not the sort of "entitlement" out of which a property interest is created.

* * *

Responden[t] * * * does not assert that she has any common-law or contractual entitlement to enforcement. If she was given a statutory entitlement, we would expect to see some indication of that in the statute itself. Although Colorado's statute spoke of "protected person[s]" such as respondent, it did so in connection with matters other than a right to enforcement. It said that a "protected person shall be provided with a copy of [a restraining] order" when it is issued, * * * that a law enforcement agency "shall make all reasonable efforts to contact the protected party upon the arrest of the restrained person," * * * and that the agency "shall give [to the protected person] a copy" of the report it submits to the court that issued the order * * *. Perhaps most importantly, the statute spoke directly to the protected person's power to "initiate contempt proceedings against the restrained person if the order [was] issued in a civil action or request the prosecuting attorney to initiate contempt proceedings if the order [was] issued in a criminal action." * * * The protected person's express power to "initiate" civil contempt proceedings contrasts tellingly with the mere ability to "request" initiation of criminal contempt proceedings—and even more dramatically with the complete silence about any power to "request" (much less demand) that an arrest be made.

* * *

[I]t is by no means clear that an individual entitlement to enforcement of a restraining order could constitute a "property" interest for purposes of the Due Process Clause. Such a right would not, of course, resemble any traditional conception of property. Although that alone does not disqualify it from due process protection * * * the right to have a restraining order enforced does not "have some ascertainable monetary value," as * * * our [other] property-as-entitlement" cases have implicitly required. * * * Perhaps most radically, the alleged property interest here arises *incidentally*, not out of some new species of government benefit or service, but out of a function that government actors have always performed—* * * arresting people who they have probable cause to believe have committed a criminal offense.

We conclude, therefore, that respondent did not, for purposes of the Due Process Clause, have a property interest in police enforcement of the restraining order against her husband. It is accordingly unnecessary to address the Court of Appeals' determination * * * that the town's custom or policy prevented the police from giving her due process when they deprived her of that alleged interest. * * *

* * *

The judgment of the Court of Appeals is

Reversed.

Justice SOUTER, with whom Justice BREYER joins, concurring.

* * *

[I]n every instance of property recognized by this Court as calling for federal procedural protection, the property has been distinguishable from the procedural obligations imposed on state officials to protect it. Whether welfare benefits, * * * attendance at public schools, * * * utility services, * * * public employment, * * * professional licenses, * * * and so on, the property interest recognized in our cases has always existed apart from state procedural protection before the Court has recognized a constitutional claim to protection by federal process. To accede to Gonzales's argument would therefore work a sea change in the scope of federal due process, for she seeks federal process as a substitute simply for state process. * * * There is no articulable distinction between the object of Gonzales's asserted entitlement and the process she desires in order to protect her entitlement; both amount to certain steps to be taken by the police to protect her family and herself. Gonzales's claim would thus take us beyond * * * any * * * recognized theory of Fourteenth Amendment due process, by collapsing the distinction between property protected and the process that protects it, and would federalize every mandatory state-law direction to executive officers whose performance on the job can be vitally significant to individuals affected.

* * *

Justice STEVENS, with whom Justice GINSBURG joins, dissenting.

* * *

The central question in this case is * * * whether, as a matter of Colorado law, respondent had a right to police assistance comparable to the right she would have possessed to any other service the government or a private firm might have undertaken to provide. * * *

There was a time when our tradition of judicial restraint would have led this Court to defer to the judgment of more qualified tribunals in seeking the correct answer to that difficult question of Colorado law. Unfortunately, although the majority properly identifies the "central state-law question" in this case as "whether Colorado law gave respondent a right to police enforcement of the restraining order," * * * it has chosen to ignore our settled practice by providing its *own* answer to that question. * * *

The majority's decision to plunge ahead with its own analysis of Colorado law imprudently departs from this Court's longstanding policy of paying "deference [to] the views of a federal court as to the law of a State within its jurisdiction." * * * This policy is not only efficient, but it reflects "our belief that district courts and courts of appeal are better schooled in and more able to interpret the laws of their respective States." * * *

* * *

Even if the Court had good reason to doubt the Court of Appeals' determination of state law, it would, in my judgment, be a far wiser course to certify the question to the Colorado Supreme Court. Powerful considerations support certification in this case. First, principles of federalism and comity favor giving a State's high court the opportunity to answer important questions of state law, particularly when those questions implicate uniquely local matters such as law enforcement and might well require the weighing of policy considerations for their correct resolution. * * * Second, by certifying a potentially dispositive state-law issue, the Court would adhere to its wise policy of avoiding the unnecessary adjudication of difficult questions of constitutional law. * * * Third, certification would promote both judicial economy and fairness to the parties. After all, the Colorado Supreme Court is the ultimate authority on the meaning of Colorado law, and if in later litigation it should disagree with this Court's provisional state-law holding, our efforts will have been wasted and respondent will have been deprived of the opportunity to have her claims heard under the authoritative view of Colorado law. * * *

* * *

Three flaws in the Court's rather superficial analysis of the merits highlight the unwisdom of its decision to answer the state-law question [on its own]. First, the Court places undue weight on the various statutes throughout the country that seemingly mandate police enforcement but are generally understood to preserve police discretion. As a result, the Court gives short shrift to the unique case of "mandatory arrest" statutes in the domestic violence context; States passed a wave of these statutes in the 1980's and 1990's with the unmistakable goal of eliminating police discretion in this area. Second, the Court's formalistic analysis fails to take seriously the fact that the Colorado statute at issue in this case was enacted for the benefit of the narrow class of persons who are beneficiaries of domestic restraining orders, and that the order at issue in this case was specifically intended to provide protection to respondent and her children. Finally, the Court is simply wrong to assert that a citizen's interest in the government's commitment to provide police enforcement in certain defined circumstances does not resemble any "traditional conception of property" * * *; in fact, a citizen's property interest in such a commitment is just as concrete and worthy of protection as her interest in any other important service the government or a private firm has undertaken to provide.

* * *

* * * This Court has "made clear that the property interests protected by procedural due process extend well beyond actual ownership of real estate, chattels, or money." * * * The "types of interests protected as 'property' are varied and, as often as not, intangible, 'relating to the whole domain of social and economic fact.'" * * * Logan v. Zimmerman Brush Co., 455 U.S. 422, 430, 102 S.Ct. 1148 (1982); see also Perry v. Sindermann, 408 U.S. 593, 601, 92 S.Ct. 2694 (1972) ("'[P]roperty' interests subject to procedural due process protection are not limited by a few rigid, technical forms. Rather, 'property' denotes a broad range of interests that are secured by 'existing rules or understandings'"). Thus, our cases have found "property" interests in a number of state-conferred benefits and services, including welfare benefits, Goldberg v. Kelly, 397 U.S. 254, 90 S.Ct. 1011 (1970); disability benefits, Mathews v. Eldridge, 424 U.S. 319, 96 S.Ct. 893 (1976); public education, Goss v. Lopez, 419 U.S. 565, 95 S.Ct. 729 (1975); utility services, Memphis Light, Gas & Water Div. v. Craft, 436 U.S. 1, 98 S.Ct. 1554 (1978); government employment, Cleveland Bd. of Ed. v. Loudermill, 470 U.S. 532, 105 S.Ct. 1487 (1985); as well as in other entitlements that defy easy categorization, see, e.g., Bell v. Burson, 402 U.S. 535, 91 S.Ct. 1586 (1971) (due process requires fair procedures before a driver's license may be revoked pending the adjudication of an accident claim) * * *.

Police enforcement of a restraining order is a government service that is no less concrete and no less valuable than other government services, such as education. The relative novelty of recognizing this type of property interest is explained by the relative novelty of the domestic violence statutes creating a mandatory arrest duty; before this innovation, the unfettered discretion that characterized police enforcement defeated any citizen's "legitimate claim of entitlement" to this service. Novel or not, respondent's claim finds strong support in the principles that underlie our due process jurisprudence. In this case, Colorado law *guaranteed* the provision of a certain service, in certain defined circumstances, to a certain class of beneficiaries, and respondent reasonably relied on that guarantee. As we observed in [*Board of Regents* v. *Roth*], "[i]t is a purpose of the ancient institution of property to protect those claims upon which people rely in their daily lives, reliance that must not be arbitrarily undermined." 408 U.S., at 577, 92 S.Ct., at 2709. Surely, if respondent had contracted with a private security firm to provide her and her daughters with protection from her husband, it would be apparent that she possessed a property interest in such a contract. Here, Colorado undertook a comparable obligation, and respondent—with restraining order in hand—justifiably relied on that undertaking. Respondent's claim of entitlement to this promised service is no less legitimate than the other claims our cases have upheld, and no less concrete than a hypothetical agreement with a private firm. The fact that it is based on a statutory enactment and a judicial order entered for her special protection, rather than on a formal contract, does not provide a principled basis for refusing to consider it "property" worthy of constitutional protection.

Because respondent had a property interest in the enforcement of the restraining order, state officials could not deprive her of that interest without observing fair procedures. Her description of the police behavior in this case and the department's callous policy of failing to respond properly to reports of restraining order violations clearly alleges a due process violation. At the very least, due process requires that the relevant state decisionmaker *listen* to the claimant and then *apply the relevant criteria* in reaching his decision. The failure to observe these minimal procedural safeguards creates an unacceptable risk of arbitrary and "erroneous deprivation[s]" * * *.

* * *

CHAPTER 8

DUE PROCESS OF LAW

A. DUE PROCESS AND THE FEDERAL SYSTEM: THE SELECTIVE INCORPORATION OF THE BILL OF RIGHTS INTO THE FOURTEENTH AMENDMENT

The Jury Trial Guarantee: A Case Study of Incorporation

▶ **Insert at p. 498 following the first paragraph**

Regardless of any constitutional ambiguities about minimal jury size or the margin necessary for conviction, it is worth emphasizing that—unless the defendant chooses to have a bench trial (that is, have the judge determine the facts necessary for conviction)—the Sixth Amendment requires that the *jury* determine *every* element of the crime with which the defendant is charged beyond a reasonable doubt. As the Supreme Court made clear in *Apprendi* v. *New Jersey* (see Text, p. 887), this also includes proof of "any fact that increases the penalty for a crime beyond the prescribed statutory minimum." In other words, any fact—other than the fact of a prior conviction—used to *enhance* the punishment of a crime beyond what the statute ordinarily specifies must also be proved to a jury beyond a reasonable doubt. The Court recently reaffirmed this holding in Blakely v. Washington, 542 U.S. 296, 124 S.Ct. 2531 (2004), where Justice Scalia, speaking for the Court, pointed out that it was not merely a matter of respecting *Apprendi* as precedent but reflected "the need to give intelligible content to the fundamental constitutional right of jury trial."

The Court's ruling in *Blakely* was significant: It immediately triggered the question whether the Sixth Amendment permits a federal district judge to find facts, not reflected in a jury's verdict or admitted by a defendant, that enhance a criminal penalty under the existing federal mandatory sentencing guidelines. The guidelines, originally authorized by the Sentencing Reform Act of 1984 and upheld in 1989 against a delegation-of-power challenge (see Text, p. 146), prescribed minimum and maximum sentences for federal crimes. The guidelines also required judges to tack on additional time if certain features of the crime or the defendant's background were proved to the judge (factors not essential to establishing the defendant's guilt for the crime). Sentences above and below the guidelines were open to challenge and had to be specially justified. The effect of following *Blakely* thus would be to require the jury to pass upon *every* factor governing the punishment decision as well as that of the defendant's guilt. Consequently, the existing mandatory federal sentencing guidelines would be unconstitutional and defendants upon whom enhanced punishments had been imposed could demand resentencing.

This logical conclusion was confirmed by the Supreme Court's ruling the very next Term in United States v. Booker, 543 U.S. —, 125 S.Ct. 738 (2005). The five-Justice majority reaching this conclusion was the same as in *Apprendi* and *Blakely*: Stevens, Scalia, Souter, Thomas, and Ginsburg. Although federal sentencing guidelines that were suggestive or advisory would have been constitutional, it was their mandatory quality that ran afoul of the Sixth Amendment.

But the Court split differently on the remedy. Four members of the majority voted to simply graft the Sixth Amendment requirement on to the Sentencing Reform Act and say that judges could apply the mandatory sentences in the guidelines, provided each fact pertinent to punishment was proved to a jury beyond reasonable doubt. To some, the retroactive impact of this holding conjured up the nightmare of widespread resentencing. However, Justice Ginsburg joined the four dissenters (Rehnquist, O'Connor, Kennedy, and Breyer) to create a different—remedial—majority that recognized a much smaller pool of successful convict-petitioners. The remedial majority reasoned that only a very small number of sentences imposed were invalid—those pronounced on defendants who had been convicted following a jury trial (since defendants who waived trial by jury waived the right to object to judicial enhancements) and, of those, only the ones imposed on defendants who had received sentences longer than "could have lawfully been imposed by reference to facts found by the jury or admitted by the defendant." In the five-month period right after the decision in *Booker*, the Supreme Court vacated judgment in more than 700 cases and remanded them for resentencing. Worth noting is the fact that federal district courts in the aftermath of *Booker* have stuck pretty much as they did before to the ranges in the federal sentencing guidelines. 73 U.S. Law Week 2569.

Although there is some sentiment in Congress for adopting a wait-and-see approach to find out what federal judges will in fact do, a House subcommittee has approved "*Booker*-fix" legislation (HR 1528) that would establish mandatory minimums by simply prohibiting federal judges from relying on any of a laundry list of mitigating circumstances to depart from the floor specified in the guidelines. The legislation is opposed by the U.S. Judicial Conference. And additional legislation is in the works which also has about it the unmistakable air of mandatory minimums. The House has already passed, by a 279-144 vote, so-called "gangbusters" legislation imposing stiff minimum sentences for gang-related activities. The bill (HR 1279) redefines a gang as at least three (before it was "at least five") individuals who have committed at least two crimes together, one of which is a violent crime. Certain gang-related crimes, such as kidnapping, aggravated sexual assault, and maiming, would trigger a sentence of at least 30 years. Gang-related activity resulting in death would bring life imprisonment or the death penalty. Congressional Quarterly Weekly Report, May 16, 2005, p. 1315. Another bill before Congress would impose stiffer minimum sentences for federal drug offenses. A third, proposed in the wake of an attack in Chicago on the family of a federal judge, would impose stiffer minimum sentences for courthouse crimes. New York Times, May 11, 2005, p. A16.

B. THE RIGHT TO COUNSEL

The Right to Counsel at Trial

▶ **Insert at p. 517 at the end of the chart**

OTHER CASES ON THE EFFECTIVE ASSISTANCE OF COUNSEL--CONTINUED		
CASE	RULING	VOTE
Wiggins v. Smith, 539 U.S. 510, 123 S.Ct. 2527 (2003)	Defendant's lawyer at penalty phase of his murder trial violated the requirements of *Strickland* v. *Washington* (Text, p. 515) when the attorney chose to fight the death penalty on grounds the defendant was not directly responsible for the victim's death rather than offer evidence of the defendant's very "troubled history." Evidence, readily available to the attorney, showed the defendant had no history of violence, had undergone severe physical and sexual abuse by his mother and, while in a foster home, had endured rape, was left alone for days, was forced to beg for food, and was often beaten.	7-2; Justices Scalia and Thomas dissented.
Florida v. Nixon, 543 U.S. —, 125 S.Ct. 551 (2004)	A defense attorney clearly has a duty to discuss trial strategy with his client. But when defendant in a murder case neither consents nor objects to strategy of concentrating effort on winning leniency for the defendant at the penalty phase of the trial (rather than contesting the defendant's guilt), the lawyer's representation of his client cannot be said to "f[a]ll below an objective standard of reasonableness." The attorney's performance cannot be presumed to be either deficient or prejudicial.	8-0; Chief Justice Rehnquist did not participate.

OTHER CASES ON THE EFFECTIVE ASSISTANCE OF COUNSEL--CONTINUED		
CASE	RULING	VOTE
Rompilla v. Beard, 545 U.S. —, 125 S.Ct. 2456 (2005)	"[E]ven when a capital defendant's family members and the defendant himself have suggested that no mitigating evidence is available, his lawyer is bound to make reasonable efforts to obtain and review material that counsel knows the prosecution will probably rely on as evidence of aggravation in the sentencing phase of trial." In this case, defense lawyers failed to investigate "pretty obvious signs" that the defendant had a troubled childhood and suffered from mental illness and alcoholism. The defense instead just relied on the defendant's own account that he had a conflicted childhood.	5-4; Chief Justice Rehnquist and Justices Scalia, Kennedy, and Thomas dissented.

▶ **Insert at p. 517 following the first paragraph**

Although a criminal defendant cannot have a lawyer forced on him if he chooses to go it alone at trial, can he be medicated against his will in order to be able to stand trial? There is no question that government has the authority to forcibly medicate an inmate who is dangerous to himself and others, and the Court so held in Washington v. Harper, 492 U.S. 210, 110 S.Ct. 1028 (1990). Invariably, however, this is treated as a civil matter. If a criminal defendant needs drugs to have his dangerousness controlled, the issue of medicating him so that he will be competent to stand trial usually becomes moot. But what if the defendant is not dangerous and the offense charged is a serious, but nonviolent, crime? In Sell v. United States, 539 U.S. 166, 123 S.Ct. 2174 (2003), the Court observed that forced medication in these circumstances solely for the purpose of rendering the defendant competent to stand trial "may be rare." In order to justify the administration of drugs to a nondangerous mentally ill defendant charged with a nonviolent felony, the Court held the government would have to prove: (1) that its interest in bringing him to trial is *important* (that is, weighing his lengthy confinement for mental illness against the need to try him, the government would have to show that there was a serious need to prosecute now); (2) that the forced medication of the defendant would *significantly further* that interest; (3) that involuntary medication was necessary because *no less-intrusive option* was available; and (4) that administering the medication was *medically appropriate* (not medically risky). In the absence of such showings, forced administration of antipsychotic drugs to an unwilling criminal defendant accused of a nonviolent offense unconstitutionally deprives him of his "liberty" under the Fifth Amendment to reject medical treatment. Such determinations have to be made on a case-by-case basis. In this case Sell, a psychotic and delusional dentist, had been charged with insurance fraud.

The Pretrial Right to Counsel

▶ Insert at p. 524 following *Miranda* v. *Arizona*

Generally, failing to give the *Miranda* warnings—let alone deliberately failing to give them—invalidates a confession. But what if police deliberately fail to give the warnings, the suspect confesses, then police give the warnings in the hope that the suspect will repeat her incriminating statements, she waives those rights, and she confesses again? Does giving the warnings at the second stage of a deliberate two-step interrogation approach cure the officers' failure to give them at the start? A bare majority of the Justices, in Missouri v. Seibert, 542 U.S. 600, 124 S.Ct. 2601 (2004), answered "No." The consensus (there was no Opinion of the Court) was that *Miranda* warnings given mid-interrogation were ineffective (because the questioning was nearly continuous) and thus a confession repeated after the warnings were given was inadmissible at trial.

For a discussion of Illinois legislation requiring the taping of all homicide-related interrogations and confessions, see p. 101 of this Supplement.

▶ Insert at p. 524 following the first paragraph of text

In *Dickerson*, discussed in the Text, the Court not only reaffirmed the vitality of its ruling in *Miranda* but made it clear that the *Miranda* warnings were a *constitutional* requirement, not merely a preventive rule to reduce the risk of coerced confessions. As a matter of Fifth Amendment law, *Miranda* thus makes a coerced confession inadmissible at a criminal trial. But what if a confession is coerced from a suspect without giving the *Miranda* warnings, may the suspect sue under the federal civil rights statute, 42 U.S.C.A. § 1983, to collect damages for the violation? A badly fragmented Supreme Court in Chavez v. Martinez, 528 U.S. 760, 123 S.Ct. 1994 (2003), answered "No." A plurality reasoned that the constitutional prohibition that "[n]o person * * * shall be compelled *in any criminal case* to be a *witness* against himself" (emphasis added) "at the very least requires the initiation of legal proceedings" and "police questioning does not constitute a [criminal] 'case' any more than a private investigator's precomplaint activities constitute a 'civil case.'" Writing for the plurality, Justice Thomas concluded "The text of the Self-Incrimination Clause cannot support the * * * view that * * * compulsive questioning, without more, violates the Constitution." He continued, "It is well established that the government may compel witnesses to testify at trial or before a grand jury, on pain of contempt, so long as the witness is not the target of the criminal case in which he testifies. * * * We have long permitted the compulsion of incriminating testimony so long as those statements (or evidence derived from those statements) cannot be used against the speaker in any criminal case."

In this case, Chavez, a police officer, without giving the *Miranda* warnings, grilled Martinez (who had been shot by police and was blinded and paralyzed from the waist down) while he was receiving emergency treatment by hospital personnel. Martinez, who was in severe pain, protested, but Chavez persisted until he had secured several damaging admissions. The plurality added, "Our views on the proper scope of the Fifth Amendment's Self-Incrimination Clause do not mean that police torture or other abuse that results in a confession is constitutionally permissible so long as the statements are not used at trial; it simply means that the Fourteenth Amendment's Due Process Clause, rather than the Fifth Amendment's Self-Incrimination Clause, would govern the inquiry in those cases and provide relief in appropriate circumstances." In light of *Rochin* v. *California* (see Text, p. 490), this would turn on whether police engaged in conduct that "shocks the conscience." In the plurality's view, Chavez's misconduct was neither "egregious" nor "conscience-shocking."

Finally, although a suspect's youth and inexperience in dealing with the police are factors that legitimately might be taken into account in deciding whether an individual had been subjected to "custodial interrogation" (thus triggering application of the *Miranda* rules), such factors need not specifically be considered by a state court in reaching its conclusion that the suspect's participation was voluntary rather than compelled. See Yarborough v. Alvarado, 541 U.S. 652, 124 S.Ct. 2140 (2004). In order to exercise federal habeas corpus jurisdiction over a state prisoner, the Court said it would have to be shown that the state courts' conclusion the suspect was voluntarily present was *unreasonable*. The Court conceded there was a good case for saying that the questioning here amounted to "custodial interrogation," but the fact that the state courts' conclusion may be arguable did not make it unreasonable. The test, the Court pointed out, is whether a reasonable person would have felt free to stop talking and was free to leave or whether the officer used or threatened to use force to assure the suspect's continued presence. It argued neither was the case here. On the other hand, the 17-year-old had been brought to the police station by his parents (he did not arrive by himself), they were told the interview would last about 30 minutes and it lasted two hours, and they were not allowed to be present during the questioning. The dissenters (Justices Stevens, Souter, Ginsburg, and Breyer) found it difficult to imagine a clearer case of custodial interrogation in which the youth and inexperience of the suspect figured prominently.

▶ Insert at p. 533 following note on the "Fruit of the Poisonous Tree" Doctrine

A confession is testimonial evidence because a suspect is knowingly providing evidence of his guilt by his own words. Presumably, this is constitutionally offensive for at least two reasons: because it demeans the individual by treating him as a means to and end and because coerced statements are unreliable. But what if the police rely upon un-*Miranda*zed statements to find physical evidence? Is physical evidence found as a result of inadmissible statements made by the defendant also inadmissible at trial? The Court's answered "No" in United States v. Patane, 542 U.S. 630, 124 S.Ct. 2620 (2004).

In *Patane*, a gun was admitted as evidence at defendant's trial on charges of possession of a firearm by a felon. Patane had been arrested for violating a restraining order protecting his ex-girlfriend. During his arrest, Patane cut the police off as they began to read him his rights, saying he knew them already. They then asked him if he owned a gun. After he said he did and where it was, they searched for and found it. The government argued that Patane had voluntarily answered the question and, since *his* interruption had halted their reading of the *Miranda* warnings, the evidence was admissible. Patane contended—and the appeals court agreed—that the full warnings had not been read and that the lead obtained from that error made the gun inadmissible.

A five-Justice majority held that it would not exclude the physical evidence as "fruit of the poisonous tree." The *Miranda* rules protect against the admission of coerced incriminating statements because they may be unreliable and to deter police misconduct in securing confessions, but these arguments do not hold in the case of physical evidence. Unlike testimonial evidence, the reliability of physical evidence is the same however it is secured. Nor does the admission of physical evidence run the risk of also putting into evidence against the defendant any incriminating statements he made. Justices Stevens, Souter, Ginsburg, and Breyer were of the view that the "fruit of the poisonous tree" doctrine should be applied regardless. In their view, "giving an evidentiary advantage to those who ignore *Miranda* * * * adds an important inducement for interrogators to ignore the rule * * *."

D. CONFRONTATION AND CROSS-EXAMINATION

▶ Insert at p. 554 following *Maryland* v. *Craig*

Justice Scalia emphasized the absoluteness of the Sixth Amendment right to confront witnesses in Crawford v. Washington, 541 U.S. 36, 124 S.Ct. 1354 (2004), saying, "Testimonial statements of witnesses absent from trial have been admitted only where the declarant is unavailable, and only where the defendant has had a prior opportunity to cross-examine." In Ohio v. Roberts, 448 U.S. 56, 100 S.Ct. 2531 (1980), the Court had ruled that an unavailable witness's out-of-court statement could be admitted as long as it met adequate standards of reliability. This exception to the right to confront witnesses was particularly controversial in child abuse prosecutions, such as *Maryland* v. *Craig* (see Text p. 550). Overruling *Roberts*, the Court held that there was no reliability exception to the Sixth Amendment's right of confrontation. The Sixth Amendment guarantees the right to confront and cross-examine opposing witnesses, nothing less. Justice Scalia added, "Dispensing with confrontation because testimony is obviously reliable is akin to dispensing with jury trial because a defendant is obviously guilty. This is not what the Sixth Amendment prescribes."

E. CRUEL AND UNUSUAL PUNISHMENT

The Death Penalty

▶ **Insert at p. 583 following the chart**

OTHER CASES ON THE IMPOSITION OF CAPITAL PUNISHMENT--CONTINUED		
CASE	RULING	VOTE
Roper v. Simmons, 543 U.S. —, 125 S.Ct. 1183 (2005)	Imposing capital punishment on offenders who were under 18 years of age when they committed their crimes violates the Eighth and Fourteenth Amendments. Because of their susceptibility to immature and irresponsible conduct, the negative effect of peer and other outside pressure, and the less-fixed nature of their personality traits, individuals under 18 are now widely regarded as categorically less blameworthy than adults so that imposing the death penalty on them is grossly disproportionate. Objective indicators of this consensus are the rejection of capital punishment for those under 18 by 30 states, its infrequent use in the 20 states that retained it, and the clear trend among those to abolish it. Moreover, the weight of international opinion is overwhelmingly against it.	5-4; Chief Justice Rehnquist and Justices O'Connor, Scalia, and Thomas dissented.
Deck v. Missouri, 544 U.S. —, 125 S.Ct. 2007 (2005)	The Due Process Clauses of the Fifth and Fourteenth Amendments forbid routine visible shackling of defendants during the penalty phase, as well as the guilt phrase, of a capital trial. Use of visible shackles with respect to a particular defendant is constitutionally permissible only if it is "justified by an essential state interest," such as courtroom security.	7-2; Justices Scalia and Thomas dissented.

Chapter 8 Due Process of Law

The Supreme Court has grant cert. in Kansas v. Marsh, 544 U.S. —, 125 S.Ct. 2517 (2005), to address the question whether a state law violates the Eighth and Fourteenth Amendment if it provides the death penalty in cases where the jury finds that the aggravating circumstances of the crime do not outweigh but are found merely equal to the mitigating circumstances. The Kansas Supreme Court by a 4-3 vote held that requiring the death penalty where the factors for and against the imposition of the death penalty in a given case balanced each other constituted cruel and unusual punishment. See State v. Marsh, 278 Kan. 520, 102 P.3d 445 (2003). The U.S. Supreme Court was also asked to consider whether the state supreme court's decision adequately rested on an independent state constitutional ground.

The Colorado Supreme Court has set aside the death sentence because a juror took a copy of the Bible into the jury room. The court concluded that this exposed jury deliberation on the death penalty to extraneous prejudicial information. People v. Harlan, 109 P.3d 616 (Colo. 2005).

▶ Insert at p. 583 following the paragraph

In a remarkable showing of bipartisanship and in the face of substantial law-enforcement lobbying against it, the Illinois General Assembly overwhelmingly passed legislation requiring audio or video taping of all homicide-related interrogations and confessions. The measure cleared the Illinois House by a vote of 109-7 and passed the state Senate unanimously. It was a direct response to the death penalty scandal that moved Gov. George Ryan to impose the moratorium on capital punishment noted in the Text. Chicago Tribune, May 9, 2003, pp. 1, 25; July 17, 2003, sec. 2., pp. 1, 7.

▶ Insert at p. 584 following the first paragraph

Under the Justice For All Act of 2004, 118 Stat. 2260, courts would assume that federal inmates have a right to DNA testing within three years of conviction and five years of the law's enactment. DNA testing could be ordered if an inmate asserts, under penalty of perjury, that he is innocent. Application for DNA testing later than this would be presumed too late unless the inmate could show good cause for the delay. The government is forbidden to destroy DNA evidence in federal criminal cases while the defendant remains in prison. The law authorizes $151 million annually for five years to help states and localities speed up processing of biological crime scene evidence and $5 million annually to the states until 2009 to help meet the cost of post-conviction DNA programs. Annual grants of $30 million for five years are earmarked for helping with medical personnel costs and DNA sample preservation expense. Annual grants of $75 million are authorized to improve the representation of defendants in capital cases and improve the representation of the public in state capital cases. The law also guarantees specific rights to the victims of crime: the right to be reasonably protected from the accused, the right to be reasonably heard at proceedings, the right to full and timely restitution, the right to proceedings without unreasonable delay, and the opportunity to assert these rights in federal district court on appeal.

The Supreme Court will hear argument at its October 2005 Term on whether DNA evidence constitutes a "truly persuasive showing of actual innocence" sufficient to entitle a state inmate to federal habeas corpus relief under *Herrera v. Collins* (see Text, 583). This case is the Court's first opportunity to consider the impact of DNA evidence on the constitutional right to a fair trial. A federal appeals court rejected the claim of federal habeas relief by a vote of 8-7. House v. Bell, 386 F.3d 668 (6th Cir. en banc, 2004), *cert. granted*, 545 U.S. —, 125 S.Ct. 2991 (2005).

Mandatory Life Imprisonment

▶ Insert at p. 589 following the second paragraph

The prediction that, given the current composition of the Court, challenges to noncapital sentences under the Eighth Amendment's proportionality principle would be in for rough sledding was borne out by the Justices' review of California's "three strikes" law. In the following *Ewing* case, the plurality's application of the "gross disproportionality" standard announced in *Harmelin,* in combination with the disavowal that the Amendment contains any proportionality principle at all by Justices Scalia and Thomas, assured the state a relatively easy victory.

EWING V. CALIFORNIA
Supreme Court of the United States, 2003
538 U.S. 11, 123 S.Ct. 1179, 155 L.Ed.2d 108

BACKGROUND & FACTS Gary Ewing walked into the pro shop of an El Segundo, California golf course and walked out with three golf clubs valued at nearly $400 apiece. They were concealed in the leg of his pants. A shop employee called police and Ewing was arrested. He subsequently pleaded guilty to the theft. Although his shoplifting could have constituted a misdemeanor, in light of Ewing's past criminal record the trial judge decided the offense should remain a felony. This conviction was his fourth in a series of strikes under the state's "three strikes and you're out" law and triggered much more severe punishment than would have been the case had the theft offense been considered by itself. As a newly-convicted felon with two or more "serious" or "violent" previous felony offenses, Ewing received a prison term of 25 years to life in accordance with the law. He appealed on the grounds that such a sentence was out of all proportion to the offense and violated the Eighth Amendment. A state court of appeal rejected his argument and affirmed the sentence. The California Supreme Court denied review, and Ewing then successfully petitioned the U.S. Supreme Court for certiorari.

Justice O'CONNOR announced the judgment of the Court and delivered an opinion in which THE CHIEF JUSTICE [REHNQUIST] and Justice KENNEDY join.

In this case, we decide whether the Eighth Amendment prohibits the State of California from sentencing a repeat felon to a prison term of 25 years to life under the State's "Three

Strikes and You're Out" law.

* * *

California's current three strikes law consists of two virtually identical statutory schemes "designed to increase the prison terms of repeat felons." * * * When a defendant is convicted of a felony, and he has previously been convicted of one or more prior felonies defined as "serious" or "violent" * * * sentencing is conducted pursuant to the three strikes law. Prior convictions must be alleged in the charging document, and the defendant has a right to a jury determination that the prosecution has proved the prior convictions beyond a reasonable doubt. * * *

If the defendant has one prior "serious" or "violent" felony conviction, he must be sentenced to "twice the term otherwise provided as punishment for the current felony conviction." * * * If the defendant has two or more prior "serious" or "violent" felony convictions, he must receive "an indeterminate term of life imprisonment." * * * Defendants sentenced to life under the three strikes law become eligible for parole on a date calculated by reference to a "minimum term," which is the greater of (a) three times the term otherwise provided for the current conviction, (b) 25 years, or (c) the term determined by the court pursuant to [the statute] for the underlying conviction, including any enhancements. * * *

Under California law, certain offenses may be classified as either felonies or misdemeanors. These crimes are known as "wobblers." Some crimes that would otherwise be misdemeanors become "wobblers" because of the defendant's prior record. For example, petty theft, a misdemeanor, becomes a "wobbler" when the defendant has previously served a prison term for committing specified theft-related crimes. * * * Other crimes, such as grand theft, are "wobblers" regardless of the defendant's prior record. * * * Both types of "wobblers" are triggering offenses under the three strikes law only when they are treated as felonies. Under California law, a "wobbler" is presumptively a felony and "remains a felony except when the discretion is actually exercised" to make the crime a misdemeanor. * * *

In California, prosecutors may exercise their discretion to charge a "wobbler" as either a felony or a misdemeanor. Likewise, California trial courts have discretion to reduce a "wobbler" charged as a felony to a misdemeanor either before preliminary examination or at sentencing to avoid imposing a three strikes sentence. * * * In exercising this discretion, the court may consider "those factors that direct similar sentencing decisions," such as "the nature and circumstances of the offense, the defendant's appreciation of and attitude toward the offense, ... [and] the general objectives of sentencing." * * *

* * *

The Eighth Amendment, which forbids cruel and unusual punishments, contains a "narrow proportionality principle" that "applies to noncapital sentences." Harmelin v. Michigan, 501 U.S. 957, 996-997, 111 S.Ct. 2680 (1991).

* * *

* * * The Eighth Amendment does not require strict proportionality between crime and sentence. Rather, it forbids only extreme sentences that are 'grossly disproportionate' to the crime." * * *

* * *

[L]egislatures enacting three strikes laws made a deliberate policy choice that individuals who have repeatedly engaged in serious or violent criminal behavior, and whose conduct has not been deterred by more conventional approaches to punishment, must be isolated from society in order to protect the public safety. Though three strikes laws may be relatively new, our tradition of deferring to state legislatures in making and implementing such important policy decisions is longstanding. * * *

* * *

When the California Legislature enacted the three strikes law, it made a judgment that protecting the public safety requires incapacitating criminals who have already been convicted of at least one serious or violent crime. Nothing in the Eighth Amendment prohibits California from making that choice. * * *

California's justification is no pretext. Recidivism is a serious public safety concern in California and throughout the Nation. According to a recent report, approximately 67 percent of former inmates released from state prisons were charged with at least one "serious" new crime within three years of their release. * * *. In particular, released property offenders like Ewing had higher recidivism rates than those released after committing violent, drug, or public-order offenses. * * * Approximately 73 percent of the property offenders released in 1994 were arrested again within three years, compared to approximately 61 percent of the violent offenders, 62 percent of the public-order offenders, and 66 percent of the drug offenders. * * *

* * *

The State's interest in deterring crime also lends some support to the three strikes law. We have long viewed both incapacitation and deterrence as rationales for recidivism statutes: "[A] recidivist statute['s] ... primary goals are to deter repeat offenders and, at some point in the life of one who repeatedly commits criminal offenses serious enough to be punished as felonies, to segregate that person from the rest of society for an extended period of time." Rummel [v. Estelle, 463 U.S.,] at 284, 100 S.Ct. 1133. Four years after the passage of California's three strikes law, the recidivism rate of parolees returned to prison for the commission of a new crime dropped by nearly 25 percent. * * *

To be sure, California's three strikes law has sparked controversy. Critics have doubted the law's wisdom, cost-efficiency, and effectiveness in reaching its goals. * * * This criticism is appropriately directed at the legislature, which has primary responsibility for making the difficult policy choices that underlie any criminal sentencing scheme. We do not sit as a "superlegislature" to second-guess these policy choices. It is enough that the State of California has a reasonable basis for believing that dramatically enhanced sentences for habitual felons "advance[s] the goals of [its] criminal justice system in any substantial way." * * *

* * * The gravity of [Ewing's] offense was not merely "shoplifting three golf clubs." Rather, Ewing was convicted of felony grand theft for stealing nearly $1,200 worth of

merchandise after previously having been convicted of at least two "violent" or "serious" felonies. Even standing alone, Ewing's theft should not be taken lightly. * * *

* * *

Ewing's sentence is justified by the State's public-safety interest in incapacitating and deterring recidivist felons, and amply supported by his own long, serious criminal record. Ewing has been convicted of numerous misdemeanor and felony offenses, served nine separate terms of incarceration, and committed most of his crimes while on probation or parole. His prior "strikes" were serious felonies including robbery and three residential burglaries. To be sure, Ewing's sentence is a long one. But it reflects a rational legislative judgment, entitled to deference, that offenders who have committed serious or violent felonies and who continue to commit felonies must be incapacitated. The State of California "was entitled to place upon [Ewing] the onus of one who is simply unable to bring his conduct within the social norms prescribed by the criminal law of the State." Rummel [v. Estelle, 445 U.S.,] at 284, 100 S.Ct. 1133. * * *

We hold that Ewing's sentence of 25 years to life in prison, imposed for the offense of felony grand theft under the three strikes law, is not grossly disproportionate and therefore does not violate the Eighth Amendment's prohibition on cruel and unusual punishments. The judgment of the California Court of Appeal is affirmed.

It is so ordered.

Justice SCALIA, concurring in the judgment.

In my concurring opinion in Harmelin v. Michigan, 501 U.S. 957, 984, 985, 111 S.Ct. 2680 (1991), I concluded that the Eighth Amendment's prohibition of "cruel and unusual punishments" was aimed at excluding only certain *modes* of punishment, and was not a "guarantee against disproportionate sentences." * * *

Proportionality—the notion that the punishment should fit the crime—is inherently a concept tied to the penological goal of retribution. "[I]t becomes difficult even to speak intelligently of 'proportionality,' once deterrence and rehabilitation are given significant weight," * * *—not to mention giving weight to the purpose of California's three strikes law: incapacitation. * * *

[W]hat [the plurality] * * * reads into the Eighth Amendment is not the unstated proposition that all punishment should be reasonably proportionate to the gravity of the offense, but rather the unstated proposition that all punishment should reasonably pursue the multiple purposes of the criminal law. That formulation would make it clea[r] * * * that the plurality is not applying law but evaluating policy.

Because I agree that petitioner's sentence does not violate the Eighth Amendment's prohibition against cruel and unusual punishments, I concur in the judgment.

Justice THOMAS, concurring in the judgment.

I agree with Justice SCALIA's view that the proportionality test * * * is incapable of judicial application. * * * In my view, the Cruel and Unusual Punishments Clause of the Eighth Amendment contains no proportionality principle. * * *

* * *

Justice STEVENS, with whom Justice SOUTER, Justice GINSBURG and Justice BREYER join, dissenting.

* * * The concurrences prompt this separate writing to emphasize that proportionality review is not only capable of judicial application but also required by the Eighth Amendment.

* * * Faithful to the [Eighth] Amendment's text, this Court has held that the Constitution directs judges to apply their best judgment in determining the proportionality of fines, * * * bail, * * * and other forms of punishment, including the imposition of the death sentence * * *. It "would be anomalous indeed" to suggest that the Eighth Amendment makes proportionality review applicable in the context of bail and fines but not in the context of other forms of punishment, such as imprisonment. * * * Rather, by broadly prohibiting excessive sanctions, the Eighth Amendment directs judges to exercise their wise judgment in assessing the proportionality of all forms of punishment.

The absence of a black-letter rule does not disable judges from exercising their discretion in construing the outer limits on sentencing authority that the Eighth Amendment imposes. After all, judges are "constantly called upon to draw ... lines in a variety of contexts," * * * and to exercise their judgment to give meaning to the Constitution's broadly phrased protections. For example, the Due Process Clause directs judges to employ proportionality review in assessing the constitutionality of punitive damages awards on a case-by-case basis. * * * Also, although the Sixth Amendment guarantees criminal defendants the right to a speedy trial, the courts often are asked to determine on a case-by-case basis whether a particular delay is constitutionally permissible or not. * * *

* * * I think it clear that the Eighth Amendment's prohibition of "cruel and unusual punishments" expresses a broad and basic proportionality principle that takes into account all of the justifications for penal sanctions. It is this broad proportionality principle that would preclude reliance on any of the justifications for punishment to support, for example, a life sentence for overtime parking. * * *

* * *

Justice BREYER, with whom Justice STEVENS, Justice SOUTER, and Justice GINSBURG join, dissenting.

The constitutional question is whether the "three strikes" sentence imposed by California upon repeat-offender Gary Ewing is "grossly disproportionate" to his crime. * * * In Solem v. Helm, 463 U.S. 277, 103 S.Ct. 3001 (1983), the Court found grossly disproportionate a somewhat longer sentence imposed on a recidivist offender for triggering criminal conduct that was somewhat less severe. In my view, the differences are not determinative, and the Court should reach the same ultimate conclusion here.

* * *

* * * Ewing's sentence on its face imposes one of the most severe punishments available upon a recidivist who subsequently engaged in one of the less serious forms of criminal conduct. * * * I do not deny the seriousness of shoplifting, which * * * costs retailers in the range of $30 billion annually. * * * But

consider that conduct in terms of the factors that this Court mentioned in *Solem*—the "harm caused or threatened to the victim or society," the "absolute magnitude of the crime," and the offender's "culpability." * * * In respect to all three criteria, the sentence-triggering behavior here ranks well toward the bottom of the criminal conduct scale.

* * * Nor is there evidence presented here that the law enforcement community believes lengthy prison terms necessary adequately to deter shoplifting. To the contrary, well-publicized instances of shoplifting suggest that the offense is often punished without any prison sentence at all. On the other hand, shoplifting is a frequently committed crime; but "frequency," standing alone, cannot make a critical difference. Otherwise traffic offenses would warrant even more serious punishment.

This case, of course, involves shoplifting engaged in by a *recidivist*. One might argue that *any* crime committed by a recidivist is a serious crime potentially warranting a 25-year sentence. But this Court rejected that view in *Solem*, and in *Harmelin* * * * Our cases make clear that, in cases involving recidivist offenders, we must focus upon "the [offense] that triggers the life sentence," with recidivism playing a "relevant," but not necessarily determinative, role. * * * And here * * * that offense is among the less serious, while the punishment is among the most serious. * * *

[S]ome objective evidence suggests that many experienced judges would consider Ewing's sentence disproportionately harsh. The United States Sentencing Commission * * * * does not include shoplifting (or similar theft-related offenses) among the crimes that might trigger especially long sentences for recidivists * * *.

* * *

Believing Ewing's argument a strong one, sufficient to pass the threshold, I turn to the comparative analysis. A comparison of Ewing's sentence with other sentences requires answers to two questions. First, how would other jurisdictions (or California at other times, *i.e.*, without the three strikes penalty) punish the *same offense conduct*? Second, upon what other conduct would other jurisdictions (or California) impose the *same prison term*? Moreover, since hypothetical punishment is beside the point, the relevant prison time, for comparative purposes, is *real* prison time, *i.e.*, the time that an offender must *actually serve*.

* * *

The upshot is that comparison of other sentencing practices, both in other jurisdictions and in California at other times (or in respect to other crimes), validates what an initial threshold examination suggested. Given the information available, given the state and federal parties' ability to provide additional contrary data, and given their failure to do so, we can assume for constitutional purposes that the following statement is true: Outside the California three strikes context, Ewing's recidivist sentence is virtually unique in its harshness for his offense of conviction, and by a considerable degree.

* * *

I can find no * * * special criminal justice concerns that might justify this sentence. The most obvious potential justification for bringing Ewing's theft within the ambit of the statute is administrative. California must draw some kind of workable line between conduct that will trigger, and conduct that will not trigger, a "three strikes" sentence. "But the fact that a line has to be drawn somewhere does not justify its being drawn anywhere." Pearce v. Commissioner, 315 U.S. 543, 558, 62 S.Ct. 754 (1942) (Frankfurter, J., dissenting). The statute's administrative objective would seem to be one of separating more serious, from less serious, triggering criminal conduct. Yet the statute does not do that job particularly well.

* * *

Most "wobbler" statutes classify the same criminal conduct either as a felony or as a misdemeanor, depending upon the actual punishment imposed, * * * which in turn depends primarily upon whether "the rehabilitation of the convicted defendant" either does or does not "require" * * * "incarceration in a state prison as a felon." * * * In such cases, the felony/misdemeanor classification turns primarily upon the nature of the offender, not the comparative seriousness of the offender's conduct.

* * *

Neither do I see any other way in which inclusion of Ewing's conduct (as a "triggering crime") would further a significant criminal justice objective. One might argue that those who commit several *property* crimes should receive long terms of imprisonment in order to "incapacitate" them, *i.e.*, to prevent them from committing further crimes in the future. But that is not the object of this particular three strikes statute. Rather, as the plurality says, California seeks " 'to reduce *serious* and *violent* crime.'" * * * The statute's definitions of both kinds of crime include crimes against the person, crimes that create danger of physical harm, and drug crimes. * * * They do not include even serious crimes against property, such as obtaining large amounts of money, say, through theft, embezzlement, or fraud. Given the omission of vast categories of property crimes—including grand theft unarmed—from the "strike" definition, one cannot argue, on *property-crime-related incapacitation grounds,* for inclusion of Ewing's crime among the triggers.

* * *

* * * Ewing's sentence (life imprisonment with a minimum term of 25 years) is grossly disproportionate to the triggering offense conduct—stealing three golf clubs—Ewing's recidivism notwithstanding.

* * *

Prisoners' Rights

▶ Insert at p. 592 following the first paragraph

Emphasizing that prison regulations need bear only a rational relationship to legitimate penological interests and that substantial deference is due the judgment of prison administrators charged with defining the goals of a correctional system and choosing the best means for achieving them, the Court in Overton v. Bazzetta, 539 U.S. 126, 123 S.Ct. 2162 (2003), sustained numerous visitation restrictions imposed on inmates in Michigan's prisons. Inmates with two or more drug violations were restricted to visits only by clergy and attorneys but could apply to have broader visitation privileges restored after two years. Other regulations restricted visits to inmates by children, depending on whether the children were directly related to the inmate, whether parental rights had been taken away, or whether they were accompanied by an adult. Still other restrictions banned visits by relatives who were former prison inmates unless the warden approved. All of these the state justified based on its concern for security in light of the escalating number of visitors to its corrections facilities and substance abuse among inmates. The Court, 9-0, rejected the contention that any of these restrictions violated the Eighth Amendment by imposing cruel and unusual conditions of confinement or infringed any associational rights protected by the First Amendment.

A similar posture of deference to prison administrators was also apparent in the Court's review of procedures governing the assignment of certain convicts to "supermax" prisons. These are maximum security institutions with highly restrictive conditions designed to segregate the most dangerous inmates (those who head gangs, lead riots, participate in organized crime, etc.) from the general prison population. "Supermax" confinement entails solitary confinement, deprivation of almost any stimuli and all human contact, very few opportunities for visitation, and the monitoring of virtually every aspect of life. Placement in "supermax" confinement is for an indefinite period and disqualifies an inmate from parole. In Wilkinson v. Austin, 545 U.S. —, 125 S.Ct. 2384 (2005), the Court unanimously held that there was no deprivation of due process where the Ohio prison system provided: (1) multiple levels of review for any decision recommending "supermax" confinement; (2) review of any decision to so confine an inmate within 30 days of the decision; (3) notice of the factual basis for the decision; and (4) a fair opportunity to rebut the decision. But no other attributes of an adversary hearing, such as the right to call witnesses, were required. While the Court acknowledged that inmates possessed a "liberty" interest in not being placed in "supermax" confinement erroneously, nonetheless important governmental interests in protecting the safety of other inmates, prison personnel, and the public, and the expense, burden, and delay associated with adding other adversarial protections weighed against recognizing more procedural guarantees.

The Supreme Court has agreed to consider at its October 2005 Term whether state prisoners with disabilities can sue for damages under the Americans With Disabilities Act. The inmate, a paraplegic, argued that he could not maneuver his wheelchair in his small cell and was deprived of access to a toilet, a shower, and his bed. United States v. Georgia, 545 U.S. —125 S.Ct. 2256 (2005).

Confining Dangerous Persons Other than Upon Criminal Conviction

▶ Insert at p. 597 following the second paragraph

The Supreme Court upheld both Alaska and Connecticut's Megan's Laws. In the Alaska case, which follows, the statute was challenged on grounds its retroactive application violated the Ex Post Facto Clause. In the Connecticut case (see p. 114 of this Supplement), the state law, it was argued, denied due process to sexual offenders who could show they no longer posed a danger.

SMITH v. DOE
Supreme Court of the United States, 2003
538 U.S. 84, 123 S.Ct. 1140, 155 L.Ed.2d 164

BACKGROUND & FACTS Within two years of the 1994 sexual assault and murder of seven-year-old Megan Kanka in New Jersey, every state enacted a version of "Megan's Law," which requires the registration of convicted sex offenders and public notification of their whereabouts. The Alaska law requires the registration of any "sex offender or child kidnapper" present in the state and that anyone being released from state custody for commission of these offenses register at least 30 days prior to his release. In addition to the offender's name, the information to be provided includes his address, place of employment, all aliases, identifying features, vehicle license number, and treatment history. Registration is required for 15 years, except that repeat offenders and anyone convicted of an aggravated sex offense must register for life and provide verification of this information quarterly. The Alaska law is effective retroactively, so that offenders convicted before the law was enacted are subject to its provisions.

John Doe I was convicted of sexually abusing a 14-year old and John Doe II pleaded no-contest to a finding that he had abused his daughter when she was between 9 and 11 years old. Both, aggravated sex offenders, convicted before the Alaska Megan's Law was enacted, challenged its retroactive application as a violation of the Ex Post Facto Clause of the Constitution. A federal district court so held and judgment in the plaintiffs' favor was affirmed by a federal appeals court. The Alaska Commissioner of Public Safety and the state attorney general successfully sought review by the U.S. Supreme Court.

Justice KENNEDY delivered the opinion of the Court.

The Alaska Sex Offender Registration Act requires convicted sex offenders to register with law enforcement authorities, and much of the information is made public. We must decide whether the registration requirement is a retroactive punishment prohibited by the *Ex Post Facto* Clause.

* * *

* * * We must "ascertain whether the legislature meant the statute to establish 'civil' proceedings." Kansas v. Hendricks, 521 U.S. 346, 361, 117 S.Ct. 2072 (1997). If the intention of the legislature was to impose punishment, that ends the inquiry. If, however, the intention was to enact a regulatory scheme that is civil and nonpunitive, we must further examine whether the statutory scheme is "'so punitive either in purpose or effect as to negate [the State's] intention' to deem it 'civil.'" * * * Because we "ordinarily defer to the legislature's stated intent," * * * "'only the clearest proof' will suffice to override legislative intent and transform what has been denominated a civil remedy into a criminal penalty" * * *.

* * *

* * * Here, the Alaska Legislature

expressed the objective of the law in the statutory text itself. The legislature found that "sex offenders pose a high risk of reoffending," and identified "protecting the public from sex offenders" as the "primary governmental interest" of the law. * * * The legislature further determined that "release of certain information about sex offenders to public agencies and the general public will assist in protecting the public safety." * * * In this case, as in *Hendricks*, "[n]othing on the face of the statute suggests that the legislature sought to create anything other than a civil ... scheme designed to protect the public from harm." * * *

* * *

Other formal attributes of a legislative enactment, such as the manner of its codification or the enforcement procedures it establishes, are * * * [indicators] of the legislature's intent. * * * In this case these factors are open to debate. The notification provisions of the Act are codified in the State's "Health, Safety, and Housing Code," * * * confirming our conclusion that the statute was intended as a nonpunitive regulatory measure. * * * The Act's registration provisions, however, are codified in the State's criminal procedure code, and so might seem to point in the opposite direction. These factors, though, are not dispositive. The location and labels of a statutory provision do not by themselves transform a civil remedy into a criminal one. * * *

* * *

[Moreover,] [t]he policy to alert convicted offenders to the civil consequences of their criminal conduct does not render the consequences themselves punitive. When a State sets up a regulatory scheme, it is logical to provide those persons subject to it with clear and unambiguous notice of the requirements and the penalties for noncompliance. The Act requires registration either before the offender's release from confinement or within a day of his conviction (if the offender is not imprisoned). Timely and adequate notice serves to apprize individuals of their responsibilities and to ensure compliance with the regulatory scheme. Notice is important, for the scheme is enforced by criminal penalties. * * * Invoking the criminal process in aid of a statutory regime does not render the statutory scheme itself punitive.

* * *

We conclude * * * that the intent of the Alaska Legislature was to create a civil, nonpunitive regime.

* * *

Some colonial punishments * * * were meant to inflict public disgrace. Humiliated offenders were required "to stand in public with signs cataloguing their offenses." * * *

Any initial resemblance to early punishments is, however, misleading. Punishments such as whipping, pillory, and branding inflicted physical pain and staged a direct confrontation between the offender and the public. Even punishments that lacked the corporal component, such as public shaming, humiliation, and banishment, involved more than the dissemination of information. They either held the person up before his fellow citizens for face-to-face shaming or expelled him from the community. * * * By contrast, the stigma of Alaska's Megan's Law results not from public display for ridicule and shaming but from the dissemination of accurate information about a criminal record, most of which is already public. Our system does not treat dissemination of truthful information in furtherance of a legitimate governmental objective as punishment. * * * The publicity may cause adverse consequences for the convicted defendant, running from mild personal embarrassment to social ostracism. In contrast to the colonial shaming punishments, however, the State does not make the publicity and the resulting stigma an integral part of the objective of the regulatory scheme.

The fact that Alaska posts the information on the Internet does not alter our conclusion. It must be acknowledged that notice of a criminal conviction subjects the offender to public shame, the humiliation increasing in proportion to the extent of the publicity. And the geographic reach of the Internet is greater than anything which could have been designed in colonial times. These facts do not render Internet notification punitive. The purpose and the principal effect of notification are to inform the public for its own safety, not to humiliate the offender. Widespread public access is necessary for the efficacy of the scheme, and the attendant humiliation is but a collateral consequence of a valid regulation.

The State's Web site does not provide the public with means to shame the offender by, say, posting comments underneath his record. An individual seeking the information must take the initial step of going to the Department of Public Safety's Web site, proceed to the sex offender registry, and then look up the desired information. The process is more analogous to a visit to an official archive of criminal records than it is to a scheme forcing an offender to appear in public with some visible badge of past criminality. * * *

* * *

* * * The Act's obligations are less harsh than the sanctions of occupational debarment, which we have held to be nonpunitive. * * * The Act does not restrain activities sex offenders may pursue but leaves them free to change jobs or residences.

* * *

Although the public availability of the information may have a lasting and painful impact on the convicted sex offender, these consequences flow not from the Act's registration and dissemination provisions, but from the fact of conviction, already a matter of public record. * * *

* * *

The duration of the reporting requirements is not excessive. Empirical research on child molesters, for instance, has shown that, "[c]ontrary to conventional wisdom, most reoffenses do not occur within the first several years after release," but may occur "as late as 20 years following release." * * *

* * *

* * * Alaska's * * * [law] establish[es] a civil regulatory scheme. The Act is nonpunitive, and its retroactive application does not violate the *Ex Post Facto* Clause. The judgment of the Court of Appeals for the Ninth Circuit is reversed, and the case is remanded for further proceedings consistent with this opinion.

It is so ordered.

Justice SOUTER, concurring in the judgment.

I agree with the Court that Alaska's Sex Offender Registration Act does not amount to an *ex post facto* law. * * *

* * *

To me, the indications of punitive character * * * and the civil indications weighed heavily by the Court are in rough equipoise. * * * What tips the scale for me is the presumption of constitutionality normally accorded a State's law. That presumption gives the State the benefit of the doubt in close cases like this one, and on that basis alone I concur in the Court's judgment.

Justice STEVENS, dissenting [in *Smith v. Doe*, but concurring in *Connecticut Dept. of Public Safety v. Doe*].

* * *

* * * In my opinion, a sanction that (1) is imposed on everyone who commits a criminal offense, (2) is not imposed on anyone else, and (3) severely impairs a person's liberty is punishment.

It is therefore clear to me that the Constitution prohibits the addition of these sanctions to the punishment of persons who were tried and convicted before the legislation was enacted. * * * [R]etroactive application of these statutes constitutes a flagrant violation of the protections afforded by the Double Jeopardy and *Ex Post Facto* Clauses of the Constitution.

I think it equally clear, however, that the State may impose registration duties and may publish registration information as a part of its punishment of this category of defendants. * * * [A]s a matter of procedural fairness, Alaska requires its judges to include notice of the registration requirements in judgments imposing sentences on convicted sex offenders and in the colloquy preceding the acceptance of a plea of guilty to such an offense. * * * Thus, I agree with the Court that these statutes are constitutional as applied to *post*enactment offenses. [Emphasis supplied.]

* * * [F]or those convicted of offenses committed after the effective date of such legislation, there would be no separate procedural due process violation so long as a defendant is provided a constitutionally adequate trial. * * *

Justice GINSBURG, with whom Justice BREYER joins, dissenting.

* * *

* * * I would hold Alaska's Act punitive in effect. Beyond doubt, the Act involves an "affirmative disability or restraint." * * * Alaska's Act imposes onerous and intrusive obligations on convicted sex offenders; and it exposes registrants, through aggressive public notification of their crimes, to profound humiliation and community-wide ostracism. * * *

Furthermore, the Act's requirements resemble historically common forms of punishment. * * * Its registration and reporting provisions are comparable to conditions of supervised release or parole; its public notification regimen, which permits placement of the registrant's face on a webpage under the label "Registered Sex Offender," calls to mind shaming punishments once used to mark an offender as someone to be shunned. * * *

[T]he Act retributively targets past guilt, *i.e.*, * * * it "revisit[s] past crimes [more than it] prevent[s] future ones." * * *

* * *

[T]he Act has a legitimate civil purpose: to promote public safety by alerting the public to potentially recidivist sex offenders in the community. * * * But its scope notably exceeds this purpose. The Act applies to all convicted sex offenders, without regard to their future dangerousness. And the duration of the reporting requirement is keyed not to any determination of a particular offender's risk of reoffending, but to whether the offense of conviction qualified as aggravated. The reporting requirements themselves are exorbitant: The Act requires aggravated offenders to engage in perpetual quarterly reporting, even if their personal information has not changed. * * * And meriting heaviest weight in my judgment, the Act makes no provision whatever for the possibility of rehabilitation: Offenders cannot shorten their registration or notification period, even on the clearest demonstration of rehabilitation or conclusive proof of physical incapacitation.

However plain it may be that a former sex offender currently poses no threat of recidivism, he will remain subject to long-term monitoring and inescapable humiliation.

* * *

* * * I would hold * * * [the Act's] retroactive application incompatible with the *Ex Post Facto* Clause, and would therefore affirm the judgment of the Court of Appeals.

In a companion case, Connecticut Dept. of Public Safety v. Doe, 538 U.S. 1, 123 S.Ct. 1160 (2003), the Supreme Court unanimously rejected the contention that Connecticut's Megan's Law violated the Due Process Clause of the Fourteenth Amendment because it did not provide for a hearing to determine the current dangerousness of an individual convicted of offenses that triggered the registration and notification requirements. The Court held that, even if injury to one's reputation from the public notification requirement constituted the deprivation of a liberty interest within the protection of the Fourteenth Amendment, due process did not require the government to prove a fact that was not relevant. Under the statute, proof of conviction sufficed to impose the registration and notification requirements, and the state was under no obligation to show additionally that the offender still posed a risk of reoffending.

The Ex Post Facto Clause

In *Kansas v. Hendricks* (Text, p. 593) and *Smith v. Doe* (this Supplement, p. 110), the Court heard and rejected Ex Post Facto Clause challenges. In the *Stogner* case, which follows, it heard another such attack on a state statute. The issue in this case is whether California could prosecute an episode of child sex abuse, now decades-old, by retroactively canceling the statute of limitations that barred prosecution of the offense. In the course of its opinion, the Court describes what constitutes an ex post facto law and comes to the conclusion that the state law at issue violates the constitutional prohibition. The Court's ruling in *Stogner* takes on added significance in light of the current scandal involving allegations of past child sex abuse by priests. Viewed in this light, *Stogner v. California* has special importance.

STOGNER V. CALIFORNIA
Supreme Court of the United States, 2003
539 U.S. 607, 123 S.Ct. 2446, 156 L.Ed.2d 544

BACKGROUND & FACTS In 1993 the California legislature enacted a law imposing a new statute of limitations on the prosecution of sex-related child abuse offenses. The new law permitted prosecution for those crimes where the limitation period on their prosecution had expired, if: (1) a victim has reported the allegation of abuse to the police; (2) there is "independent evidence that clearly and convincingly corroborates the victim's allegation"; and (3) the prosecution is begun within a year of the victim's report.

In 1998 a grand jury indicted Marion Stogner on a sex-related child abuse offense that occurred sometime between 1955 and 1973. The statute of limitations on prosecuting that offense at the time was three years. That period had lapsed long before this prosecution was begun. Stogner moved to dismiss the complaint on grounds the 1993 statute authorizing prosecution violated the Ex Post Facto Clause of the Constitution. A state trial court agreed, but its dismissal of the complaint was reversed on appeal. The U.S. Supreme Court ultimately granted certiorari.

Justice BREYER delivered the opinion of the Court.

* * *

The Constitution's two *Ex Post Facto* Clauses prohibit the Federal Government and the States from enacting laws with certain retroactive effects. See Art. I, § 9, cl. 3 (Federal Government); Art. I, § 10, cl. 1 (States). The law at issue here created a new criminal limitations period that extends the time in which prosecution is allowed. It authorized criminal prosecutions that the passage of time had previously barred. Moreover, it was enacted after prior limitations periods for Stogner's alleged offenses had expired. Do these features of the law, taken together, produce the kind of retroactivity that the Constitution forbids? * * *

First, the new statute threatens the kinds of harm that * * * the *Ex Post Facto* Clause seeks to avoid. Long ago the Court pointed out that the Clause protects liberty by preventing governments from enacting statutes with "manifestly *unjust and oppressive* " retroactive effects. Calder v. Bull, 3 U.S. (3 Dall.) 386, 391, 1 L.Ed. 648 (1798). Judge Learned Hand later wrote that extending a limitations period after the State has assured "a man that he has become safe from its pursuit ... seems to most of us unfair and dishonest." Falter v. United States, 23 F.2d 420, 426 (2d Cir. 1928) * * *. In such a case, the government has refused "to play by its own rules," Carmell v. Texas, 529 U.S. 513, 533, 120 S.Ct. 1620 (2000). It has deprived the defendant of the "fair warning" * * * that might have led him to preserve exculpatory evidence. * * * And a Constitution that permits such an extension, by allowing legislatures to pick and choose when to act retroactively, risks both "arbitrary and potentially vindictive legislation" * * * Weaver v. Graham, 450 U.S., at 29, 101 S.Ct. 960 (1981).

Second, the kind of statute at issue falls literally within the categorical descriptions of *ex post facto* laws set forth by Justice Chase more than 200 years ago in *Calder* v. *Bull* * * *—a categorization that this Court has recognized as providing an authoritative account of the scope of the *Ex Post Facto* Clause. * * * He wrote: "I will state what laws I consider *ex post facto* laws, within the words and the intent of the prohibition. 1st. Every law that makes an action done before the passing of the law, and which was innocent when done, criminal; and punishes such action. *2d. Every law that aggravates a crime, or makes it greater than it was, when committed.* 3d. Every law that changes the punishment, and inflicts a greater punishment, than the law annexed to the crime, when committed. *4th. Every law that alters the legal rules of evidence, and receives less, or different, testimony, than the law required at the time of the commission of the offence, in order to convict the offender. All these, and similar laws, are manifestly unjust and oppressive.*"* * * (emphasis altered from original).

* * *

The second category * * * describes California's statute as long as those words are understood as Justice Chase understood them—i.e., as referring to a statute that "inflict[s] *punishments*, where the party was not, by *law*, liable to *any punishment*" * * *. After (but not before) the original statute of limitations had expired, a party such as Stogner was not "liable to any punishment." California's new statute therefore "aggravated" Stogner's alleged crime, or made it "greater than it was, when committed" * * *.

* * *

* * * California's law [may fall] * * * within * * * [Justice Chase's fourth category] as well. * * *

Significantly, a statute of limitations reflects a legislative judgment that, after a certain time, *no quantum of evidence is sufficient to convict.* * * * [Emphasis supplied.] And that judgment typically rests, in large part, upon evidentiary concerns—for example, concern that the passage of time has eroded memories or made witnesses or other evidence unavailable. * * *

* * *

Third, likely for the reasons just stated, numerous legislators, courts, and commentators have long believed it well settled that the *Ex Post Facto* Clause forbids resurrection of a time-barred prosecution. Such sentiments appear already to have been widespread when the Reconstruction Congress of 1867—the Congress that drafted the 14th Amendment—rejected a bill that would have revived time-barred prosecutions for treason that various Congressmen wanted brought against Jefferson Davis and "his coconspirators" * * *.

* * *

In sum, California's law subjects an individual such as Stogner to prosecution long after the State has, in effect, granted an amnesty, telling him that he is "at liberty to return to his country ... and that from henceforth he may cease to preserve the proofs of his innocence" * * *. It retroactively withdraws a complete defense to prosecution after it has already attached, and it does so in a manner that allows the State to withdraw this defense at will and with respect to individuals already identified. * * *

We conclude that a law enacted after expiration of a previously applicable limitations period violates the *Ex Post Facto* Clause when it is applied to revive a previously time-barred prosecution. The California court's judgment to the contrary is

Reversed.

Justice KENNEDY, with whom THE CHIEF JUSTICE [REHNQUIST], Justice SCALIA, and Justice THOMAS join, dissenting.

* * * A law which does not alter the definition of the crime but only revives prosecution does not make the crime "greater than it was, when committed." * * *

* * *

* * * The California statute challenged by petitioner changes only the timespan within which the action against him may be filed; it does not alter the criminal quality assigned to the offense.

The Court's opinion renders the second *Calder* category unlimited and the surrounding categories redundant. A law which violates the first *Calder* category would also violate the Court's conception of category two, because such a law would "inflic[t] punishments, where the party was not, by law, liable to any punishment." * * * The Court's new definition not only distorts the original meaning of the second *Calder* category, but also threatens the coherence of the overall *ex post facto* scheme.

* * *

The majority seems to suggest that retroactive extension of expired limitations periods is "'arbitrary and potentially vindictive legislation'" * * * but * * * [t]he California statute can be explained as motivated by legitimate concerns about the continuing suffering endured by the victims of childhood abuse.

The California Legislature noted that "young victims often delay reporting sexual abuse because they are easily manipulated by offenders in positions of authority and trust, and because children have difficulty remembering the crime or facing the trauma it can cause." * * * The concern is amply supported by empirical studies. * * *

* * *

When a child molester commits his offense, he is well aware the harm will plague the victim for a lifetime. * * * The victims whose interests [the new statute] takes into consideration have been subjected to sexual abuse within the confines of their own homes and by people they trusted and relied upon for protection. A familial figure of authority can use a confidential relation to conceal a crime. The violation of this trust inflicts deep and lasting hurt. Its only poor remedy is that the law will show its compassion and concern when the victim at last can find the strength, and know the necessity, to come forward. When the criminal has taken distinct advantage of the tender years and perilous position of a fearful victim, it is the victim's lasting hurt, not the perpetrator's fictional reliance, that the law should count the higher. The victims whose cause is now before the Court have at last overcome shame and the desire to repress these painful memories. They have reported the crimes so that the violators are brought to justice and harm to others is prevented. The Court now tells the victims their decision to come forward is in vain.

The gravity of the crime was known, and is being measured, by its wrongfulness when committed. It is a common policy for States to suspend statutes of limitations for civil harms against minors, in order to "protec[t] minors during the period when they are unable to protect themselves." * * * [I]t is fictional for the Court to say, in the given context, the new policy somehow alters the magnitude of the crime. The wrong was made clear by the law at the time of the crime's commission. The criminal actor knew it, even reveled in it. It is the commission of the then-unlawful act that the State now seeks to punish. The gravity of the crime is left unchanged by altering a statute of limitations of which the actor was likely not at all aware.

* * *

The Court's stretching of *Calder's* second category contradicts the historical understanding of that category, * * * misapprehends the purposes of the *Ex Post Facto* Clause[,] * * * [and] disregards the interests of those victims of child abuse who have found the courage to face their accusers and bring them to justice. The Court's opinion harms not only our *ex post facto* jurisprudence but also these and future victims of child abuse, and so compels my respectful dissent.

CHAPTER 9

OBTAINING EVIDENCE

B. WARRANTLESS SEARCHES AND SEIZURES

Consent

▶ **Insert at p. 624 following** *United States* **v.** *Drayton*

Drayton, like Court rulings before it, made clear that consent is to be imputed in light of the totality of the circumstances, not by any automatic rule. There may be lack of consent to a search or interrogation even if the individual makes no attempt to leave or does not refuse to cooperate. Lack of consent, the Court has said, could be inferred from any of the following circumstances: "the threatening presence of several officers, the display of a weapon by an officer, some physical touching of the citizen, or the use of language or tone of voice indicating that compliance with the officer's request might be compelled."

In Kaupp v. Texas, 538 U.S. 626, 123 S.Ct. 1843 (2003), the Court's most recent case along these lines, the defendant, a 17 year old, was implicated in statements about the murder of a 14-year-old girl by the victim's older teenage half-brother who had been having sexual relations with her. After failing to obtain a warrant to question Kaupp, police went to his residence in the middle of the night, awakened him with a flashlight, and told him "we have to talk," to which he replied "Okay." They then handcuffed him and led him, clad only in a T-shirt and boxer shorts, out of the house and into to a patrol car. All of this, despite the fact that the victim's half-brother had failed polygraph examinations three times, while Kaupp had successfully passed his. In a per curiam opinion, the Court unanimously held that, in the absence of probable cause (or even reasonable suspicion) that Kaupp was implicated, merely reading him the *Miranda* warnings was insufficient. As the Court repeated from a previous decision, "'*Miranda* warnings, *alone* and *per se*, cannot always * * * break * * * the causal connection between the * * * [Fourth Amendment violation] and the confession.'"

But what if two joint occupants of a property differ in their willingness to grant consent to a search? Is there at least an automatic rule here? The answer may depend on whether both are physically present when the police seek to search the property. In United States v. Matlock, 415 U.S. 164, 94 S.Ct. 988 (1974), the Supreme Court (over dissents by Justices Douglas, Brennan, and Marshall) held that, if the consenting individual was physically present but the non-consenting occupant was not, consent would be deemed to have been given. But what if both are present and they disagree about consenting to the search—admittedly a rare event? The Supreme Court has granted cert. in Georgia v. Randolph, 278 Ga. 614, 604 S.E.2d 835 (2004), *cert. granted*, 544 U.S. —, 125 S.Ct. 1840 (2005), to address the question. Currently, there is a conflict between federal and state courts on the answer. The minority view, adopted by the Georgia Supreme Court, is that if a co-owner of the property is physically present and refuses consent, then consent has not been given. Since, generally speaking, the U.S. Supreme Court reverses when it grants cert., the odds favor the majority view.

Search Incident to Arrest

▶ Insert at p. 627 following the chart

OTHER CASES ON ARRESTS, SEARCHES, AND DETENTIONS IN AND ABOUT THE HOME --CONTINUED		
CASE	RULING	VOTE
Muehler v. Mena, 543 U.S. —, 125 S.Ct. 1465 (2005)	In the circumstances of this case, federal officers did not violate the Fourth Amendment when they detained the resident in handcuffs for 2-3 hours in the garage while they searched the house for deadly weapons and a wanted gang member pursuant to a search warrant. The handcuffing was justified as minimizing any risk to the officers' safety and did not depend upon the weightiness of the grounds for the search. Nor did questioning the resident about her immigration status during the search implicate any protected Fourth Amendment interest.	9-0.

▶ Insert at p. 628 following the last sentence in the first paragraph

Thus, in United States v. Banks, 540 U.S. 31, 124 S.Ct. 521 (2003), after knocking and announcing, federal agents were constitutionally justified in waiting only 15-20 seconds before entering to execute a search warrant for possession of cocaine.

Motor Vehicles

▶ **Insert at p. 634 following the chart on Automobile Searches**

OTHER CASES ON AUTOMOBILE SEARCHES--CONTINUED		
CASE	RULING	VOTE
Maryland v. Pringle, 540 U.S. 366, 124 S.Ct. 795 (2003)	After pulling a vehicle over for speeding, obtaining consent to search the car, and finding drugs and money in the glove box, police were justified in arresting all three occupants of the car. Since none offered any explanation or said they knew anything about the money or cocaine, the officer had probable cause to believe that "any or all three * * * had knowledge of, and exercised dominion and control over, the cocaine."	9-0.
Thornton v. United States, 541 U.S. 615, 124 S.Ct. 2127 (2004)	When an officer has made a lawful custodial arrest of the occupant of a vehicle, a search of the passenger compartment is justified as incident to the arrest, and it makes no difference whether the occupant was inside or outside the car when the officer initiated contact. Police apprehended defendant in a parking lot after his license tag seemed to match that of a different car. He was sweaty, smacking his lips, and rambling. He consented to a patdown that turned up drugs, and a search of the car produced a handgun.	9-0.
Illinois v. Caballes, 543 U.S. —, 125 S.Ct. 834 (2005)	Following a routine traffic stop, police may walk a dog trained to sniff out drugs around the vehicle without having any particularized suspicion that the car contains narcotics. Since the dog alerts only to contraband, the practice cannot "compromise any legitimate interest in privacy."	6-2; Justices Souter and Ginsburg dissented. Chief Justice Rehnquist did not participate.

Street Stops

▶ **Insert at p. 657 following the chart**

OTHER CASES DRAWING UPON *TERRY* V. *OHIO*--CONTINUED		
CASE	RULING	VOTE
Hiibel v. Sixth Judicial District Court of Nevada, 542 U.S. 177, 124 S.Ct. 2451 (2004)	An individual can be punished for refusing to disclose his name if he is detained by the police, in the words of a Nevada statute, "under circumstances which reasonably indicate that the person has committed, is committing or is about to commit a crime." The statute did not require the person to produce a driver's license or any other document. Disclosing one's name did not constitute testimonial evidence and thus did not fall within the protection of the Fifth Amendment guarantee against self-incrimination.	5-4; Justices Stevens, Souter, Ginsburg, and Breyer dissented.

Border Searches

▶ **Insert at p. 658 following the second paragraph**

The Supreme Court reaffirmed these border search principles most recently in United States v. Flores-Montano, 541 U.S. 149, 124 S.Ct. 1582 (2004). In that case, the Justices unanimously upheld customs officials' actions in removing and disassembling the gas tank of a station wagon on the off-chance drugs might be concealed in it. Whether the officers' search was random, routine, or just based on a hunch made no constitutional difference. Although an intrusive body search, might present a justifiable occasion for greater constitutional scrutiny, the expectation of privacy in a vehicle, especially one searched at the border, is much less. If a border search was conducted in a manner that resulted in serious damage to property or its destruction that, too, might trigger heightened examination, but here the removal and assembly of the gas tank could be redressed simply by reassembling and reattaching it, at no deprivation of any property interest to the owner. On its facts, this was an easy Fourth Amendment case for the Court.

CHAPTER 9 OBTAINING EVIDENCE   123

C. CURRENT CONTROVERSIES IN SEARCH AND SEIZURE LAW

▶ **Insert at p. 668 following the chart**

In a pair of close rulings, courts have held the line against random drug testing where states have conditioned the receipt of benefits on such searches. In State ex rel. Ohio AFL-CIO v. Ohio Bureau of Workers Compensation, 97 Ohio St.3d 504, 780 N.E.2d 981 (2002), the Ohio Supreme Court by a 4-3 majority ruled that the state could not permit employers to require that anyone injured on the job be tested for the use of drugs and alcohol. And a federal district court struck down a Michigan regulation that required random drug testing of persons receiving welfare benefits. The federal Temporary Assistance for Needy Families Act authorized the states to drug-test welfare recipients. The state argued that such testing was justified by the "special need" to protect children from drugs, but the district court found the practice rested only on a "public safety" interest and that, by itself, could not constitute a "special need." See Marchwinski v. Howard, 113 F.Supp.2d 1134 (E.D.Mich. 2000), ultimately affirmed by an evenly divided (6-6) federal appeals court sitting en banc, 2003 WL 1870916 (6th Cir. 2002).

▶ **Insert at p. 680 after the first paragraph**

Distinguishable from the facts in *City of Indianapolis* v. *Edmond* were those in Illinois v. Lidster, 540 U.S. 419, 124 S.Ct. 885 (2004), upholding the constitutionality of a roadblock established for informational purposes rather than to directly catch offenders. In Justice Breyer's works, "The stop's primary law enforcement purpose was *not* to determine whether a vehicle's occupants were committing a crime, but to ask * * * [them], as members of the public, for their help in providing information about a crime in all likelihood committed by others." In *Lidster*, police stopped cars *to gather information* about a fatal hit-and-run accident that occurred a week earlier. The officers handed out flyers and asked motorists if they had been in the area at the time of the accident and if they had seen anything. After his vehicle had been stopped, Lidster was arrested and subsequently convicted of driving while intoxicated. Speaking for a six-Justice majority, Justice Breyer noted that the informational stop "significant[ly]" advanced "important investigatory needs" and was "appropriately tailored," occurring as it did a week after the hit-and-run accident, on the same highway, near the accident site, and at about the same time of night. "Most importantly," he went on to observe, "the stop only minimally interfered" with Fourth Amendment rights, since it entailed only a short wait in line, a brief request for information, was a general inquiry, and created little or no cause for anxiety and alarm.

D. WIRETAPPING AND EAVESDROPPING

▶ **Insert at p. 693 following *Katz* v. *United States***

Whatever check-and-balance assumption underlay the Supreme Court's decisions in *Berger* and *Katz* about the necessity of judicial supervision of electronic surveillance, it is clear that this is belied by reality. Recent figures released by the Administrative Office of U.S. Courts show that state and federal judges approved 1,710 applications for wire, oral, or electronic communications taps in 2004. Four states (New York, California, New Jersey, and Florida) accounted for three-quarters of the surveillance orders. This did not include 1,754 terror-related investigations under the Foreign Intelligence Surveillance Act (FISA) (see Text, p. 700). During 2004, federal taps increased 26% and state-approved surveillance 13%. By far the largest number of non-terror related taps—1308—related to drug investigations, 121 were for gambling and racketeering activities, and 48 were for homicides and assaults. Most surveillance sought to intercept communications on portable devices, such as cellphones and pagers. This surveillance resulted in 4,506 arrests and 634 convictions. But most startling of all: Although wiretaps in the U.S. jumped 19% in 2004, *not a single court denied an application to tap.* See www.cnn.com/2005/LAW/04/28/increased.wiretaps.ap/index.html.

▶ Insert at p. 701 following the second paragraph of text

Section 215 of the PATRIOT Act requiring Internet service companies to provide personal information about their subscribers and barring them from disclosing to anyone the fact that they have received such an order from the government has been struck down by a federal district court. In Doe v. Ashcroft, 334 F.Supp.2d 471 9S.D.N.Y. 2004), the court ruled that subpoenaing such information by way of a so-called "national security letter," without any review by a court, was a violation of both the First and Fourth Amendments. New York Times, Sept. 30, 2004, p. A23. Nonetheless, the House voted to extend the library and wiretap provisions of the PATRIOT Act for another 10 years. Moreover, the House voted to require that the FBI director *personally* approve demands for library records and bookstore sales slips. See p. 45 of this Supplement

▶ Insert at p. 703 at the end of the page

Section 213 of the USA PATRIOT Act, which finds its source in the 1978 foreign intelligence surveillance statute, permits federal agents to search the homes of suspected terrorists and spies with secret Federal Intelligence Surveillance Court approval but without any prior notice to the suspect. This provision is commonly referred to as the "sneak and peek law." In July 2003, Rep. C. L. Otter (R-Id.) introduced an amendment to the annual appropriations bill for the federal departments of Commerce, Justice, and State that would have denied funding to conduct any "sneak and peek" activities. The Otter Amendment garnered bipartisan support and passed the House of Representatives by a surprising margin of 309-118. The measure, dubbed the "Terrorist Tipoff Amendment" by the Justice Department which strongly opposed it, was also not in the bill that made permanent most of the provisions of the USA PATRIOT Act.

CHAPTER 10

THE RIGHT OF PRIVACY

Abortion

▶ Insert at p. 719 following *Roe* v. *Wade*

Congress has enacted the Unborn Victims of Violence Act, 118 Stat. 568. The law provides that when someone commits a federal crime of violence against a pregnant woman and the fetus is injured or killed, the offender would be guilty of the same offense as if the injury had occurred to the mother. This is in addition to punishing whatever injury the woman has sustained. The House of Representatives passed the bill by a vote of 254-163 on Feb. 26, 2004, and it cleared the Senate by a margin of 61-38 a month later. Proponents of the measure said it was intended to deter attacks on pregnant women, but pro-choice advocates argued that it was really aimed at elevating the legal status of the fetus and thus undercutting the premise of the Court's abortion decisions since *Roe* v. *Wade* that a fetus is not a person. The law defines an "unborn child" as "a member of the species homo sapiens, at any stage of development, who is carried in the womb." See Congressional Quarterly Weekly Report, Mar. 27, 2004, pp. 744-746.

▶ Insert at p. 734 following *Planned Parenthood of Southeastern Pennsylvania v. Casey*

Parental notification laws at issue in *Casey* and other rulings have withstood constitutional challenge so long as they contain a judicial by-pass permitting a judge to let the young pregnant woman decide for herself if she is deemed sufficiently mature, but what if such laws fail to contain a health exception as well? The Supreme Court has granted cert. in Ayotte v. Planned Parenthood of Northern New England, 544 U.S. —, 125 S.Ct. 2294 (2005), to hear argument on the constitutionality of New Hampshire's parental notification requirement which does not contain an exception permitting the performance of the procedure to preserve the health of the pregnant woman. The federal appeals court struck down the parental notification requirement on precisely that ground. See Planned Parenthood of Northern New England v. Heed, 390 F.3d 53 (1st Cir. 2004). The appeal is a matter of some controversy because the current New Hampshire governor, John Lynch, a Democrat, sides with the appeals court and opposes the appeal. He has said he never would have signed the statute containing the requirement had he been governor at the time. Ayotte, the current state attorney general, is a holdover from the previous Republican administration. It is unclear whether there will be consequences: the attorney general in New Hampshire is appointed by the governor, although the appointment must be confirmed by a five-member commission. See http://abcnews.go.com/US/wireStory?id=810155.

▸ Insert at p. 738 following *Stenberg* v. *Carhart*

In a slap at the Supreme Court's decision, Congress passed the Partial-Birth Abortion Ban Act, 117 Stat. 1201, which became law in November 2003. The legislation is very similar to the state law struck down in *Stenberg* v. *Carhart*. The Senate passed the measure by a vote of 64-33 and it won House approval by a margin of 282-139. In its consideration of the bill, the Senate specifically rejected a call to return the bill to committee with instructions to have it rewritten to address "constitutional issues raised by the Supreme Court['s]" ruling. About 30 states have enacted "partial birth" bans and abortion rights supporters have mounted successful legal challenges in 20 of them. As the term is used in the legislation, a "partial birth" abortion is a procedure in which the fetus is terminated after its head is outside the body of the mother or, in a breech procedure, where "any part of the fetal trunk past the navel is outside the body of the mother." It is estimated that less than 2 percent of abortions fall in this category and this late-pregnancy procedure usually involves fatally deformed fetuses. While performance of the procedure is permitted to save the *life* of the mother, the law does not exempt "partial birth" abortions performed only to protect the *health* of the mother. A federal district court sitting in San Francisco struck down the ban in Planned Parenthood Federation of America v. Ashcroft, 320 F.Supp.2d 957 (N.D.Cal. 2004), for precisely that reason. The court also concluded that the language of the statute was unconstitutionally vague and thus provided inadequate notice of what conduct it forbade and invited arbitrary enforcement. These defects amounted to imposing an "undue burden" on reproductive choice, that is they created "a substantial obstacle in the path of a woman seeking an abortion of a nonviable fetus." Federal courts in two other cases have agreed, see National Abortion Rights Federation v. Ashcroft, 330 F.Supp.2d 436 (S.D.N.Y. 2004); Cathcart v. Ashcroft, 331 F.Supp.2d 805 (D.Neb. 2004), *affirmed*, 2005 WL 1592942 (8th Cir. 2005).

A strategy employed by some government officials who are ardent opponents of so-called partial-birth abortion is to subpoena the medical records of patients who have had the procedure performed. In one high-profile demand for such records, the Kansas attorney general asserted the material was being subpoenaed to prosecute criminal cases (such as statutory rape and incest). New York Times, Feb. 25, 2005, pp. A1, A17. But attempts by the U.S. Department of Justice to procure such files have been blocked by the federal courts. In Northwestern Memorial Hospital v. Ashcroft, 362 F.3d 923 (7th Cir. 2004), a federal appeals court held that the subpoena imposed an undue burden on the hospital when the probative value of the records was weighed against patients' fears of identification and the consequent harm to the hospital. See also Planned Parenthood of America v. Ashcroft, 2004 WL 432222 (N.D. Calif. 2004). Another district court agreed to enforce the subpoena, but only if patients' names and all identifying information were deleted, see National Abortion Federation v. Ashcroft, 2004 WL 555701 (S.D.N.Y. 2004).

▸ Insert at p. 740 following note on Anti-abortion Protests and Racketeering

As explained in the Text, *NOW* v. *Scheidler* held that militant anti-abortion groups, such as Operation Rescue, which interfere with patients' access to medical services, could be sued under the federal anti-racketeering law. RICO authorizes both criminal proceedings and civil actions. To collect triple damages in civil suits, plaintiffs must show "a pattern of racketeering activity," which can be established by proof of at least two actions that violate state or federal law. The National Organization for Women and two abortion facilities sued Operation Rescue and individual defendants for violating the federal Hobbs Act, 18 U.S.C.A. § 1951(a), which punishes anyone who "in any way or degree obstructs, delays, or affects commerce or movement of any article or commodity in commerce, by robbery or extortion or attempts or conspires so to do, or commits or threatens physical violence to any person or property in furtherance of a plan or purpose to do so * * *."

Plaintiffs alleged over 20 violations each of the Hobbs Act, of state extortion law, of attempting or conspiring to violate either or both, of the federal Travel Act, and of instances of attempting to violate the Travel Act. Plaintiffs argued that the defendants were members of a nationwide conspiracy to shut down abortion clinics through a pattern of intimidating activity that amounted to extortion. In Scheidler v. National Organization of Women, 537 U.S. 393, 123 S.Ct. 1057 (2003), the Supreme Court held that the defendants did not commit extortion because, regardless of their intimidating tactics, they did not "obtain" property from the plaintiffs. Although it was undisputed that Operation Rescue and the individual defendants disrupted and shut down the clinics, those acts did not violate the Hobbs Act because extortion requires that the perpetrators acquire property, not merely deprive the owners of its use. The defendants did not pursue or receive "something of value" from the plaintiffs. The Court refused to construe the statute expansively because adequate notice of what it is the law punishes, implicit in due process, requires that criminal statutes be interpreted strictly.

Following remand after the 2003 decision, the Supreme Court has yet again granted cert., see Scheidler v. National Organization of Women, 545 U.S. —, 125 S.Ct. 2991 (2005); Operation Rescue v. National Organization of Women, 545 U.S. —, 125 S.Ct. 2991 (2005). The question presented this time is whether on remand the appeals court correctly held—in conflict with two other federal appellate courts—"that the Hobbs Act can be read to punish acts or threats of violence against 'any person or property' in a manner that 'in any way or degree * * * affects commerce,' even if such acts or threats of violence are wholly unconnected to either extortion or robbery." Presumably, the Court will hear argument at its upcoming October 2005 Term.

If NOW were to win the third round and also on remand, it is conceivable that the damages could bankrupt Operation Rescue and the other defendants. The prospect that bankruptcy might be used to escape paying any damages in case of an adverse judgment moved Sen. Charles Schumer (D-N.Y.) to propose an amendment during passage of The Bankruptcy Abuse Prevention and Consumer Protection Act of 2005, 119 Stat. 23, that would preclude violent protesters from using such a strategy. The amendment was defeated on a largely party-line vote of 46-53. Congressional Quarterly Weekly Report, Mar. 14, 2005, pp. 652, 667.

Privacy and Other Lifestyle Issues

▶ **Insert at p. 755 at the bottom of the page**

After granting cert. in the *Lawrence* case, as noted in the Text, the Supreme Court answered in the affirmative the question "Should *Bowers v. Hardwick* be overruled?" In his opinion for a majority of the Court in *Lawrence*, Justice Kennedy makes it clear that the right to privacy, which the *Griswold* decision once anchored in the marital relationship, now extends to all persons *as individuals*, not because of their membership in a particular social group. The effect of the Court's ruling, which was to strike down the existing sodomy laws in Texas and 11 other states (see Text, p. 756), drew a predictably shrill response from Justice Scalia in dissent and predictions of the direst consequences. By its ruling in *Lawrence*, the Court rendered pp. 749-756 of the Text little more than a historical curiosity.

LAWRENCE V. TEXAS
Supreme Court of the United States, 2003
539 U.S. 558, 123 S.Ct. 2472, 156 L.Ed.2d 508

BACKGROUND & FACTS Houston police responded to a report of a weapons disturbance at a private residence. When they entered an apartment, they found John Lawrence and Tyron Garner engaged in a sexual act. Lawrence and Garner were arrested, held in custody overnight, and charged with violating a provision of the Texas Penal Code that punished "sexual intercourse with another individual of the same sex." A trial court convicted them and imposed a fine of $200 each in addition to $141 in court costs. Lawrence and Garner appealed, arguing that the state law violated both the Equal Protection and Due Process Clauses of the Fourteenth Amendment. A state appellate court affirmed the convictions and the U.S. Supreme Court granted their petitions for certiorari.

Justice KENNEDY delivered the opinion of the Court.

Liberty protects the person from unwarranted government intrusions into a dwelling or other private places. In our tradition the State is not omnipresent in the home. And there are other spheres of our lives and existence, outside the home, where the State should not be a dominant presence. Freedom extends beyond spatial bounds. Liberty presumes an autonomy of self that includes freedom of thought, belief, expression, and certain intimate conduct. The instant case involves liberty of the person both in its spatial and more transcendent dimensions.

The question before the Court is the validity of a Texas statute making it a crime for two persons of the same sex to engage in certain intimate sexual conduct.

* * *

We conclude the case should be resolved by determining whether the petitioners were free as adults to engage in the private conduct in the exercise of their liberty under the Due Process Clause of the Fourteenth Amendment to the Constitution. For this inquiry we deem it necessary to reconsider the Court's holding in *Bowers*.

[Although] [t]here are broad statements of the substantive reach of liberty under the Due Process Clause in earlier cases, * * * the most pertinent beginning point is our decision in Griswold v. Connecticut, 381 U.S. 479, 85 S.Ct. 1678 (1965).

In *Griswold* the Court invalidated a state law prohibiting the use of drugs or devices of contraception and counseling or aiding and abetting the use of contraceptives. The Court described the protected interest as a right to privacy and placed emphasis on the marriage relation and the protected space of the marital bedroom. * * *

After *Griswold* it was established that the right to make certain decisions regarding sexual conduct extends beyond the marital relationship. In Eisenstadt v. Baird, 405 U.S. 438, 92 S.Ct. 1029 (1972), the Court invalidated a law prohibiting the distribution of contraceptives to unmarried persons. The case was decided under the Equal Protection Clause, * * * but with respect to unmarried persons, the Court went on to state the fundamental proposition that the law impaired the exercise of their personal rights[:] * * * "It is true that in *Griswold* the right of privacy in question inhered in the marital relationship.... If the right of privacy means anything, it is the right of the *individual,* married or single, to be free from unwarranted governmental intrusion into matters so fundamentally affecting a person as the decision whether to bear or beget a child." * * *

The opinions in *Griswold* and *Eisenstadt* were part of the background for the decision in Roe v. Wade, 410 U.S. 113, 93 S.Ct. 705 (1973). * * * *Roe* recognized the right of a woman to make certain fundamental decisions affecting her destiny and confirmed once more that the protection of liberty under the Due Process Clause has a substantive dimension of fundamental significance in defining the rights of the person.

* * * Both *Eisenstadt* and * * * *Roe* confirmed that the reasoning of *Griswold* could not be confined to the protection of rights of married adults. This was the state of the law with respect to some of the most relevant cases when the Court considered *Bowers v. Hardwick.*

* * *

The Court began its substantive discussion in *Bowers* as follows: "The issue presented is whether the Federal Constitution confers a fundamental right upon homosexuals to engage in sodomy and hence invalidates the laws of the many States that still make such conduct illegal and have done so for a very long time." * * * That statement, we now conclude, discloses the Court's own failure to appreciate the extent of the liberty at stake. To say that the issue in *Bowers* was simply the right to engage in certain sexual conduct demeans the claim the individual put forward, just as it would demean a married couple were it to be said marriage is simply about the right to have sexual intercourse. The laws involved in *Bowers* and here are, to be sure, statutes that purport to do no more than prohibit a particular sexual act. Their penalties and purposes, though, have more far-reaching consequences, touching upon the most private human conduct, sexual behavior, and in the most private of places, the home. The statutes do seek to control a personal relationship that, whether or not entitled to formal recognition in the law, is within the liberty of persons to choose without being punished as criminals.

This, as a general rule, should counsel against attempts by the State, or a court, to define the meaning of the relationship or to set its boundaries absent injury to a person or abuse of an institution the law protects. It suffices for us to acknowledge that adults may choose to enter upon this relationship in the confines of their homes and their own private lives and still retain their dignity as free persons. When sexuality finds overt expression in intimate conduct with another person, the conduct can be but one element in a personal bond that is more enduring. The liberty protected by the Constitution allows homosexual persons the right to make this choice.

[*Bowers*] * * * misapprehended the claim of liberty there presented to it, and thus stat[ed] the claim to be whether there is a fundamental right to engage in consensual sodomy * * *.

At the outset it should be noted that there is no longstanding history in this country of laws directed at homosexual conduct as a distinct matter. * * * [E]arly American sodomy laws were not directed at homosexuals as such but instead sought to prohibit nonprocreative sexual activity more generally. * * *

Laws prohibiting sodomy do not seem to have been enforced against consenting adults acting in private. A substantial number of sodomy prosecutions and convictions for which there are surviving records were for predatory acts against those who could not or did not consent, as in the case of a minor or the victim of an assault. * * *

* * *

[F]ar from possessing "ancient roots," * * * American laws targeting same-sex couples did not develop until the last third of the 20th century. The reported decisions concerning the prosecution of consensual, homosexual sodomy between adults for the years 1880-1995 are not always clear in the details, but a significant number involved conduct in a public place. * * *

It was not until the 1970's that any State singled out same-sex relations for criminal prosecution, and only nine States have done so. * * *

In summary, the historical grounds relied upon in *Bowers* are more complex than the majority opinion and the concurring opinion by Chief Justice Burger indicate. Their historical premises are not without doubt and, at the very least, are overstated.

It must be acknowledged, of course, that the Court in *Bowers* was making the broader point that for centuries there have been powerful voices to condemn homosexual conduct as immoral. The condemnation has been shaped by religious beliefs, conceptions of right and acceptable behavior, and respect for the traditional family. For many persons these are not trivial concerns but profound and deep convictions accepted as ethical and moral principles to which they aspire and which thus determine the course of their lives.

These considerations do not answer the question before us, however. The issue is whether the majority may use the power of the State to enforce these views on the whole society through operation of the criminal law. * * *

* * * In all events we think that our laws and traditions in the past half century are of most relevance here. These references show an emerging awareness that liberty gives substantial protection to adult persons in deciding how to conduct their private lives in matters pertaining to sex. * * *

This emerging recognition should have been apparent when *Bowers* was decided. * * * In 1961 Illinois changed its laws to * * * [decriminalize sexual acts between individuals of the same sex;] [o]ther States soon followed. * * *

* * *

Of even more importance, almost five years before *Bowers* was decided the European Court of Human Rights considered a case with parallels to *Bowers* and to today's case. * * * The court held that the laws proscribing the conduct were invalid under the European Convention on Human Rights. Dudgeon v. United Kingdom, 45 Eur. Ct. H.R. (1981) ¶; 52. Authoritative in all countries that are members of the Council of Europe (21 nations then, 45 nations now), the decision is at odds with the premise in *Bowers* that the claim put forward was insubstantial in our Western civilization.

In our own constitutional system the deficiencies in *Bowers* became even more apparent in the years following its announcement. The 25 States with laws prohibiting the relevant conduct referenced in the *Bowers* decision are reduced now to 13, of which 4 enforce their laws only against homosexual conduct. * * *

Two principal cases decided after *Bowers* cast its holding into even more doubt. In Planned Parenthood of Southeastern Pa. v. Casey, 505 U.S. 833, 112 S.Ct. 2791 (1992), the Court reaffirmed the substantive force of the liberty protected by the Due Process Clause. The *Casey* decision again confirmed that our laws and tradition afford constitutional protection to personal decisions relating to marriage, procreation, contraception, family relationships, child rearing, and education. * * * In explaining the respect the Constitution demands for the autonomy of the person in making these choices, we stated as follows: "These matters, involving the most intimate and personal choices a person may make in a lifetime, choices central to personal dignity and autonomy, are central to the liberty protected by the Fourteenth Amendment. At the heart of liberty is the right to define one's own concept of existence, of meaning, of the universe, and of the mystery of human life. Beliefs about these matters could not define the attributes of personhood were they formed under compulsion of the State." * * *

Persons in a homosexual relationship may seek autonomy for these purposes, just as heterosexual persons do. The decision in *Bowers* would deny them this right.

The second post-*Bowers* case of principal relevance is Romer v. Evans, 517 U.S. 620, 116 S.Ct. 1620 (1996). There the Court struck down class-based legislation directed at homosexuals as a violation of the Equal Protection Clause. *Romer* invalidated an amendment to Colorado's constitution which named as a solitary class persons who were homosexuals, lesbians, or bisexual either by "orientation, conduct, practices or relationships," * * * and deprived them of protection under state antidiscrimination laws. We concluded that the provision was "born of animosity toward the class of persons affected" and further that it had no rational relation to a legitimate governmental purpose. * * *

* * *

Equality of treatment and the due process right to demand respect for conduct protected by the substantive guarantee of liberty are linked in important respects, and a decision on the latter point advances both interests. If protected conduct is made criminal and the law which does so remains unexamined for its substantive validity, its stigma might remain even if it were not enforceable as drawn for equal protection reasons. When homosexual conduct is made criminal by the law of the State, that declaration in and of itself is an invitation to subject homosexual persons to discrimination both in the public and in the private spheres. The central holding of *Bowers* has been brought in question by this case, and it should be addressed. Its continuance as precedent demeans the lives of homosexual persons.

* * *

The foundations of *Bowers* have sustained serious erosion from our recent decisions in *Casey* and *Romer*. * * *

* * * The right the petitioners seek in this case has been accepted as an integral part of human freedom in many other countries. There has been no showing that in this country the governmental interest in circumscribing personal choice is somehow more legitimate or urgent.

* * *

Bowers was not correct when it was decided, and it is not correct today. It ought not to remain binding precedent. *Bowers* v. *Hardwick* should be and now is overruled.

The present case does not involve minors. It does not involve persons who might be injured or coerced or who are situated in relationships where consent might not easily be refused. It does not involve public conduct or prostitution. It does not involve whether the government must give formal recognition to any relationship that homosexual persons seek to enter. * * * The petitioners are entitled to respect for their private lives. The State cannot demean their existence or control their destiny by making their private sexual conduct a crime. Their right to liberty under the Due Process Clause gives them the full right to engage in their conduct without intervention of the government. * * * The Texas statute furthers no legitimate state interest which can justify its intrusion into the personal and private life of the individual.

* * *

The judgment of the Court of Appeals for the Texas Fourteenth District is reversed, and the case is remanded for further proceedings not inconsistent with this opinion.

It is so ordered.

Justice O'CONNOR, concurring in the judgment.

The Court today overrules Bowers v. Hardwick, 478 U.S. 186, 106 S.Ct. 2841 (1986). I joined *Bowers,* and do not join the Court in overruling it. Nevertheless, I agree with the Court that Texas' statute banning same-sex sodomy is unconstitutional. * * * Rather than relying on the substantive component of the Fourteenth Amendment's Due Process Clause, as the Court does, I base my conclusion on the Fourteenth Amendment's Equal Protection Clause.

* * *

* * * Sodomy between opposite-sex partners * * * is not a crime in Texas. * * * Texas treats the same conduct differently based solely on the participants. Those harmed by this law are people who have a same-sex sexual orientation and thus are more likely to engage in * * * [the prohibited] behavior * * *.

The Texas statute makes homosexuals unequal in the eyes of the law by making particular conduct—and only that conduct—subject to criminal sanction. * * *

* * *

This case raises a different issue than *Bowers:* whether, under the Equal Protection Clause, moral disapproval is a legitimate state interest to justify by itself a statute that bans homosexual sodomy, but not heterosexual sodomy. It is not. Moral disapproval of this group, like a bare desire to harm the group, is an interest that is insufficient to satisfy rational basis review under the Equal Protection Clause. * * * Indeed, we have never held that moral disapproval, without any other asserted state interest, is a sufficient rationale under the Equal Protection Clause to justify a law that discriminates among groups of persons.

Moral disapproval of a group cannot be a legitimate governmental interest under the Equal Protection Clause because legal classifications must not be "drawn for the purpose of disadvantaging the group burdened by the law." * * * Texas' invocation of moral disapproval as a legitimate state interest proves nothing more than Texas' desire to criminalize homosexual sodomy. But the Equal Protection Clause prevents a State from creating "a classification of persons undertaken for its own sake." * * * And because Texas so rarely enforces its sodomy law as applied to private, consensual acts, the law serves more as a statement of dislike and disapproval against homosexuals than as a tool to stop criminal behavior. * * *

* * *

A State can of course assign certain consequences to a violation of its criminal law. But the State cannot single out one identifiable class of citizens for punishment that does not apply to everyone else, with moral disapproval as the only asserted state interest for the law. * * *

Whether a sodomy law that is neutral both in effect and application * * * would violate the substantive component of the Due Process Clause is an issue that need not be decided today. I am confident, however, that so long as the Equal Protection Clause requires a sodomy law to apply equally to the private consensual conduct of homosexuals and heterosexuals alike, such a law would not long stand in our democratic society. * * *

Justice SCALIA, with whom THE CHIEF

JUSTICE [REHNQUIST] and Justice THOMAS join, dissenting.

* * *

Most of * * * today's opinion has no relevance to its actual holding—that the Texas statute "furthers no legitimate state interest which can justify" its application to petitioners under rational-basis review. * * * [T]he Court simply describes petitioners' conduct as "an exercise of their liberty" * * * and proceeds to apply an unheard-of form of rational-basis review that will have far-reaching implications beyond this case. * * *

* * *

Today's approach to *stare decisis* invites us to overrule an erroneously decided precedent (including an "intensely divisive" decision) *if*: (1) its foundations have been "eroded" by subsequent decisions,* * * (2) it has been subject to "substantial and continuing" criticism, and (3) it has not induced "individual or societal reliance" that counsels against overturning * * *. The problem is that *Roe* itself—which today's majority surely has no disposition to overrule—satisfies these conditions to at least the same degree as *Bowers*.

* * *

* * * State laws against bigamy, same-sex marriage, adult incest, prostitution, masturbation, adultery, fornication, bestiality, and obscenity are likewise sustainable only in light of *Bowers*' validation of laws based on moral choices. Every single one of these laws is called into question by today's decision; the Court makes no effort to cabin the scope of its decision to exclude them from its holding. * * * The impossibility of distinguishing homosexuality from other traditional "morals" offenses is precisely why *Bowers* rejected the rational-basis challenge. "The law," it said, "is constantly based on notions of morality, and if all laws representing essentially moral choices are to be invalidated under the Due Process Clause, the courts will be very busy indeed." * * *

What a massive disruption of the current social order, therefore, the overruling of *Bowers* entails. Not so the overruling of *Roe*, which would simply have restored the regime that existed for centuries before 1973, in which the permissibility of and restrictions upon abortion were determined legislatively State-by-State. *Casey*, however, chose to base its *stare decisis* determination on a different "sort" of reliance. "[P]eople," it said, "have organized intimate relationships and made choices that define their views of themselves and their places in society, in reliance on the availability of abortion in the event that contraception should fail." * * * This falsely assumes that the consequence of overruling *Roe* would have been to make abortion unlawful. It would not; it would merely have *permitted* the States to do so. Many States would unquestionably have declined to prohibit abortion, and others would not have prohibited it within six months (after which the most significant reliance interests would have expired). Even for persons in States other than these, the choice would not have been between abortion and childbirth, but between abortion nearby and abortion in a neighboring State.

* * *

[The Texas sodomy statute] undoubtedly

imposes constraints on liberty. So do laws prohibiting prostitution, recreational use of heroin, and, for that matter, working more than 60 hours per week in a bakery. But there is no right to "liberty" under the Due Process Clause, though today's opinion repeatedly makes that claim. * * * The Fourteenth Amendment *expressly allows* States to deprive their citizens of "liberty," *so long as "due process of law" is provided* * * *.

Our opinions applying the doctrine known as "substantive due process" hold that the Due Process Clause prohibits States from infringing *fundamental* liberty interests, unless the infringement is narrowly tailored to serve a compelling state interest. * * * We have held repeatedly, in cases the Court today does not overrule, that *only* fundamental rights qualify for this so-called "heightened scrutiny" protection—that is, rights which are " 'deeply rooted in this Nation's history and tradition'" * * *. All other liberty interests may be abridged or abrogated pursuant to a validly enacted state law if that law is rationally related to a legitimate state interest.

Bowers held, first, that criminal prohibitions of homosexual sodomy are not subject to heightened scrutiny because they do not implicate a "fundamental right" under the Due Process Clause * * *.

The Court today does not overrule this holding. Not once does it describe homosexual sodomy as a "fundamental right" * * *.

* * *

The Court's description of "the state of the law" at the time of *Bowers* only confirms that *Bowers* was right. * * * The Court points to Griswold v. Connecticut, 381 U.S. 479, 481-482, 85 S.Ct. 1678 (1965). But that case *expressly disclaimed* any reliance on the doctrine of "substantive due process," and grounded the so-called "right to privacy" in penumbras of constitutional provisions *other than* the Due Process Clause. Eisenstadt v. Baird, 405 U.S. 438, 92 S.Ct. 1029 (1972), likewise had nothing to do with "substantive due process"; it invalidated a Massachusetts law prohibiting the distribution of contraceptives to unmarried persons solely on the basis of the Equal Protection Clause. Of course *Eisenstadt* contains well known dictum relating to the "right to privacy," but this referred to the right recognized in *Griswold*—a right penumbral to the *specific* guarantees in the Bill of Rights, and not a "substantive due process" right.

Roe v. Wade recognized that the right to abort an unborn child was a "fundamental right" protected by the Due Process Clause. * * * The *Roe* Court, however, made no attempt to establish that this right was "'deeply rooted in this Nation's history and tradition'"; instead, it based its conclusion that "the Fourteenth Amendment's concept of personal liberty ... is broad enough to encompass a woman's decision whether or not to terminate her pregnancy" on its own normative judgment that anti-abortion laws were undesirable. * * *

* * *

[T]he Court * * * says: "[W]e think that our laws and traditions in the past half century are of most relevance here. These references show *an emerging awareness* that liberty gives substantial protection to adult persons in deciding how to conduct their private lives *in matters pertaining to sex*." (emphasis added).

Apart from the fact that such an "emerging awareness" does not establish a "fundamental right," the statement is factually false. States continue to prosecute all sorts of crimes by adults "in matters pertaining to sex": prostitution, adult incest, adultery, obscenity, and child pornography. Sodomy laws, too, have been enforced "in the past half century," in which there have been 134 reported cases involving prosecutions for consensual, adult, homosexual sodomy. * * *

In any event, * * * [c]onstitutional entitlements do not spring into existence because some States choose to lessen or eliminate criminal sanctions on certain behavior. Much less do they spring into existence, as the Court seems to believe, because *foreign nations* decriminalize conduct. * * *

* * *

The Texas statute undeniably seeks to further the belief of its citizens that certain forms of sexual behavior are "immoral and unacceptable"—the same interest furthered by criminal laws against fornication, bigamy, adultery, adult incest, bestiality, and obscenity. *Bowers* held that this *was* a legitimate state interest. The Court today reaches the opposite conclusion. The Texas statute, it says, "furthers *no legitimate state interest* which can justify its intrusion into the personal and private life of the individual" (emphasis addded). The Court embraces instead Justice STEVENS' declaration in his *Bowers* dissent, that "the fact that the governing majority in a State has traditionally viewed a particular practice as immoral is not a sufficient reason for upholding a law prohibiting the practice" * * *. This effectively decrees the end of all morals legislation. If, as the Court asserts, the promotion of majoritarian sexual morality is not even a *legitimate* state interest, none of the above-mentioned laws can survive rational-basis review.

* * *

Today's opinion is the product of a Court, which is the product of a law-profession culture, that has largely signed on to the so-called homosexual agenda, by which I mean the agenda promoted by some homosexual activists directed at eliminating the moral opprobrium that has traditionally attached to homosexual conduct. * * *

* * * It is clear from this that the Court has taken sides in the culture war, departing from its role of assuring, as neutral observer, that the democratic rules of engagement are observed. Many Americans do not want persons who openly engage in homosexual conduct as partners in their business, as scoutmasters for their children, as teachers in their children's schools, or as boarders in their home. They view this as protecting themselves and their families from a lifestyle that they believe to be immoral and destructive. The Court views it as "discrimination" which it is the function of our judgments to deter. * * * [T]he Court * * * is seemingly unaware that * * * [its] attitudes * * * are not obviously "mainstream"; that in most States what the Court calls "discrimination" against those who engage in homosexual acts is perfectly legal * * *.

Let me be clear that I have nothing against homosexuals, or any other group, promoting their agenda through normal democratic means. Social perceptions of sexual and other morality change over time, and every group has the right to persuade its fellow citizens that its view of such matters is the best. That homosexuals have achieved some success in that enterprise is attested to by the fact that Texas is one of the few remaining States that criminalize private, consensual homosexual acts. But persuading one's fellow citizens is one thing, and imposing one's views in absence of democratic majority will is something else. * * * What Texas has chosen to do is well within the range of traditional democratic action, and its hand should not be stayed through the invention of a brand-new "constitutional right" by a Court that is impatient of democratic change. * * *

One of the benefits of leaving regulation of this matter to the people rather than to the courts is that the people, unlike judges, need not carry things to their logical conclusion. The people may feel that their disapprobation of homosexual conduct is strong enough to disallow homosexual marriage, but not strong enough to criminalize private homosexual acts—and may legislate accordingly. The Court today pretends that it possesses a similar freedom of action, so that we need not fear judicial imposition of homosexual marriage, as has recently occurred in Canada (in a decision that the Canadian Government has chosen not to appeal). See Halpern v. Toronto, 2003 WL 34950 (Ontario Ct.App.) * * *. At the end of its opinion—after having laid waste the foundations of our rational-basis jurisprudence—the Court says that the present case "does not involve whether the government must give formal recognition to any relationship that homosexual persons seek to enter." * * * Do not believe it. * * * Today's opinion dismantles the structure of constitutional law that has permitted a distinction to be made between heterosexual and homosexual unions, insofar as formal recognition in marriage is concerned. If moral disapprobation of homosexual conduct is "no legitimate state interest" for purposes of proscribing that conduct and if * * * "[w]hen sexuality finds overt expression in intimate conduct with another person, the conduct can be but one element in a personal bond that is more enduring," * * * what justification could there possibly be for denying the benefits of marriage to homosexual couples exercising "[t]he liberty protected by the Constitution"? * * *

* * *

But *Lawrence* has been held not to protect against a state ban on sex toys. In Williams v. Attorney General of Alabama, 378 F.3d 1232 (11th Cir. 2004), a divided federal appeals court held the sale of devices whose purpose was genital stimulation was not within the right to sexual privacy recognized by the Supreme Court. The Supreme Court denied cert., 544 U.S. —, 125 S.Ct. 1335 (2005).

▶ **Insert at p. 763 following *United States* v. *Oakland Cannabis Buyers' Cooperative***

As the Text explains, the *Oakland Cannabis* case arose out of the federal government's opposition to successful voter initiatives in California and Arizona authorizing medical prescriptions for the individual use of marijuana by patients for whom more conventional drugs failed to control the pain and side-effects associated with the treatment of illnesses such as cancer. But federal efforts to undermine the result of the states' democratic process went further. The Clinton and Bush administrations then sought to muzzle physicians who even *recommended* the medical use of marijuana to patients because, it was asserted, such recommendations would lead to illegal use and imperil the war on drugs. On First Amendment grounds, several physicians who professionally recommended medical marijuana sued to enjoin federal officials from revoking their federal license to prescribe controlled substances and from conducting any investigations that might lead to such a revocation. The doctors argued that such retaliation, or the threat of it, infringed their right to communicate with patients. A federal district court agreed and subsequently enjoined the federal government. The injunction, however, did not limit the government's ability to investigate physicians who aided and abetted the actual distribution and possession of marijuana.

On appeal, the federal government lost. In Conant v. Walters, 309 F.3d 629 (9th Cir. 2002), the federal appellate court began from the premise that "[b]eing a member of a regulated profession does not * * * result in a surrender of First Amendment rights" and observed that "[t]he Supreme Court has recognized that physician speech is entitled to First Amendment protection because of the significance of the doctor-patient relationship." The court went on to observe that "[t]he government policy * * * strike[s] at core First Amendment interests * * * [because an] integral component of the practice of medicine is the communication between a doctor and a patient" which must remain frank and open. Punishment for "recommending" the medical use of marijuana was unconstitutional because the term did not have "the requisite 'narrow specificity.'" It cited *Thomas v. Collins* (see Text, p. 791) as precedent for the vulnerability of regulations that fail to distinguish precisely between discussion and advocacy. As the court explained, "[W]hether a doctor-patient discussion of medical marijuana constitutes a 'recommendation' depends largely on the meaning a patient attributes to the doctor's words." In closing, the court added, "Our decision is consistent with the principles of federalism that have left states as the primary regulators of professional conduct." The Supreme Court subsequently denied cert., 540 U.S. 946, 124 S.Ct. 387 (2003).

This does not mean that the cause of medical marijuana emerged triumphant, however. California patients growing and possessing marijuana for medical purposes challenged Congress's authority under the Commerce Clause to regulate the private cultivation and therapeutic use. Turning the tables on conservatives with an ironic dual-federalist argument, they asserted that, if the reach of the Commerce Clause was not long enough to permit Congress to criminalize possession of firearms at school (see Text, p. 328), it would hardly permit criminalizing the cultivation and use of marijuana in one's own home. Although the most states' rights-oriented Justices agreed, a majority of the Court did not. See *Gonzales v. Raich* at p. 46 of this Supplement. Nor did the House of Representatives which, on a vote of 161-264, turned down an amendment to the 2006 appropriations bill for the Justice Department that would have withheld funding to enforce federal drug laws against patients in states with medical marijuana laws. Congressional Quarterly Weekly Report, June 20, 2005, pp. 1648, 1664.

The Right to Die

▶ **Insert at p. 764 following the third full paragraph**

NOTE—THE UNENDING CASE OF TERRI SCHIAVO

In 1990, Terri Schiavo, then 27 years old, collapsed in her Florida home from heart failure. The heart attack was not fatal but resulted in brain damage that left her unconscious. She had no written living will. Eight years later, her husband, Michael Schiavo, petitioned a state guardianship court to authorize the termination of life-support procedures. The petition was opposed by her parents, Robert and Mary Schindler. After a trial at which both sides presented evidence, the court held that there was clear and convincing evidence both that Terri Schiavo was in a "persistent vegetative state" and that, were she competent to make her own decision, she would chose to discontinue life-support. Although this decision was affirmed on appeal, the Schindlers attacked the final court order, alleging the misrepresentation of certain facts and asserting that they had new evidence. In the appeals and reconsiderations that followed, the courts over and over upheld the termination of life-support. In the process, the case became a *cause célèbre* of right-to-life advocates.

As a consequence of politicizing the issue, the Florida Legislature enacted a law to give Governor Jeb Bush "authority to issue a one-time stay to prevent the withholding of nutrition and hydration from a patient" in the instance where someone challenged the withholding of nutrition and hydration from a family member who "as of October 15, 2003" was in a persistent vegetative state, had life-sustaining measures withheld, and failed to provide any advance directive to terminate life-support—all factors that described the Schiavo case. The governor's subsequent order was challenged by Michael Schiavo, Terri's court-recognized guardian, and a state circuit court held that the law was unconstitutional because it violated the right of privacy, amounted to a delegation of legislative power, and encroached upon the very nature of judicial power. On appeal in Bush v. Schiavo, 885 So.2d 321 (Fla. 2004), the state supreme court unanimously agreed that the state law was unconstitutional on separation-of-powers grounds because, "as applied in this case, it resulted in an executive order that effectively reversed a properly rendered final judgment and thereby constituted an unconstitutional encroachment on the power that has been reserved for the independent judiciary." In short, the court concluded that the statute unlawfully permitted the governor to substitute his judgment in place of that already rendered by the constituted judicial process. Moreover, the state supreme court pointed out that the legislature had provided no meaningful guidance for the governor to make his decision. The U.S. Supreme Court denied certiorari, 543 U.S. —, 125 S.Ct. 1086 (2005). Following further motions by the Schindlers to prevent life-support from being discontinued, a state trial court and intermediate appellate court reaffirmed the final court decree ending life-support. In re Guardianship of Schiavo, — So.2d — (Fla.App. 2d Dist. 2005), 2005 WL 600377.

But there was more to come. Congressional Republicans, seeking to side-step the state courts and use a federal court to achieve a different outcome, called members of the House and Senate back into session from Easter Recess to vote on legislation to give a federal district court jurisdiction in the case. Labeled an act "for the relief of the parents of Theresa Marie Schiavo," the bill gave the parents the right to sue in the U.S. District Court for the Middle District of Florida. It empowered the federal court "to issue such declaratory and injunctive relief as may be necessary to protect the rights of Theresa Marie Schiavo under the Constitution and laws of the United States relating to the withholding of food, fluids or medical treatment necessary to sustain her life." Injunctive relief would extend to reinserting the feeding tube which had been disconnected following the last state court decision. Because the bill provided that the federal court hearing the case would hear it *de novo*—that is, anew—all of the previous state court decisions in effect would be legally disregarded. On March 19, 2005, the Senate passed the measure by a voice vote. In action the next day, the House passed the bill by a vote of 203-58 with virtually all Republicans supporting the legislation and those Democrats who participated breaking about evenly. See Congressional Quarterly Weekly Report, Mar. 21, 2005, pp. 704-706; Mar. 28, 2005, pp. 778-784.

Public opinion polling suggests that those 157 members of the House who did not vote may have more accurately reflected public sentiment. ABC News reported that 70% of the public thought it was inappropriate for Congress to intervene in the case compared with 19% who thought Congress did the right thing. Worse yet, there was strong evidence that the public took a dim view of the motives of officials behind the legislative effort: 67% of the public thought the intervention was motivated by trying to turn the situation to political advantage. On the question of whether the removal of Terri Schiavo's feeding tube was the right thing to do, 63% said it was, 28% disagreed. More problematic, still, for the law's supporters were poll results that showed those who "strongly" disapproved Congress's action out-numbered those who "strongly" favored the law by two to one. Disapproval of Congress's action, it seemed, was both high and deep. Poll results from CBS News reflected much the same sentiment: 82% opposed congressional and presidential involvement and 74% took a dim view of the underlying motives. The Gallup Poll subsequently reported that President Bush's approval ratings also took a hit—down 7 points to 45% from a week earlier, the lowest point to that date of his presidency.

The legal battle then reverted to the courts. On the same day President George W. Bush signed the two-page law, 119 Stat. 15, the Schindlers were in federal district court moving for a temporary injunction to reinsert the feeding tube while the parties litigated the merits of the case. The following day, the federal district court denied the motion on grounds that, while the Schindlers could show irreparable harm if the tube was not temporarily reinserted, they had not shown a substantial likelihood of prevailing on the constitutional merits. On appeal, a panel of the Eleventh U.S. Circuit Court of Appeals, held 2-1 that the district judge did not abuse his discretion in finding that the Schindlers had failed to show a substantial constitutional case. See Schiavo ex rel. Schindler v. Schiavo, 357 F.Supp.2d 1378 (M.D.Fla. 2005), *affirmed*, 403 F.3d 1223 (11th Cir. 2005). On a petition for rehearing en banc—that is, by the entire complement of appeals judges for the Eleventh Circuit—the vote was 10-2 against. Further, on a petition for relief to Justice Kennedy, who then referred the matter to the U.S. Supreme Court, the Justices for the fifth time declined to hear the case. 544 U.S. —, 125 S.Ct. 1692 (2005). The appeal to Justice Kennedy, as Circuit Justice for the Eleventh Circuit, had been supported by an *amicus curiae* brief filed by Republican leaders of the U.S. House arguing that the law Congress passed required the feeding tube to be reinserted until all constitutional issues were litigated and settled. Citing a plain reading of the law, withdrawal of a previous version of the bill, and a colloquy on the Senate floor during passage which clearly showed an understanding to the contrary, the federal district court had already rejected the argument that Congress had intended to impose an automatic temporary stay on terminating life-support. (At one point, a congressional committee even attempted to use its subpoena power, ordering Terry Schiavo to appear at a hearing, to delay the court-ordered removal of the feeding tube, see p. 15 of this Supplement.)

In the meantime, a bill to re-institute life-support, which passed the Florida House, was voted down in the state Senate, and efforts by Governor Jeb Bush to have the state physically take custody of Terri Schiavo were rebuffed by a Florida circuit court. Bush and the state's department of social services had argued there was new evidence from a neurologist who said he believed that Terri Schiavo has been misdiagnosed. The doctor, strongly identified with various right-to-life causes, however, had never conducted a physical examination of her. New York Times, Mar. 24, 2005, pp. A1, A16. There were more unsuccessful rounds of petitions and appeals in both federal and state courts, this time in which the Schindlers asserted Terri Schiavo "tried to say 'I want to live' just minutes before the feeding tube was removed a week [earlier.] The parents sa[id] Schiavo said "Ahhhhh' and 'Waaaaaa' when asked to repeat the phrase 'I want to live.'" New York Times, Mar. 27, 2005, p. A16. See Schiavo ex rel. Schindler v. Schiavo, 358 F.Supp.2d 1161 (M.D.Fla. 2005), *affirmed*, 403 F.3d 1289 (11th Cir. 2005).

Perhaps the most stunning rebuke to the federal legislation came from a most unexpected source—Judge Stanley F. Birch, a federal appeals judge appointed by President George W. Bush's father and one noted for his conservative views on social issues. "Specially concurring" in yet another denial of rehearing en banc by the 11th Circuit, Judge Birch wrote: "If the Act only provided for jurisdiction consistent with Article III[,] * * * [it] would not be in violation of the principles of separation of powers. [But the Act] goes further * * * [and] provides that the district court: (1) shall engage in 'de novo' review of Mrs. Schiavo's constitutional and federal claims; (2) shall not consider whether these claims were previously 'raised, considered, or decided in State court proceedings'; (3) shall not engage in 'abstention in favor of State court proceedings'; and (4) shall not decide the case on the basis of 'whether remedies available in the State courts have been exhausted.' * * * Because these provisions constitute legislative dictation of how a federal court should exercise its judicial functions * * *, the Act invades the province of the judiciary and violates the separation of powers principle." Taking aim at the criticism that judges who refused to achieve the congressionally-desired outcome in the *Schiavo* case were "activist judges" (meaning the sort of judge "who decides the outcome of a controversy before him according to personal conviction"), Judge Birch left the clear impression that it was Congress and the President who were the "activists." He concluded, "By arrogating vital judicial functions to itself, * * * Congress violated core constitutional separation principles" and thus acted "demonstrably at odds with our Founding Fathers' blueprint for the governance of a free people—our Constitution." Schiavo ex rel. Schindler v. Schiavo, 404 F.3d 1270

(11th Cir. 2005).

By the time it was all over, there had been more than two dozen court decisions in the case, all of which sided with Michael Schiavo in his effort to bring the matter to a close. It made the constitutional claim that there had been a lack of due process seem truly ironic. In the view of Andrew Cohen, legal analyst for CBS News: "What makes this case so unusual, so startling even, is the length and extent to which officials in the other two branches of government were willing to go to try to circumnavigate the dictates of the law on behalf of a single individual. Capitol Hill's tailor-made legislation * * * was just the most visible example of this special treatment. The President's decision to interrupt his vacation [to fly back to the White House to sign the legislation] was the most curious example. Governor Bush's attempt to take custody of Terri Schiavo on the flimsiest of abuse allegations, and upon the conclusion of a doctor who did not evaluate her, was the most serious." Cohen concluded: "Astonishingly, all of these actions took place after the courts had reached their final conclusions over matters entirely within the jurisdiction of the courts to decide. They all took place after the other two branches should have recognized that judges and not politicians get to decide individual cases." See Andrew Cohen, "The Courts Push Back," March 24, 2005, at http://www.cbsnews.com/stories/2005/03/24/opinion/courtwatch/main682992.shtml.

Political snarling by right-wing members of Congress continued on after Terri Schiavo's eventual death on March 31. House Republican leader Tom DeLay threatened retribution and did not rule out impeachment for those federal judges who "thumbed their nose at Congress and the President." In other statements, he went on to decry a "Judicial War of Faith" because of judicial "invention of rights to abortion and prohibitions on school prayer." Federal courts, he charged, had "run amok." Senator John Cormyn (R-Tex.) went so far as to suggest that "judicial activism" was one of the motivating factors behind recent physical attacks on judges (although all the available evidence showed the slayings were prompted by adverse verdicts and avoiding punishment for criminal offenses). An aide to one Senator thought that "mass impeachments" might be necessary. New York Times, Apr. 1, 2005, pp. A1, A16; Apr. 8, 2005, p. A15.

In his nineteenth annual Report on the Federal Judiciary, an ailing Chief Justice Rehnquist took notice of "several bills introduced in the last Congress that would limit the jurisdiction of the federal courts to decide constitutional challenges to certain kinds of government actions." He responded, "[O]ur Constitution has struck a balance between judicial independence and accountability, giving individual judges secure tenure but making the federal Judiciary subject ultimately to the popular will because judges are appointed and confirmed by elected officials." The real crisis facing the federal courts, he pointed out, was the grossly inadequate level of funding voted by Congress, which left "too few judges handling too few cases in too few courtrooms inundated with too many criminal defendants and civil litigants." Andrew Cohen, "Rehnquist's Punch Line Overlooked," www.cbsnews.com/stories/2005/01/05/opinion/courtwatch/main664789.shtml. Less modulated was the response of others who saw DeLay's attack in particular as an attempt to deflect attention from mounting allegations that had committed many serious ethics violations.

◆ Insert at p. 774 at the end of the note on Oregon's Death with Dignity Law

Judge Jones's ruling was affirmed by a divided federal appeals court in Oregon v. Ashcroft, 368 F.3d 1118 (9th Cir. 2004). The appellate court opinion sounded a stern rebuke to the Attorney General for putting the statute to a use unintended by Congress. Speaking for the appeals panel, Judge Richard C. Tallman wrote, "The attorney general's unilateral attempt to regulate medical practices historically entrusted to state lawmakers interferes with the democratic debate about physician-assisted suicide and far exceeds the scope of his authority under federal law." The majority made it clear that this case was not about whether physician-assisted suicide is "inconsistent with the public interest or constitutes legitimate medical practice" but "simply about who gets to decide." The court's answer was that the states do. The majority seemed to concede that if Congress chose to override the Oregon law it legitimately could, but the present statute did not authorize that. The Supreme Court has granted cert. and will hear argument at its upcoming Term. Gonzales v. Oregon, 544 U.S. —, 125 S.Ct. 1299 (2005).

CHAPTER 11

FREEDOM OF SPEECH

B. TIME, PLACE, AND MANNER LIMITATIONS

Speech in a "Public Forum"

▸ **Insert at p. 824 at the end of the note**

A decade later, New York City was still found to be prosecuting individuals under the anti-begging ordinance declared unconstitutional in *Loper*, as if the decision hadn't happened and even though the city council had long since passed a new ordinance limiting prosecutions to "aggressive" or "threatening" panhandling. In 2003 and 2004 alone, some 140 individuals had been arrested on charges under the illegal ordinance, 129 of them in the Bronx. Police officials said they would take steps to put an immediate end to the practice and advocates for the homeless have filed a class action to overturn prosecutions under the old law. New York Times, June 10, 2005, p. A21.

▸ **Insert at p. 825 after the discussion of *City of Chicago* v. *Morales***

In another attempt to keep likely perpetrators of crime away, Cincinnati passed an ordinance banning from a high-crime neighborhood—tagged a "drug exclusion zone"—anyone who had been arrested or convicted of certain drug offenses. The ordinance barred drug traffickers, for example, from neighborhood streets, sidewalks, and other "public ways" for 90 days and excluded persons convicted of drug offenses for a year. In State v. Burnett, 755 N.E.2d 857 (Ohio, 2001), *cert. denied*, 535 U.S. 1034, 122 S.Ct. 1790 (2002), the Ohio Supreme Court held the ordinance unconstitutional on grounds it infringed a right to intra-state travel. The ordinance was also struck down by federal courts as well, but on grounds it violated both the right to travel and freedom of association. See Johnson v. City of Cincinnati, 119 F.Supp.2d 735 (S.D. Ohio 2000), *affirmed*, 310 F.3d 484 (6th Cir. 2002), *cert. denied*, 539 U.S. 915, 123 S.Ct. 2276 (2003).

▸ **Insert at p. 837 following the first full paragraph**

The subject of the following note, allegedly a "compelled subsidy," is closely akin to the issue raised in the *Southworth* case. Just as government cannot constitutionally coerce an individual to express a point of view (see *West Virginia State Board of Education* v. *Barnette*, Text, p. 858) or even to reveal one he or she would prefer to keep personal, a private organization, such as a union, cannot compel its members to pay for the dissemination of opinions with which its members may disagree and which have no direct relationship to their basis for joining the group. But what if government compels businessmen to support industry advertising with which they disagree? Is this legitimate economic regulation by the government or does it trample the First Amendment rights of individual businessmen?

NOTE—IF BEEF "I[S] WHAT'S FOR DINNER," WHO'S PAYING FOR IT?

Familiar television and print advertisements of a few years ago touted the idea of consuming a succulent steak—or even having a hamburger—with the trademark line, "Beef—it's what's for dinner." But this bit of promotion and marketing was not advertising copy put out by an industry trade association but the federal government.

In the Beef Promotion and Research Act of 1985, Congress adopted a federal policy of promoting and marketing beef and beef products to be paid for by an assessment on the sales and importation of cattle. The Secretary of Agriculture implements this policy through a Cattlemen's Beef Promotion and Research Board (Beef Board) made up of a geographically representative group of beef producers and importers nominated by their trade associations. The Beef Board then convenes an Operating Committee made up of 20 members, half of whom are comprised of Beef Board members and half representatives named by state beef councils. The Secretary imposes a $1-a-head assessment (or checkoff) on all sales and importation of cattle. Proceeds of the checkoff go to fund promotional campaigns and other beef-related projects. The law provides that the Secretary or his authorized agent must approve all projects and promotional matter.

Two associations whose members pay the checkoff and individuals who raise and sell cattle and thus also pay the assessment sued the Secretary of Agriculture challenging the program on First Amendment grounds, arguing that they were legally compelled to pay for speech with which they disagreed. The plaintiffs preferred advertising that promoted the superiority of American beef, or grain-fed beef, or certified Angus or Hereford beef, as distinguished from generic beef. A federal district and appellate court agreed and struck down the program on First Amendment grounds.

Following a referendum by beef producers to support the program and make it permanent, the Secretary collected more than $1 billion through the checkoff. A substantial portion of those proceeds were spent on the promotional campaign highlighted by the trademark line "Beef—it's what's for dinner." Copy for that campaign, as for other funded projects, was approved by the Secretary.

In Johanns v. Livestock Marketing Association, 544 U.S. —, 125 S.Ct. 2055 (2005), the Supreme Court reversed the judgment and sustained the advertising program. Speaking for the Court, Justice Scalia wrote:

We have sustained First Amendment challenges to allegedly compelled expression in two categories of cases: true "compelled speech" cases, in which an individual is obliged personally to express a message he disagrees with, imposed by the government; and "compelled subsidy" cases, in which an individual is required by the government to subsidize a message he disagrees with, expressed by a private entity. * * *

* * *

In * * * [the second category of cases,] the speech was, or was presumed to be, that of an entity other than the government itself. [These cases dealt with union dues or student activity fees the proceeds of which were used to subsidize views with which the contributors disagreed, see *Board of Regents of University of Wisconsin System v. Southworth*, Text, p. 836; Abood v. Detroit Board of Education, 431 U.S. 209, 97 S.Ct. 1782 (1977)]. * * * Our compelled-subsidy cases have consistently respected the principle that "[c]ompelled support of a private association is fundamentally different from compelled support of government." * * * "Compelled support of government"—even those programs of government one does not approve—is of course perfectly constitutional, as every taxpayer must attest. And some government programs involve, or entirely consist of, advocating a position. * * *

* * *

The message set out in the beef promotions is from beginning to end the message established by the Federal Government. Congress has directed the implementation of a "coordinated program" of promotion, "including paid advertising, to advance the image and desirability of beef and beef products." * * * Congress and the Secretary have also specified, in general terms, what the promotional campaigns shall contain * * * and what they shall not * * *.

[T]he Secretary exercises final approval authority over every word used in every promotional campaign. All proposed promotional messages are reviewed by Department officials both for substance and for wording, and some proposals are rejected or rewritten by the Department. * * * [O]fficials of the Department also attend and participate in the open meetings at which proposals are developed. * * *

* * *

[R]espondents * * * contend that crediting the advertising to "America's Beef Producers" impermissibly uses not only their money but also their seeming endorsement to promote a message with which they do not agree. Communications cannot be "government speech," they argue, if they are attributed to someone other than the government; and the person to whom they are attributed, when he is, by compulsory funding, made the unwilling instrument of communication, may raise a First Amendment objection.

* * *

Whether the *individual* respondents who are beef producers would be associated with speech labeled as coming from "America's Beef Producers" is a question on which the trial record is altogether silent. We have only the funding tagline itself * * * that, standing alone, is not sufficiently specific to convince a reasonable factfinder that any particular beef producer, or all beef producers, would be tarred with the content of each trademarked ad. * * *

Justice Breyer, concurring, acceded to the majority's view even though he "remain[ed] of the view that the assessments * * * are best described [simply] as a form of economic regulation." Speaking for the three dissenters, Justice Souter "t[ook] the view that if government relies on the government-speech doctrine to compel specific groups to fund speech with targeted taxes, it must make itself politically accountable by indicating that the content actually is a government message * * *." He continued:

[T]he requirement of effective public accountability means the ranchers ought to prevail, it being clear that the Beef Act does not establish an advertising scheme subject to effective democratic checks. The reason for this is simple: the ads are not required to show any sign of being speech by the Government, and experience * * * demonstrates how effectively the Government has masked its role in producing the ads. Most obviously, many of them include the tag line, "[f]unded by America's Beef Producers," * * * which all but ensures that no one reading them will suspect that the message comes from the National Government. * * * [R]eaders would most naturally think that ads urging people to have beef for dinner were placed and paid for by the beef producers who stand to profit when beef is on the table. No one hearing a commercial for Pepsi or Levi's thinks Uncle Sam is the man talking behind the curtain. Why would a person reading a beef ad think Uncle Sam was trying to make him eat more steak? Given the circumstances, it is hard to see why anyone would suspect the Government was behind the message unless the message came out and said so.

* * *

[E]xpression that is not ostensibly governmental, which government is not required to embrace as publicly as it speaks, cannot constitute government speech sufficient to justify enforcement of a targeted subsidy to broadcast it. * * *

CHAPTER 11 FREEDOM OF SPEECH

In another controversy involving a claim of compelled speech, law schools have mounted a constitutional challenge to the so-called Solomon Amendment which denies federal funding to institutions of higher education if they exclude military recruiters. The case, in which the Supreme Court has granted cert., is summarized at p. 204 of this Supplement.

▶ **Insert at p. 858 following the chart**

OTHER CASES ON TIME, PLACE, AND MANNER LIMITATIONS GENERALLY-- CONTINUED		
CASE	RULING	VOTE
Virginia v. Hicks, 539 U.S. 113, 123 S.Ct. 2191 (2003)	City housing authority's unwritten rule that requires any nonresident first obtain permission before leafleting or demonstrating in public housing was not overbroad. On its face and as generally applied, it did not abridge any appreciable amount of protected speech. Prosecution of a nonresident for trespassing after he was warned not to return did not violate the First Amendment.	9-0.

C. SYMBOLIC SPEECH

Compelling the Flag Salute

▶ **Insert at p. 864 following *West Virginia State Board of Education* v. *Barnette***

Pennsylvania law requires that students in public and private schools throughout the state begin the school day with the Pledge of Allegiance or National Anthem and requires school officials to notify the parents of any students who refused to salute the flag. Not surprisingly in light of *Barnette*, a federal appeals court, in The Circle School v. Pappert, 381 F.3d 172 (3rd Cir. 2004), has ruled that this violates the First Amendment.

Flag Burning and Nude Dancing: Whether to Apply the *O'Brien* Test

▶ **Insert at p. 879 following the third paragraph**

For the sixth time in a decade, the House has passed the Flag Desecration Amendment. The proposed amendment, whose wording is the same as that indicated in the Text, passed by a 286-130 vote; more than the two-thirds majority required but its lowest level of support yet. Although the proposed amendment has never made it past the Senate—it fell four votes short the last time—the addition of four Republican seats following the November 2004 election have markedly increased its prospects. Congressional Quarterly Weekly Report, June 27, 2005, pp. 1742, 1766.

Cross Burning and Hate Speech

▶ **Insert at p. 886 following *R.A.V.* v. *City of St. Paul***

To the majority in R.A.V., it was the "political correctness" of the ordinance that ran afoul of the First Amendment—the prohibition on certain forms of symbolic speech. To the four concurring Justices, it was the possibility of conviction because the speaker had used symbols that merely caused offense or resentment by women and particular minorities. But what if a law prohibited cross-burning because the speaker had the intent to intimidate, and setting the cross afire put the victim in fear of bodily harm? Would this constitute conduct still punishable under *Brandenburg* as "advocacy directed to inciting or producing imminent lawless action and * * * likely to incite or produce such action"? Or would the fact that the law dealt only with cross-burning still render it constitutionally vulnerable, whatever the speaker's intent?

In Virginia v. Black, 538 U.S. 343, 123 S.Ct. 1536 (2003), the Court held that government could specifically punish cross-burning with the intent to intimidate. Indeed, the state law in question would have been sustained, except that it contained a provision that the "burning of a cross shall be prima facie evidence of an intent to intimidate a person or group of persons." In other words, the statute provided that the burning of a cross itself was sufficient for conviction unless rebutted by other evidence.

Speaking for Chief Justice Rehnquist and Justices Stevens and Breyer, Justice O'Connor explained: "[T]he prima facie provision strips away the very reason why a State may ban cross burning with the intent to intimidate. * * * [It] permits a jury to convict in every cross-burning case in which defendants exercise their constitutional right not to put on a defense. And even where a defendant like Black presents a defense, the prima facie evidence provision makes it more likely that the jury will find an intent to intimidate regardless of the particular facts of the case. The provision permits the Commonwealth to arrest, prosecute, and convict a person based solely on the fact of cross burning itself." Because of this, the statute had a chilling effect on core speech protected by the First Amendment. Since the state supreme court struck down the entire statute on the grounds that, like the ordinance in R.A.V., it was content-based, the Court vacated the judgments in the cases consolidated for hearing with Black's and remanded the matter to give the state supreme court a chance to construe the cross-burning statute in a manner that would save it.

Although agreeing that, consistent with *R.A.V.*, cross-burning with the intent to intimidate could be prohibited, Justice Scalia objected both to declaring the provision unconstitutional on its face and to taking into account, in assessing its chilling effect, the risk of arrest and prosecution as well as that of conviction. Justice Thomas thought that, given the lengthy and unambiguous history of cross-burning as a means of terrorizing groups targeted by the Klan, it was "conduct" not "speech," and the likelihood of infringing expression protected by the First Amendment was so low that burning a cross could legitimately constitute prima facie evidence of intimidation. On the other hand, Justice Souter, speaking also for Justices Kennedy and Ginsburg, concluded (as had a bare majority of the Virginia Supreme Court) that this statute was indistinguishable from the ordinance invalidated in *R.A.V.*—both enactments were flatly unconstitutional because they specifically singled out cross-burning for punishment and thus censored expression based on its content.

D. Campaign Finance Reform, Corporate Speech, and Party Patronage

Campaign Finance Reform

▶ **Insert at p. 898 following the fourth paragraph**

Because Congress required expedited consideration of any constitutional challenges to the Bipartisan Campaign Reform Act (BCRA), also called the McCain-Feingold Act after its Senate sponsors, the Supreme Court interrupted its annual summer recess to hear a day of oral argument on the constitutionality of the statute. The purpose of fast-tracking the suits was to get the rules settled before the onset of the 2004 presidential and congressional campaigns. Two months into its October 2003 Term, the Court handed down its decision on the constitutionality of several provisions of the BCRA in McConnell v. Federal Election Commission, 540 U.S. 96, 124 S.Ct. 619 (2003). The ruling was hailed by advocates of campaign-finance reform as "a landmark decision" because the Court upheld the most important provisions of the law. Although the Justices' votes varied somewhat with the particular provision at issue, the dominant 5-4 decision pattern pitted Justices Stevens, O'Connor, Souter, Ginsburg, and Breyer against Chief Justice Rehnquist and Justices Scalia, Kennedy, and Thomas. Because Justice O'Connor had agreed with the opponents of campaign finance regulation in several previous decisions, hers was regarded as the critical fifth vote in this case.

The heart of McCain-Feingold is the law's ban on the solicitation, receipt, or expenditure of "soft money" by the national political parties. The BCRA also prohibits the transfer of any soft money by the national parties to state or local parties for use in the election of any federal officeholder. Previous campaign finance regulation that survived constitutional scrutiny limited only "hard money," that is money used to specifically advocate the election or defeat of a named candidate, usually identified by magic words, such as "vote for," "elect," "defeat," or "reject." All else was regarded as "soft money." This umbrella term included money for such things as get-out-the-vote drives and so-called "issue ads" (media messages, often simplistic and aggressively negative that did not name names but usually had the desired effect of helping or hindering a candidate by sharply contrasting positions on public policy). The BCRA aimed at keeping soft money out of party hands in federal elections. Interest groups through PACs (political action committees), however, were still free to acquire and spend funds on issue ads, but the Act required corporations, unions, and interest groups (1) to identify themselves in their advertisements, (2) to register with broadcasters as the sponsors of the ads (and such records were to be publicly available), and (3) to refrain from any collusion with the political parties in the production or airing of the ads. McCain-Feingold treated any expenditures of PACs which were coordinated with any candidate as the equivalent of "hard money," and therefore subject to the existing limitations under federal election law. The provision of the BCRA forbidding contributions by any individual under 18 (to guard against end-runs by adults who might try to from channel money through their children) was struck down, while other provisions of the law, such as the "millionaires amendment" (which set higher limits for candidates facing wealthy opponents who were bankrolling their own campaigns) and the indexing of limitations on contributions according to inflation, were not reached by the Court.

Since *McConnell* was widely-regarded as a possible occasion for overruling *Buckley* and thus could have resulted in the complete deregulation of campaign finance on First Amendment grounds, you might expect that this case would warrant more extensive coverage. Moreover, the deferential tone of the Stevens-O'Connor opinion was surprising; it tip-toed around the use of strict scrutiny and stood in sharp contrast to previous campaign finance decisions. But there are several reasons why *McConnell* may not be the "landmark decision" it seems: First, the opinions present a kind of maze (the Opinion of the Court is spread over three separate opinions written by four different Justices) in which a highly-fragmented Court appears to show less agreement on what to say and takes longer to say it than *Buckley* v. *Valeo* nearly 30 years ago. The opinions in *McConnell* consume nearly 300 pages in the *U.S. Reports* (four pages more than *Buckley*) and convey an impression that the Court has returned to the days when the Justices delivered seriatim opinions. Second, the heart of the ruling turns on a 5-4 majority and Justice O'Connor has announced her retirement, so *McConnell's* footing seems shaky. And even if the decision in *McConnell* has durability, McCain-Feingold did little to put a lid on the *amount* independent political groups can spend.

E. Commercial Speech

▶ Insert at p. 927 after the second paragraph

The Supreme Court has long recognized that organizational fundraising—and its personal counterpart, begging (see Text, p. 823)—is protected speech within the meaning of the First Amendment. Because appeals for money by groups and associations very frequently entail some form of issue advocacy, it was thought that organizational fundraising was, constitutionally speaking, nearly beyond meaningful government regulation. A perennial problem with charitable fundraising, however, is high overhead costs, with the consequence that comparatively little money finally goes to the cause in whose name the money was solicited. This is particularly true when fundraising is done by telemarketing companies operating under contract with the charity. Many members of the public regard high overhead costs as a form of theft, and in response to the clamor that a lid be put on expenses associated with solicitations, governments attempted to set a maximum percentage of the money raised that can go to defray overhead costs. Some jurisdictions identified excessive overhead costs as a type of fraud. In a series of cases decided during the 1980s, the Court held that state and local governments could not impose a ceiling on fundraising costs and could not simply define fraud as exceeding those limits. The Court ruled that laws "barring fees in excess of a prescribed level, effectively imposed prior restraints on fundraising, and were therefore incompatible with the First Amendment."

In Illinois ex rel. Madigan v. Telemarketing Associates, Inc., 538 U.S. 600, 123 S.Ct. 1829 (2003), the Court was confronted with what it saw as a distinctly different situation. In this case, a telemarketing outfit had contracted with a Vietnam veterans organization to raise money with the result that 15% or less of the proceeds went to the charity. The state attorney general charged the telemarketing firm with violating Illinois' fraud statute, not because it kept 85% of the money raised, but because it deliberately misled the public. Telemarketing Associates informed the people it called that "a significant amount of each dollar donated would be paid to [the veterans organization] for its [charitable] purposes while in fact the [fundraisers] knew that * * * 15 cents or less of each dollar" would actually go to the charity. Writing for a unanimous Court, Justice Ginsburg said, "While bare failure to disclose that information directly to potential donors does not suffice to establish fraud, when nondisclosure is accompanied by intentionally misleading statements designed to deceive the listener, the First Amendment leaves room for a fraud claim." She continued:

> [I]n contrast to a prior restraint on solicitation, or a regulation that imposes on fundraisers an uphill burden to prove their conduct lawful, in a properly tailored fraud action the State bears the full burden of proof. False statement alone does not subject a fundraiser to fraud liability. * * * [T]o prove a defendant liable for fraud, the complainant must show that the defendant made a false representation of a material fact knowing that the representation was false; further, the complainant must demonstrate that the defendant made the representation with the intent to mislead the listener, and succeeded in doing so. * * *

Moreover, "As an additional safeguard responsive to First Amendment concerns, an appellate court could independently review the trial court's findings" of fact instead of simply deferring to them. She concluded, "What the First Amendment and our case law emphatically do not require * * * is a blanket exemption from fraud liability for a fundraiser who intentionally misleads in calls for donations."

▶ Insert at p. 927 following the second paragraph

In 2003, the Federal Trade Commission went one step further and put in place a do-not-call registry of telephone subscribers who did not want to be bothered with telemarketing calls, whether automated or personal. A federal district court ruled that existing legislation did not authorize the commission to set up such a registry, US Security v. Federal Trade Commission, 282 F.Supp.2d 1285 (W.D.Okla. 2003), but this action was later reversed by a federal appeals court in Mainstream Marketing Services, Inc. v. Federal Trade Commission, 358 F.3d 1228 (10th Cir. 2004), *cert. denied*, 543 U.S. —, 125 S.Ct. 47 (2004). Congress speedily passed legislation the same day as the district court's adverse ruling by impressive majorities explicitly empowering the FTC to act. The House vote was 412-8; the Senate vote was 95-0. See Congressional Quarterly Weekly Report, Dec. 13, 2003, p. 3138.

CHAPTER 12

FREEDOM OF THE PRESS

▶ **Insert at p. 931 following the excerpt by Chief Justice Burger**

The concentration of power in large media corporations bothered others as well. So when the Federal Communications Commission announced in June 2003 that it was going to relax the rules and allow media companies to own several newspapers and broadcasting stations serving the same market, there was a major effort in Congress to overrule the FCC and prevent such acquisitions. Legislators split roughly along the same lines as divided the commissioners (Republicans in favor and Democrats opposed). However, the legislation never got off the ground; nor, for that matter, did the commission's rules. After issuing a temporary restraining order that put the new rules on hold, a federal appeals court subsequently told the FCC to rewrite many of them, although it upheld the commission's authority. See Prometheus Radio Project v. Federal Communications Commission, 373 F.3d 372 (3d Cir. 2004), *cert. denied*, 545 U.S. —, 125 S.Ct. 2904 (2005). One of the largest media conglomerates, the Gannett Company, currently publishes 101 daily papers and owns 22 television stations. Other large media corporations, whose expansion has been delayed by the court decision, include News Corporation (which runs the Fox Entertainment Group, Fox Television, and the *New York Post*), and Viacom (which owns CBS). See New York Times, June 25, 2004, pp. C1, C4.

A. CENSORSHIP AND PRIOR RESTRAINT

The Right to Publish

▶ **Insert at p. 935 following *Near v. Minnesota***

In light of the disfavor with which *Near* viewed a permanent injunction against all future speech, it was with more than a little anticipation that Court watchers awaited the Court's decision this past Term in Tory v. Cochran, 544 U.S. —, 125 S.Ct. 2108 (2005). The case involved a challenge to an injunction sought by Johnnie Cochran, best known for his role as O. J. Simpson's lawyer in the football player's double murder trial (see Text, p. 1028). Cochran secured the injunction to silence Ulysses Tory, a disgruntled former client who hounded the attorney claiming (falsely, it was determined) that he owed him money. Tory had complained to the local bar association, had written Cochran letters demanding the payment of $10 million, and had engaged in various forms of public protest: picketing Cochran's law office with several confederates, holding up signs containing numerous insults, threats, and obscenities and chanting the same. The California courts found Tory's claim to be without foundation and enjoined the various forms expression which it held to be libelous and slanderous.

The Supreme Court had granted cert. to consider "[w]hether a permanent injunction as a remedy in a defamation action, preventing all future speech about an admitted public figure, violates the First Amendment." Before the Court could decide the case, however, Cochran died, but the injunction did not automatically lapse. Cochran's widow was allowed to intervene in his place, arguing that her interest in the law practice kept the issue alive. The Court failed to reach the question for which cert. had been granted, concluding that "the injunction ha[d] now lost its underlying rationale." Justice Breyer, speaking for the Court, continued: "Since picketing Cochran and his law offices while engaging in injunction-forbidden speech could no longer achieve the objectiv[e] * * * (coercing Cochran to pay a 'tribute for desisting in this activity'), * * * the grounds for the injunction are much diminished, if they have not disappeared altogether. Consequently, the injunction, as written, now amounts to an overly broad prior restraint upon speech, lacking plausible justification. * * * As such, the Constitution forbids it." Were an "appropriate party" to ask for relief along these lines in the future, there would be time then to consider the matter. Justices Scalia and Thomas were of the view that the Court should just dismiss the writ of certiorari as improvidently granted and say no more.

▶ **Insert at p. 937 following the fourth paragraph and before the note**

Emphasizing that the First Amendment requires "prompt judicial determination" following an administrative decision to deny a license to exhibit adult materials, the Court reafffirmed the principles set out in *Freedman v. Maryland* (see Text, p. 937). In City of Littleton, Colorado v. Z. J. Gifts, 541 U.S. 774, 124 S.Ct. 2219 (2004), the Court ruled that a guarantee of just "prompt access to judicial review" was insufficient. The Court refrained from imposing any other special rules of review where local government denied a license to an adult business "as long as the courts remain sensitive to the need to prevent First Amendment harms and administer those procedures accordingly."

Confidentiality of Sources

▶ **Insert on p. 957 following the note on *In re Farber and the New York Times Co.***

In what is probably the most sensational modern case of invoking the claim of a newsman's privilege, the Supreme Court turned down the opportunity to re-examine its decision in *Branzburg v. Hayes* that there is no federal privilege protecting the confidentiality of a journalist's sources. The case dealt with civil contempt citations imposed on two reporters involved in a story about one or more Bush administration officials blowing the cover of a CIA operative in retaliation for public criticism by the agent's husband.

The controversy began with President George W. Bush's assertion in his 2003 State of the Union message that "[t]he British government has learned that Saddam Hussein recently sought significant quantities of uranium from Africa." The importance of the assertion was its direct link to the administration's later-proved-inaccurate claim that Hussein possessed weapons of mass destruction, the justification originally offered by Bush for starting the war in Iraq. Controversy over

Bush's statement flared. Former Ambassador Joseph Wilson, who said that he had been dispatched to Niger in 2002 by the CIA at Vice President Cheney's request to investigate the matter, said there was no credible evidence to support Bush's statement in an op-ed piece in the *New York Times*. In his *Chicago Sun-Times* column of July 14, 2003, Robert Novak reported that Wilson had been sent to Niger without the knowledge of the CIA director and that "two senior administration officials" told him that Wilson's selection was at the suggestion of Wilson's wife, Valerie Plame, whom Novak said was a CIA "operative on weapons of mass destruction." A few days later, the identification of Plame as "a CIA official who monitors the proliferation of weapons of mass destruction" was repeated in a *Time* magazine article, "A War on Wilson?" by Matthew Cooper. Other accounts in the media reported that "two top White House officials called at least six Washington journalists and disclosed the identity and occupation of Wilson's wife." Judith Miller, a White House correspondent for the *New York Times* who gathered material on the story but did not publish it, was also subpoenaed.

In the firestorm that followed, a special prosecutor, Patrick Fitzgerald, was appointed to investigate whether one or more administration officials had violated the Intelligence Identities Protection Act, 50 U.S.C.A. § 421, that punishes those with access to classified information who deliberately unmask a secret agent. A federal grand jury was subsequently empaneled and subpoenas served on both Cooper and Miller, who refused to disclose their sources as a matter of First Amendment privilege. After a ruling that such a constitutional privilege did not exist, citing *Branzburg*, a federal judge sentenced each to jail until they complied with the grand jury's demand. The ruling was upheld on appeal, and petitions for certiorari were filed with the Supreme Court. In re Special Counsel Investigation, 332 F.Supp.2d 26 (D.D.C. 2004), 338 F.Supp.2d 16 (D.D.C. 2004), *affirmed*, 397 F.3d 964 (D.C. Cir. 2005), *rehearing en banc denied*, 405 F.3d 17 (D.C. Cir. 2005). The attorneys general of 34 states (with shield laws) filed a brief supporting Cooper and Miller's petitions for cert. arguing that the absence of federal protection for journalistic sources undermined the laws in states that did offer some protection. New York Times, May 28, 2005, p. A8. However, the Supreme Court denied cert., Miller v. United States, 455 U.S. —, 125 S.Ct. 2977 (2005); Cooper v. United States, 455 U.S. —, 125 S.Ct. 2977 (2005). Time, Inc. later said Cooper would turn over his notes and, after being released from the promise of confidentiality by his source, he also agreed to testify. Miller, who had not been released from confidentiality by her source, went to jail. New York Times, July 1, 2005, pp. A1, A12; July 7, 2005, pp. A1, A16.

Meanwhile, inquiring minds undoubtedly want to know—what about Novak? A strange silence settled over his role. It is inconceivable Fitzgerald didn't ask him who his sources were. A possible answer is that he talked. In any case, if the journalists aren't vulnerable to prosecution under 50 U.S.C. § 421, a government employee would be, but only if he or she could be proved to have deliberately unmasked an intelligence agent knowing that the government took "affirmative measures" to keep the agent's identity secret. So, the ultimate questions, criminally speaking, are: Who did the leaking? and Did the government official(s)—who may be the journalists' sources, or be named by them,—*intentionally* out Plame? If so, Miller won't be doing time alone. In any case, that the employee might not be criminally liable doesn't answer the question whether he or she should continue to work for the government. See New York Times, July 12, 2005, pp. A1, A14.

The Right of Access

▶ **Insert on p. 972 following the first paragraph**

In another Freedom of Information Act (FOIA) case decided the same Term, the Supreme Court had occasion to interpret the Act's "personal privacy" exception. Exemption 7(c) of the law excuses the government from having to disclose "records or information compiled for law enforcement purposes" that "could reasonably be expected to constitute an unwarranted invasion of personal privacy." In the case at hand, National Archives and Records Administration v. Favish, 541 U.S. 157, 124 S.Ct. 1570 (2004), a reporter working for the conservative interest group Accuracy in Media sued to gain access to several photographs taken at the scene of Vincent Foster's suicide. Foster, former deputy White House counsel, had been found dead in a Washington, D.C. park following revelations of some early scandals in the Clinton Administration. Favish, the reporter, was still skeptical after five separate government investigations concluded that Foster's death was a suicide. The Court rejected Favish's FOIA claim to gain access to several close-up pictures of the body and revolver on the grounds that the "personal privacy" exemption was not limited to simply "the right to control information about oneself" but extended as well to include the privacy interest of "[f]amily members [who] have a personal stake in honoring and mourning their dead and objecting to unwarranted public exploitation that, by intruding on their own grief, tends to degrade the rights and respect they seek to accord to the deceased person who was once one of their own." Moreover, if the privacy exception were less broadly interpreted, "child molesters, rapists, murderers, and other violent criminals * * * [could] make FOIA requests for autopsies, photographs, and records of their deceased victims"—a prospect the Court found "gruesome."

Summarizing the purpose and scope of the FOIA and the Court's approach to interpreting the personal privacy exception contained in the law, Justice Kennedy explained:

> FOIA is often explained as a means for citizens to know "what the Government is up to." * * * This phrase should not be dismissed as a convenient formalism. It defines a structural necessity in a real democracy. The statement confirms that, as a general rule, when documents are within FOIA's disclosure provisions, citizens should not be required to explain why they seek the information. A person requesting the information needs no preconceived idea of the uses the data might serve. The information belongs to citizens to do with as they choose. Furthermore, * * * the disclosure does not depend on the identity of the requester. As a general rule, if the information is subject to disclosure, it belongs to all.

> When disclosure touches upon certain areas defined in the exemptions, however, the statute recognizes limitations that compete with the general interest in disclosure, and that, in appropriate cases, can overcome it. In the case of Exemption 7(c), the statute requires us to protect, in the proper degree, the personal privacy of citizens against the uncontrolled release of information compiled through the power of the state. The statutory direction that the information not be released if the

invasion of personal privacy could reasonably be expected to be unwarranted requires the courts to balance the competing interests in privacy and disclosure. To effect this balance and to give practical meaning to the exemption, the usual rule that the citizen need not offer a reason for requesting the information must be inapplicable.

Where the privacy concerns addressed by Exemption 7(c) are present, the exemption requires the person requesting the information to establish a sufficient reason for the disclosure. First, the citizen must show that the public interest sought to be advanced is a significant one, an interest more specific than having the information for its own sake. Second, the citizen must show the information is likely to advance that interest. Otherwise, the invasion of privacy is unwarranted.

Meanwhile, on the national security front, there has been a steep increase the number of documents classified by the government. A record 15.6 million documents were classified in 2004—approximately double the number in 2001, while the number declassified has dwindled to about a third of those declassified in 2001, and the cost has soared. See New York Times, July 3, 2005, p. 12.

▶ **Insert at p. 975 following the last paragraph in this section**

Although the House of Representatives acted earlier to end compelled disclosure of library record and bookstore sales slip information, this provision was in fact retained when the House voted subsequently to extend the USA PATRIOT Act. See p. 45 of this Supplement.

B. OBSCENITY

▶ **Insert at p. 989 following the third paragraph**

Congress responded to the constitutional defects in its punishment of "virtual child pornography" identified by the Court in Ashcroft v. Free Speech Coalition, 535 U.S. 234, 122 S.Ct. 1389 (2002). In the PROTECT Act (Prosecuting Remedies Or Tools to end the Exploitation of Children Today), 117 Stat. 650, Congress voted to reword the definition to include any visual depiction that "is a digital image, computer image, or computer generated image that is, or is indistinguishable * * * from, that of a minor engaging in sexually explicit conduct." Moreover, images of simulated—rather than actual—acts must be "lascivious" to be within the meaning of "child pornography." By "indistinguishable" in the provision just quoted, Congress means "virtually indistinguishable," that is an ordinary person viewing the image would conclude it was a picture of a real child engaged in sexual conduct. That the image was not one involving a real child could be offered as an affirmative defense to the charge, which means the burden would be on the defendant to prove that the picture was not actual. Most child pornography, however, involves pictures of real children engaged in sexual acts.

▶ **Insert at p. 998 following *National Endowment of the Arts v. Finley***

UNITED STATES V. AMERICAN LIBRARY ASSOCIATION
Supreme Court of the United States, 2003
539 U.S. 194, 123 S.Ct 2297, 156 L.Ed.2d 221

BACKGROUND & FACTS   Congress established two kinds of financial assistance to help public libraries provide their patrons with access to the Internet. One is the E-rate program which qualifies libraries to receive Internet access at a discount. Another is a program of grants under the Library Services and Technology Act (LSTA) to state agencies to link libraries with access to electronic networks and pay costs for libraries to acquire or share computer systems. Congress subsequently became concerned that library patrons of all ages would use these facilities to search for pornography on-line. Uppermost was the fear that minors might gain access or be exposed to pornographic materials or that adults searching for it would leave it displayed on computer terminals or on library printers where it might be seen by children and nonconsenting adults. To address these risks, Congress enacted the Children's Internet Protection Act (CIPA), which bars a library from receiving federal funds under either program unless the library installs a software filter to block visual images that constitute obscenity, child pornography, or material that is "harmful to minors." Upon request, the library is authorized to disable the software for an adult engaged in "bona fide research or other lawful purposes."

The American Library Association and other plaintiffs challenged the CIPA as a violation of the First Amendment. A federal district court enjoined federal enforcement of the CIPA on grounds its conditions on the receipt of federal funds were unconstitutional on their face. The federal government then successfully sought certiorari from the Supreme Court.

Chief Justice REHNQUIST announced the judgment of the Court and delivered an opinion, in which Justice O'CONNOR, Justice SCALIA, and Justice THOMAS joined.

* * *

Congress has wide latitude to attach conditions to the receipt of federal assistance in order to further its policy objectives. South Dakota v. Dole, 483 U.S. 203, 206, 107 S.Ct. 2793 (1987). But Congress may not "induce" the recipient "to engage in activities that would themselves be unconstitutional." * * *

We have held in two analogous contexts that the government has broad discretion to make content-based judgments in deciding what private speech to make available to the public. In Arkansas Ed. Television Comm'n v. Forbes, 523 U.S. 666, 672-673, 118 S.Ct. 1633 (1998), we held that public forum principles do not generally apply to a public television station's editorial judgments regarding the private speech it presents to its viewers. * * *

Similarly, in National Endowment for Arts v. Finley, 524 U.S. 569, 118 S.Ct. 2168 (1998), we upheld an art funding program that required the National Endowment for the

Arts (NEA) to use content-based criteria in making funding decisions. * * *

The principles underlying *Forbes* and *Finley* also apply to a public library's exercise of judgment in selecting the material it provides to its patrons. Just as forum analysis and heightened judicial scrutiny are incompatible with the role of public television stations and the role of the NEA, they are also incompatible with the discretion that public libraries must have to fulfill their traditional missions. Public library staffs necessarily consider content in making collection decisions and enjoy broad discretion in making them.

* * * Internet access in public libraries is neither a "traditional" nor a "designated" public forum. * * * [T]his resource—which did not exist until quite recently—has not "immemorially been held in trust for the use of the public and, time out of mind, ... been used for purposes of assembly, communication of thoughts between citizens, and discussing public questions." International Soc. for Krishna Consciousness, Inc. v. Lee, 505 U.S. 672, 679, 112 S.Ct. 2701 (1992) * * *. We have "rejected the view that traditional public forum status extends beyond its historic confines." * * * The doctrines surrounding traditional public forums may not be extended to situations where such history is lacking.

Nor does Internet access in a public library satisfy our definition of a "designated public forum." To create such a forum, the government must make an affirmative choice to open up its property for use as a public forum. * * *

* * * A public library does not acquire Internet terminals in order to create a public forum for Web publishers to express themselves, any more than it collects books in order to provide a public forum for the authors of books to speak. It provides Internet access * * * for the same reasons it offers other library resources: to facilitate research, learning, and recreational pursuits by furnishing materials of requisite and appropriate quality. * * * A library's need to exercise judgment in making collection decisions depends on its traditional role in identifying suitable and worthwhile material; it is no less entitled to play that role when it collects material from the Internet than when it collects material from any other source. Most libraries already exclude pornography from their print collections because they deem it inappropriate for inclusion. We do not subject these decisions to heightened scrutiny; it would make little sense to treat libraries' judgments to block online pornography any differently, when these judgments are made for just the same reason.

Moreover, because of the vast quantity of material on the Internet and the rapid pace at which it changes, libraries cannot possibly segregate, item by item, all the Internet material that is appropriate for inclusion from all that is not. While a library could limit its Internet collection to just those sites it found worthwhile, it could do so only at the cost of excluding an enormous amount of valuable information that it lacks the capacity to review. Given that tradeoff, it is entirely reasonable for public libraries to reject that approach and instead exclude certain categories of content, without making individualized judgments that everything they do make available has requisite and appropriate quality.

* * *

Because public libraries' use of Internet filtering software does not violate their patrons' First Amendment rights, CIPA does not induce libraries to violate the Constitution, and is a valid exercise of Congress' spending power. Nor does CIPA impose an unconstitutional condition on public libraries. Therefore, the judgment of the District Court * * * is

Reversed.

Justice KENNEDY, concurring in the judgment.

If, on the request of an adult user, a librarian will unblock filtered material or disable the Internet software filter without significant delay, there is little to this case. * * *

* * *

If some libraries do not have the capacity to unblock specific Web sites or to disable the filter or if it is shown that an adult user's election to view constitutionally protected Internet material is burdened in some other substantial way, that would be the subject for an as-applied challenge, not the facial challenge made in this case. * * *

* * *

Justice BREYER, concurring in the judgment.

* * *

In ascertaining whether the statutory provisions are constitutional, I would apply a form of heightened scrutiny * * * The Act directly restricts the public's receipt of information. * * * For that reason, we should not examine the statute's constitutionality as if it raised no special First Amendment concern—as if, like tax or economic regulation, the First Amendment demanded only a "rational basis" for imposing a restriction. * * *

At the same time, in my view, the First Amendment does not here demand application of the most limiting constitutional approach—that of "strict scrutiny." The statutory restriction in question is, in essence, a kind of "selection" restriction (a kind of editing). It affects the kinds and amount of materials that the library can present to its patrons. * * * And libraries often properly engage in the selection of materials, either as a matter of necessity (*i.e.*, due to the scarcity of resources) or by design (*i.e.*, in accordance with collection development policies). * * *

Instead, I would examine the constitutionality of the Act's restrictions here as the Court has examined speech-related restrictions in other contexts where circumstances call for heightened, but not "strict," scrutiny * * *.

In such cases the Court has asked whether the harm to speech-related interests is disproportionate in light of both the justifications and the potential alternatives. It has considered the legitimacy of the statute's objective, the extent to which the statute will tend to achieve that objective, whether there are other, less restrictive ways of achieving that objective, and ultimately whether the statute works speech-related harm that, in relation to that objective, is out of proportion. * * *

The Act's restrictions satisfy these constitutional demands. The Act seeks to restrict access to obscenity, child pornography, and, in respect to access by minors, material that is comparably harmful. These objectives are "legitimate," and indeed often "compelling." * * *

At the same time, * * * the Act allows libraries to permit any adult patron access to an "overblocked" Web site; the adult patron need only ask a librarian to unblock the specific Web site or, alternatively, ask the librarian, "Please disable the entire filter." * * *

The Act does impose upon the patron the burden of making this request. But it is difficult to see how that burden (or any delay associated with compliance) could prove more onerous than traditional library practices associated with segregating library materials in, say, closed stacks, or with interlibrary lending practices that require patrons to make requests that are not anonymous and to wait while the librarian obtains the desired materials from elsewhere. * * *

Given the comparatively small burden that the Act imposes upon the library patron seeking legitimate Internet materials, I cannot say that any speech-related harm that the Act may cause is disproportionate when considered in relation to the Act's legitimate objectives. I therefore * * * concur in the judgment.

Justice STEVENS, dissenting.

* * *

[T]he software's reliance on words to identify undesirable sites necessarily results in the blocking of thousands of pages that "contain content that is completely innocuous for both adults and minors, and that no rational person could conclude matches the filtering companies' category definitions, such as 'pornography' or 'sex.'" * * * In my judgment, a statutory blunderbuss that mandates this vast amount of "overblocking" abridges the freedom of speech protected by the First Amendment.

The effect of the overblocking is the functional equivalent of a host of individual decisions excluding hundreds of thousands of individual constitutionally protected messages from Internet terminals located in public libraries throughout the Nation. Neither the interest in suppressing unlawful speech nor the interest in protecting children from access to harmful materials justifies this overly broad restriction on adult access to protected speech. * * *

* * *

Until a blocked site or group of sites is unblocked, a patron is unlikely to know what is being hidden and therefore whether there is any point in asking for the filter to be removed. It is as though the statute required a significant part of every library's reading materials to be kept in unmarked, locked rooms or cabinets, which could be opened only in response to specific requests. Some curious readers would in time obtain access to the hidden materials, but many would not. Inevitably, the interest of the authors of those works in reaching the widest possible audience would be abridged. Moreover, because the procedures that different libraries are likely to adopt to respond to unblocking requests will no doubt vary, it is impossible to measure the aggregate effect of the statute on patrons' access to blocked sites. Unless we assume that the statute is a mere symbolic gesture, we must conclude that it will create a significant prior restraint on adult access to protected speech. * * *

* * *

[U]nlike *Finley*, the Government does not merely seek to control a library's discretion with respect to computers purchased with Government funds or those computers with Government-discounted Internet access. CIPA requires libraries to install filtering software on *every* computer with Internet access if the library receives *any* discount from the E-rate program or *any* funds from the LSTA program. * * * [U]nder this statute, if a library attempts to provide Internet service for even *one* computer through an E-rate discount, that library must put filtering software on *all* of its computers with Internet access, not just the one computer with E-rate discount.

This Court should not permit federal funds to be used to enforce this kind of broad restriction of First Amendment rights, particularly when such a restriction is unnecessary to accomplish Congress' stated goal. * * * The abridgment of speech is equally obnoxious whether a rule like this one is enforced by a threat of penalties or by a threat to withhold a benefit.

* * *

Justice SOUTER, with whom Justice GINSBURG joins, dissenting.

I agree in the main with Justice STEVENS, * * * that the blocking requirements of the Children's Internet Protection Act * * * impose an unconstitutional condition on the Government's subsidies to local libraries for providing access to the Internet * * * [but I would also conclude that the] recipient libraries * * * would violate the First Amendment's guarantee of free speech if the libraries took that action entirely on their own. * * *

* * *

[T]he unblocking provisions simply cannot be construed * * * to say that a library must unblock upon adult request, no conditions imposed and no questions asked. * * * [T]he statute says only that a library "may" unblock, not that it must. * * * In addition, it allows unblocking only for a "bona fide research or other lawful purposes," * * * and if the "lawful purposes" criterion means anything * * * it must impose some limit on eligibility for unblocking * * *.

We therefore have to take the statute on the understanding that adults will be denied access to a substantial amount of nonobscene material harmful to children but lawful for adult examination, and a substantial quantity of text and pictures harmful to no one. * * * [T]his is the inevitable consequence of the indiscriminate behavior of current filtering mechanisms, which screen out material to an extent known only by the manufacturers of the blocking software * * *.

* * * T]he restrictions on adult Internet access have no justification in the object of protecting children. Children could be restricted to blocked terminals, leaving other unblocked terminals in areas restricted to adults and screened from casual glances. And of course the statute could simply have provided for unblocking at adult request, with

no questions asked. The statute could, in other words, have protected children without blocking access for adults or subjecting adults to anything more than minimal inconvenience, just the way (the record shows) many librarians had been dealing with obscenity and indecency before imposition of the federal conditions. * * * Instead, the Government's funding conditions engage in overkill * * *.

The question for me, then, is whether a local library could itself constitutionally impose these restrictions on the content otherwise available to an adult patron through an Internet connection, at a library terminal provided for public use. The answer is no. A library that chose to block an adult's Internet access to material harmful to children (and whatever else the undiscriminating filter might interrupt) would be imposing a content-based restriction on communication of material in the library's control that an adult could otherwise lawfully see. This would simply be censorship. * * *

At every significant point, * * * the Internet blocking here defies comparison to the process of acquisition. Whereas traditional scarcity of money and space require a library to make choices about what to acquire, and the choice to be made is whether or not to spend the money to acquire something, blocking is the subject of a choice made after the money for Internet access has been spent or committed. Since it makes no difference to the cost of Internet access whether an adult calls up material harmful for children or the Articles of Confederation, blocking (on facts like these) is not necessitated by scarcity of either money or space. In the instance of the Internet, what the library acquires is electronic access, and the choice to block is a choice to limit access that has already been acquired. * * * The proper analogy * * * is not to passing up a book that might have been bought; it is either to buying a book and then keeping it from adults lacking an acceptable "purpose," or to buying an encyclopedia and then cutting out pages with anything thought to be unsuitable for all adults.

* * *

* * * I would hold in accordance with conventional strict scrutiny that a library's practice of blocking would violate an adult patron's First and Fourteenth Amendment right to be free of Internet censorship, when unjustified (as here) by any legitimate interest in screening children from harmful material. On that ground, the Act's blocking requirement in its current breadth calls for unconstitutional action by a library recipient, and is itself unconstitutional.

▶ **Insert at p. 1005 at the end of the note on the Regulation of Indecency**

Four years after its *Playboy* ruling, the Court, in Ashcroft v. American Civil Liberties Union, 542 U.S. 656, 124 S.Ct. 2783 (2004), affirmed issuing a preliminary injunction against enforcement of the Child Online Protection Act (COPA). The Court agreed with the federal court below that the plaintiffs, Internet providers and free speech advocates, were likely to prevail on the merits of their constitutional claims that the COPA was overly restrictive of legitimate free speech. A 5-4 majority of the Justices held that the government bore the burden of proof and thus far had failed to produce adequate evidence to show that criminal penalties under the COPA constituted the regulatory alternative least restrictive of free speech. However laudable and compelling the effort to make the Internet safe for minors may be, blocking and filtering software was available, and it was up to the government to show it was not effective (not just that it was imperfect). Blocking and filtering were clearly "less restrictive than COPA" because "[t]hey impose selective restrictions on speech at the receiving end, not universal restrictions on the source." Quite apart from vagueness problems with COPA's terminology—the statute punished the dissemination of material "harmful to minors"—enforcement of anything more than the least restrictive regulatory option violated the First Amendment. Said Justice Kennedy, speaking for the Court:

> Under a filtering regime, adults without children may gain access to speech they have a right to see without having to identify themselves or provide their credit card information. Even adults with children may obtain access to the same speech on the same terms simply by turning off the filter on their home computers. Above all, promoting the use of filters does not condemn as criminal any category of speech, and so the potential chilling effect is eliminated, or at least much diminished. * * * All of these things are true, moreover, regardless of how broadly or narrowly the definitions in COPA are construed.
>
> Filters also may well be more effective than COPA. First, a filter can prevent minors from seeing all pornography, not just pornography posted to the Web from America. * * * COPA does not prevent minors from having access to those foreign harmful materials. That alone makes it possible that filtering software might be more effective in serving Congress' goals. Effectiveness is likely to diminish even further if COPA is upheld, because the providers of the materials that would be covered by the statute simply can move their operations overseas. It is not an answer to say that COPA reaches some amount of materials that are harmful to minors; the question is whether it would reach more of them than less restrictive alternatives. In addition, the District Court found that verification systems may be subject to evasion and circumvention, for example by minors who have their own credit cards. * * * Finally, filters also may be more effective because they can be applied to all forms of Internet communication, including e-mail, not just communications available via the World Wide Web.
>
> That filtering software may well be more effective than COPA is confirmed by the findings of the Commission on Child Online Protection, a blue-ribbon commission created by Congress in COPA itself. * * * [N]ot only has the Government failed to carry its burden of showing the District Court that the proposed alternative is less effective, but also a Government Commission appointed to consider the question has concluded just the opposite. That finding supports our conclusion that the District Court did not abuse its discretion in enjoining the statute.

Chief Justice Rehnquist and Justices O'Connor, Scalia, and Breyer dissented.

In the latest skirmish in the battle over indecency in the media, Congress had before it a bill stiffening the penalties that can be imposed on offensive broadcasting. On March 11, 2004, the House of Representatives passed HR 3717 by a vote of 391-22 which would have made it easier for the Federal Communications Commission to fine performers as well as the holder of a broadcast license for airing indecent material. The bill removed the requirement that a warning citation must be issued first, thus giving the offender a second chance before imposing a penalty. The legislation also would have raised from $11,000 to $500,000 the maximum fine for an offense. The magnitude of the fine was to increase with the number of violations and also took into account the size of the broadcast audience. Moreover, the bill contained a three-strikes provision that mandated an FCC license revocation hearing for three-time offenders and required the commission to file annual reports with Congress about investigations into indecency violations. Although the measure enjoyed bipartisan support, it stood little chance of passage in the Senate because of the pressure of more important legislative business (such as the budget bills) and the relatively short time remaining in the 108th Congress. This dust-up followed Janet Jackson's breast-revealing conduct at the Super Bowl and a 20-minute segment of Howard Stern's radio program dealing with anal sex (for which the FCC fined Clear Channel, the station chain owner). Another impediment to passage were provisions of the Senate bill that addressed other issues as well: (1) rolling back the FCC's recent rules expanding media ownership by large companies, and (2) funding study of V-chip technology permitting viewers to block out programs with violence. See Congressional Quarterly Weekly Report, Mar. 13, 2004, pp. 635-638; New York Times, June 7, 2004, pp. C1, C8; see also Amol Sharma and Jennifer A. Dlouhy, "A New Indecency Standard: Lost in 'Terminal Vagueness?'" Congressional Quarterly Weekly Report, July 10, 2004, pp. 1668-1671.

C. LIBEL

▶ **Insert at p. 1023 following the chart**

In a noteworthy case in the developing area of Internet libel, an Ontario court has awarded damages of $125,000 plus costs to an archeologist after a native man smeared her as a "grave robber" in e-mails. While people insulting one another is hardly news on the Internet, the Ontario superior court found actual malice, saying, "The defendant's conduct in asking the recipients of his e-mail to re-disseminate to as many individuals as possible was calculated to cause the plaintiff the maximum embarrassment and professional harm and the defendant was persistent in this"—"[e]ven after the litigation was started * * *." There was "no evidence that the defendant believed that the statement was true." Madam Justice Wailan Low continued:

> Cyber-libel takes a number of forms. * * * [S]uffice it to say that there is a palpable difference between a posting on a popular website which may experience millions of "hits" on an ongoing basis and thus give rise to the existence of millions of publishees, and the sending of an e-mail to all of the publisher's acquaintances, even with the

exhortation to pass the e-mail on to others as was the case here. Clearly, the use of e-mail is far more powerful than the sending out of a multiple of hard copy letters defaming the plaintiff, but on the other hand, the e-mail medium is far less powerful than a posting on a website that has, as its initial audience, a substantially wider reach and therefore an exponentially greater potential for re-dissemination.

See Ross v. Hadley, 2004 CarswellOnt 5093 (2004).

CHAPTER 13

FREEDOM OF RELIGION

A. THE ESTABLISHMENT CLAUSE

Prayer, Bible-Reading, and Sunday Closing Laws

▶ **Insert at p. 1059 at the end of the note**

The constitutionality of displaying the Ten Commandments on government property popped up again, some 25 after the decision in *Stone* v. *Graham*, after Roy Moore, the Chief Justice of the Alabama Supreme Court (who campaigned for election to the post as "The Ten Commandments Judge"), ordered a two-and-a-half-ton granite stone marker with the Commandments to be placed in the rotunda of the state Supreme Court building. The monument was paid for by an evangelical organization. In response to a suit challenging its constitutionality, a federal district judge held the placement of the monument to be unconstitutional and ordered it removed. This judgment was affirmed on appeal. Glassroth v. Moore, 229 F.Supp.2d 1290 (M.D.Ala. 2002), *affirmed*, 335 F.3d 1282 (11th Cir. 2003), *cert. denied*, 540 U.S. 1000, 124 S.Ct. 497 (2004). When the Chief Justice refused, the district court ordered it removed within 30 days and threatened the state with a $5,000 a day fine for noncompliance. The other eight Justices of the state supreme court then ordered the stone marker removed, were themselves sued, and their action was sustained. McGinley v. Houston, 282 F.Supp.2d 1304 (M.D.Ala. 2003), *affirmed*, 361 F.3d 1328 (11th Cir. 2004) Neither the state's governor nor the attorney general backed the Chief Justice. Moore was subsequently removed from his job by a state commission for his defiance of the federal court order.

The Supreme Court, however, did grant cert. in two other recent cases that raised Establishment Clause challenges to display of the Ten Commandments on government property, one from Kentucky and one from Texas. The Court reached different conclusions in the two cases which follow, and made it clear that the context of the display matters a good deal. Along the way, the Justices revisited the contentious *Lemon* test—illuminating it, amending it, and criticizing it.

McCreary County, Kentucky v. American Civil Liberties Union
Supreme Court of the United States, 2005
545 U.S. —, 125 S.Ct. 2722, — L.Ed.2d —

BACKGROUND & FACTS   Officials in two Kentucky counties posted framed copies of the Ten Commandments in their courthouses. After the American Civil Liberties Union brought suit challenging the display as a violation of the Establishment Clause, the counties adopted similar resolutions in favor of a more extensive exhibit aimed at showing the Commandments were part of the state's "precedent legal code." Among other reasons for doing so, the resolutions noted the state legislature's acknowledgment of Jesus Christ as "the Prince of Ethics." Around the Commandments were displayed eight smaller-size documents, such as the Declaration of Independence which contained religious references (the Declaration's "endowed by their Creator" passage, for example). The common tie in the documents comprising the exhibit was their religious references.

A federal district court, citing *Lemon v. Kurtzman* (see Text, p. 1065), issued a preliminary injunction on grounds the original display lacked a secular purpose. After changing counsel, the counties revised the display once again. This time there were nine documents of equal size (among them the lyrics to "The Star Spangled Banner"). A new title, "The Foundations of American Law and Government Display" was posted with them and it was explained that the documents profoundly influenced the formation of western legal thought and the Nation. On motion by the ACLU, the district court took notice of this third display and held that the counties' asserted educational goals were unpersuasive in the face of the litigation's history. A federal appeals court affirmed, and the counties sought review by the U.S. Supreme Court.

Justice SOUTER delivered the opinion of the Court.

* * *

Twenty-five years ago in a case prompted by posting the Ten Commandments in Kentucky's public schools, this Court recognized that the Commandments "are undeniably a sacred text in the Jewish and Christian faiths" and held that their display in public classrooms violated the First Amendment's bar against establishment of religion. Stone [v. Graham, 449 U.S., at 41, 101 S.Ct., at 194]. *Stone* found a predominantly religious purpose in the government's posting of the Commandments, given their prominence as "'an instrument of religion'" * * *.

* * * When the government acts with the ostensible and predominant purpose of advancing religion, it violates that central Establishment Clause value of official religious neutrality, there being no neutrality when the government's ostensible object is to take sides. * * * By showing a purpose to favor religion, the government "sends the ... message to ... nonadherents 'that they are outsiders, not full members of the political community, and an accompanying message to adherents that they are insiders, favored members ....'" Santa Fe Independent School Dist. v. Doe, 530 U.S. 290, 309-310, 120 S.Ct. 2266 (2000) * * *.

[W]hen the government maintains Sunday closing laws, it advances religion only minimally because many working people would take the day as one of rest regardless, but if the government justified its decision with a stated desire for all Americans to honor Christ, the divisive thrust of the official action would be inescapable. This is the teaching of McGowan v. Maryland, 366 U.S. 420, 81 S.Ct. 1101 (1961), which upheld Sunday closing statutes on practical, secular grounds after finding that the government had forsaken the religious purposes behind centuries-old predecessor laws. * * *

Despite the intuitive importance of official purpose to the realization of Establishment Clause values, the Counties ask us to abandon *Lemon*'s purpose test, or at least to truncate any enquiry into purpose here. Their first argument is that * * * true "purpose" is unknowable, and its search merely an excuse for courts to act selectively and unpredictably in picking out evidence of subjective intent. * * *

* * *

[S]crutinizing purpose * * * make[s] practical sense, as in Establishment Clause analysis, where an understanding of official objective emerges from readily discoverable fact, without any judicial psychoanalysis of a drafter's heart of hearts. * * * There is * * * nothing hinting at an unpredictable or disingenuous exercise when a court enquires into purpose after a claim is raised under the Establishment Clause.

* * * In Wallace [v. Jaffree, 472 U.S. 38, 105 S.Ct. 2479 (1985)], for example, we inferred purpose from a change of wording from an earlier statute to later one, each dealing with prayer in schools. * * * And in Edwards [v. Aguillard, 482 U.S. 578, 107 S.Ct. 2573 (1987)], we relied on a statute's text and the detailed public comments of its sponsor, when we sought the purpose of a state law requiring creationism to be taught alongside evolution. * * * In other cases, the government action itself bespoke the purpose, as in [School District of] Abington [Township v. Schempp, 374 U.S. 203, 83 S.Ct. 1560 (1963)], where the object of required Bible study in public schools was patently religious * * *; in *Stone*, the Court held that the "[p]osting of religious texts on the wall serve[d] no ... educational function," and found that if "the posted copies of the Ten Commandments [were] to have any effect at all, it [would] be to induce the schoolchildren to read, meditate upon, perhaps to venerate and obey, the Commandments." * * * In each case, the government's action was held unconstitutional only because openly available data supported a commonsense conclusion that a religious objective permeated the government's action.

Nor is there any indication that the enquiry is rigged * * * to finding a religious purpose dominant every time a case is filed. In the past, the test has not been fatal very often, presumably because government does not generally act unconstitutionally, with the predominant purpose of advancing religion. * * *

* * *

Lemon said that government action must have "a secular ... purpose" * * * and after a host of cases it is fair to add that although a legislature's stated reasons will generally get deference, the secular purpose required has to be genuine, not a sham, and not merely secondary to a religious objective. * * *

[Both *Wallace* and Lynch v. Donnelly, 465 U.S. 668, 104 S.Ct. 1355 (1984)] examined and rejected claims of secular purposes that turned out to be implausible or inadequate * * *.

The Counties' second * * * [argument is that purpose] should be inferred * * * only from the latest news about the last in a series of governmental actions, however close they may all be in time and subject. But the world is not made brand new every morning, and the Counties are simply asking us to ignore perfectly probative evidence; they want an absentminded objective observer, not one presumed to be familiar with the history of the government's actions and competent to learn what history has to show * * *.

* * *

The display rejected in *Stone* had two obvious similarities to the first one in the sequence here: both set out a text of the Commandments as distinct from any traditionally symbolic representation, and each stood alone, not part of an arguably secular display. *Stone* stressed the significance of integrating the Commandments into a secular scheme to forestall the broadcast of an otherwise clearly religious message, * * * and for good reason, the Commandments being a central point of reference in the religious and moral history of Jews and Christians. They proclaim the existence of a monotheistic god (no other gods). They regulate details of religious obligation (no graven images, no sabbath breaking, no vain oath swearing). And they unmistakably rest even the universally accepted prohibitions (as against murder, theft, and the like) on the sanction of the divinity proclaimed at the beginning of the text. * * * Where the text is set out, the insistence of the religious message is hard to avoid in the absence of a context plausibly suggesting a message going beyond an excuse to promote the religious point of view. The display in *Stone* had no context that might have indicated an object beyond the religious character of the text, and the Counties' solo exhibit here did nothing more to counter the sectarian implication than the postings at issue in *Stone*. * * * What is more, at [a] ceremony for posting the framed Commandments in * * * [this case,] the county executive was accompanied by his pastor, who testified to the certainty of the existence of God. The reasonable observer could only think that the Counties meant to emphasize and celebrate the Commandments' religious message.

This is not to deny that the Commandments have had influence on civil or secular law * * *. The point is simply that the original text viewed in its entirety is an unmistakably religious statement dealing with religious obligations and with morality subject to religious sanction. When the government initiates an effort to place this statement alone in public view, a religious object is unmistakable.

Once the Counties were sued, they modified the exhibits and invited additional insight into their purpose in a display that hung for about six months. * * *

In this second display, unlike the first, the Commandments were not hung in isolation, merely leaving the Counties' purpose to emerge from the pervasively religious text of the Commandments themselves. Instead, the second version was required to include the statement of the government's purpose expressly set out in the county resolutions, and underscored it by juxtaposing the Commandments to other documents with highlighted references to God as their sole common element. The display's unstinting focus was on religious passages, showing that the Counties were posting the Commandments precisely because of their sectarian content. That demonstration of the government's objective was enhanced by serial religious references and the accompanying resolution's claim about the embodiment of ethics in Christ. Together, the display and resolution presented an indisputable, and undisputed, showing of an impermissible purpose.

* * *

After the Counties changed lawyers, they mounted a third display, without a new resolution or repeal of the old one. The result was the "Foundations of American Law and Government" exhibit, which placed the Commandments in the company of other documents the Counties thought especially significant in the historical foundation of American government. In trying to persuade the District Court to lift the preliminary injunction, the Counties cited several new purposes for the third version, including a desire "to educate the citizens of the county regarding some of the documents that played a significant role in the foundation of our system of law and government." * * *

These new statements of purpose were presented only as a litigating position * * *. Indeed, the sectarian spirit of the common resolution found enhanced expression in the third display, which quoted more of the purely religious language of the Commandments than the first two displays had done * * *. No reasonable observer could swallow the claim that the Counties had cast off the objective so unmistakable in the earlier displays.

* * *

In holding the preliminary injunction adequately supported by evidence that the Counties' purpose had not changed at the third stage, we do not decide that the Counties' past actions forever taint any effort on their part to deal with the subject matter. We hold only that purpose needs to be taken seriously under the Establishment Clause and needs to be understood in light of context; an implausible claim that governmental purpose has changed should not carry the day in a court of law any more than in a head with common sense. * * *

Nor do we have occasion here to hold that a sacred text can never be integrated constitutionally into a governmental display on the subject of law, or American history. We do not forget, and in this litigation have frequently been reminded, that our own courtroom frieze was deliberately designed in the exercise of governmental authority so as to include the figure of Moses holding tablets exhibiting a portion of the Hebrew text of the later, secularly phrased Commandments; in the company of 17 other lawgivers, most of them secular figures, there is no risk that Moses would strike an observer as evidence that the National Government was violating neutrality in religion.

The importance of neutrality as an interpretive guide is no less true now than it was when the Court broached the principle in Everson v. Board of Ed. of Ewing, 330 U.S. 1, 67 S.Ct. 504 (1947) * * *.

* * *

[T]he government may not favor one religion over another, or religion over irreligion, religious choice being the prerogative of individuals under the Free Exercise Clause. The principle has been helpful simply because it responds to one of the major concerns that prompted adoption of the Religion Clauses. The Framers and the citizens of their time intended not only to protect the integrity of individual conscience in religious matters * * * but to guard against the civic divisiveness that follows when the Government weighs in on one side of religious debate * * *.

* * *

[T]he dissent's argument for the original understanding is flawed from the outset by its failure to consider the full range of evidence showing what the Framers believed. The dissent is certainly correct in putting forward evidence that some of the Framers thought some endorsement of religion was compatible with the establishment ban * * * [but] there is also evidence supporting the proposition that the Framers intended the Establishment Clause to require governmental neutrality in matters of religion, including neutrality in statements acknowledging religion. The very language of the Establishment Clause represented a significant departure from early drafts that merely prohibited a single national religion, and, the final language instead "extended [the] prohibition to state support for 'religion' in general." * * *

The historical record, moreover, is complicated beyond the dissent's account by the writings and practices of figures * * * [such as] Thomas Jefferson and James Madison. Jefferson, for example, refused to issue Thanksgiving Proclamations because he believed that they violated the Constitution. * * * And Madison * * * criticized Virginia's general assessment tax not just because it required people to donate "three pence" to religion, but because "it is itself a signal of persecution. It degrades from the equal rank of Citizens all those whose opinions in Religion do not bend to those of the Legislative authority." * * *

The fair inference is that there was no common understanding about the limits of the establishment prohibition * * *. What the evidence does show is a group of statesmen, like others before and after them, who proposed a guarantee with contours not wholly worked out, leaving the Establishment Clause with edges still to be determined. And none the worse for that. Indeterminate edges are the kind to have in a constitution meant to endure * * *.

* * *

Historical evidence * * * supports no solid argument for changing course * * * whereas public discourse at the present time certainly raises no doubt about the value of the interpretative approach invoked for 60 years now. We are centuries away from the St. Bartholomew's Day massacre and the treatment of heretics in early Massachusetts, but the divisiveness of religion in current public life is inescapable. This is no time to deny the prudence of * * * requir[ing] the Government to stay neutral on religious belief * * *.

Given the ample support for the District Court's finding of a predominantly religious purpose behind the Counties' third display, we affirm the Sixth Circuit in upholding the preliminary injunction.

It is so ordered.

Justice O'CONNOR, concurring.

* * *

Reasonable minds can disagree about how to apply the Religion Clauses in a given case. But the goal of the Clauses is clear: to carry out the Founders' plan of preserving religious liberty to the fullest extent possible in a pluralistic society. By enforcing the Clauses, we have kept religion a matter for the individual conscience, not for the prosecutor or bureaucrat. At a time when we see around the world the violent consequences of the assumption of religious authority by government, Americans may count themselves fortunate: Our regard for constitutional boundaries has protected us from similar travails, while allowing private religious exercise to flourish.* * *

* * *

* * * When the government associates one set of religious beliefs with the state and identifies nonadherents as outsiders, it encroaches upon the individual's decision about whether and how to worship. In the marketplace of ideas, the government has vast resources and special status. * * * Allowing government to be a potential mouthpiece for competing religious ideas risks the sort of division that might easily spill over into suppression of rival beliefs. Tying secular and religious authority together poses risks to both.

Given the history of this particular display of the Ten Commandments, the Court correctly finds an Establishment Clause violation. * * * The purpose behind the counties' display is relevant because it conveys an unmistakable message of endorsement to the reasonable observer. * * *

It is true that many Americans find the Commandments in accord with their personal beliefs. But we do not count heads before enforcing the First Amendment. * * * Nor can we accept the theory that Americans who do not accept the Commandments' validity are outside the First Amendment's protections. There is no list of approved and disapproved beliefs appended to the First Amendment * * *. It is true that the Framers lived at a time when our national religious diversity was neither as robust nor as well recognized as it is now. They may not have foreseen the variety of religions for which this Nation would eventually provide a home. They surely could not have predicted new religions, some of them born in this country. But they did know that line-drawing between religions is an enterprise that, once begun, has no logical stopping point. * * * The Religion Clauses * * * protect adherents of all religions, as well as those who believe in no religion at all.

* * *

Justice SCALIA, with whom THE CHIEF JUSTICE [REHNQUIST] and Justice THOMAS join, and with whom Justice KENNEDY joins as to [parts,] dissenting.

* * *

* * * George Washington added to the form of Presidential oath prescribed by Art. II, § 1, cl. 8, of the Constitution, the concluding

words "so help me God." * * * The Supreme Court under John Marshall opened its sessions with the prayer, "God save the United States and this Honorable Court." * * * The First Congress instituted the practice of beginning its legislative sessions with a prayer. * * * The same week that Congress submitted the Establishment Clause as part of the Bill of Rights for ratification by the States, it enacted legislation providing for paid chaplains in the House and Senate. * * * The day after the First Amendment was proposed, the same Congress that had proposed it requested the President to proclaim "a day of public thanksgiving and prayer, to be observed, by acknowledging, with grateful hearts, the many and signal favours of Almighty God." * * *

These actions of our First President and Congress and the Marshall Court were not idiosyncratic; they reflected the beliefs of the period. Those who wrote the Constitution believed that morality was essential to the well-being of society and that encouragement of religion was the best way to foster morality. * * *

James Madison, in his first inaugural address, likewise placed his confidence "in the guardianship and guidance of that Almighty Being whose power regulates the destiny of nations, whose blessings have been so conspicuously dispensed to this rising Republic, and to whom we are bound to address our devout gratitude for the past, as well as our fervent supplications and best hopes for the future." * * *

Nor have the views of our people on this matter significantly changed. Presidents continue to conclude the Presidential oath with the words "so help me God." Our legislatures, state and national, continue to open their sessions with prayer led by official chaplains. The sessions of this Court continue to open with the prayer "God save the United States and this Honorable Court." Invocation of the Almighty by our public figures, at all levels of government, remains commonplace. Our coinage bears the motto "IN GOD WE TRUST." And our Pledge of Allegiance contains the acknowledgment that we are a Nation "under God." * * *

With all of this reality * * * staring it in the face, how can the Court *possibly* assert that "'the First Amendment mandates governmental neutrality between ... religion and nonreligion'" * * * and that "[m]anifesting a purpose to favor ... adherence to religion generally" * * * is unconstitutional? Who says so? Surely not the words of the Constitution. Surely not the history and traditions that reflect our society's constant understanding of those words. Surely not even the current sense of our society, recently reflected in an Act of Congress adopted *unanimously* by the Senate and with only 5 nays in the House of Representatives * * * criticizing a Court of Appeals opinion that had held "under God" in the Pledge of Allegiance unconstitutional. See Act of Nov. 13, 2002, * * * 116 Stat. 2057, 2058, 2060-2061 * * *. Nothing stands behind the Court's assertion that governmental affirmation of the society's belief in God is unconstitutional except the Court's own say-so * * *.

[W]hen the government relieves churches from the obligation to pay property taxes, when it allows students to absent themselves from public school to take religious classes, and when it exempts religious organizations from generally applicable prohibitions of religious discrimination, it surely means to bestow a benefit on religious practice—but we have approved it. * * * Indeed, * * * [in] Marsh v. Chambers, [463 U.S. 783, 103 S.Ct. 3330 (1983)], the Court upheld the Nebraska State Legislature's practice of paying a chaplain to lead it in prayer at the opening of legislative sessions. * * *

[The reason] for occasionally ignoring the neutrality principle * * * is the instinct for self-preservation, and the recognition that the Court, which "has no influence over either the sword or the purse," The Federalist No. 78, p. 412 (J. Pole ed.2005), cannot go too far down the road of an enforced neutrality that contradicts both historical fact and current practice without losing all that sustains it: the willingness of the people to accept its interpretation of the Constitution as definitive, in preference to the contrary interpretation of the democratically elected branches.

Besides appealing to the demonstrably false principle that the government cannot favor religion over irreligion, today's opinion suggests that the posting of the Ten Commandments violates the principle that the government cannot favor one religion over another. * * * That is indeed a valid principle where public aid or assistance to religion is concerned, * * * or where the free exercise of religion is at issue, * * * but it necessarily applies in a more limited sense to public acknowledgment of the Creator. If religion in the public forum had to be entirely nondenominational, there could be no religion in the public forum at all. One cannot say the word "God," or "the Almighty," one cannot offer public supplication or thanksgiving, without contradicting the beliefs of some people that there are many gods, or that God or the gods pay no attention to human affairs. With respect to public acknowledgment of religious belief, it is entirely clear from our Nation's historical practices that the Establishment Clause permits this disregard of polytheists and believers in unconcerned deities, just as it permits the disregard of devout atheists. * * *

Historical practices * * * demonstrate that there is a distance between the acknowledgment of a single Creator and the establishment of a religion. The former is, as *Marsh v. Chambers* put it, "a tolerable acknowledgment of beliefs widely held among the people of this country." * * * The three most popular religions in the United States, Christianity, Judaism, and Islam—which combined account for 97.7% of all believers—are monotheistic. * * * All of them, moreover (Islam included), believe that the Ten Commandments were given by God to Moses, and are divine prescriptions for a virtuous life. * * * Publicly honoring the Ten Commandments is thus indistinguishable, insofar as discriminating against other religions is concerned, from publicly honoring God. * * *

* * *

* * * In two respects [the Court] modifies *Lemon* to ratchet up the Court's hostility to religion. First, the Court justifies inquiry into legislative purpose, not as an end itself, but as a means to ascertain the appearance of the government action to an "'objective observer.'" * * * Under this approach, even if a government could show that its actual purpose was not to advance religion, it would presumably violate the Constitution as long as the Court's objective observer would think otherwise. * * *

* * *

Second, the Court replaces *Lemon*'s requirement that the government have "*a* secular ... purpose," * * * (emphasis added), with the heightened requirement that the secular purpose "predominate" over any purpose to advance religion. * * * [This] finds no support in our cases.

* * * By shifting the focus of *Lemon*'s purpose prong from the search for a genuine, secular motivation to the hunt for a predominantly religious purpose, the Court converts what has in the past been a fairly limited inquiry into a rigorous review of the full record. Those responsible for the adoption of the Religion Clauses would surely regard it as a bitter irony that the religious values they designed those Clauses to *protect* have now become so distasteful to this Court that if they constitute anything more than a subordinate motive for government action they will invalidate it.

* * *

On its face, the Foundations Displays manifested the purely secular purpose that the Counties asserted before the District Court: "to display documents that played a significant role in the foundation of our system of law and government." * * * That the Displays included the Ten Commandments did not transform their apparent secular purpose into one of impermissible advocacy for Judeo-Christian beliefs. * * * [W]hen the Ten Commandments appear alongside other documents of secular significance in a display devoted to the foundations of American law and government, the context communicates that the Ten Commandments are included, not to teach their binding nature as a religious text, but to show their unique contribution to the development of the legal system. * * * This is doubly true when the display is introduced by a document that informs passersby that it "contains documents that played a significant role in the foundation of our system of law and government."

* * * The acknowledgment of the contribution that religion in general, and the Ten Commandments in particular, have made to our Nation's legal and governmental heritage is surely no more of a step towards establishment of religion than was the practice of legislative prayer we approved in *Marsh* v. *Chambers*, * * * and it seems to be on par with the inclusion of a creche or a menorah in a "Holiday" display that incorporates other secular symbols * * *. The parallels between this case and *Marsh* and *Lynch* [see Text, p. 1093] are sufficiently compelling that they ought to decide this case, even under the Court's misguided Establishment Clause jurisprudence. * * *

* * *

For the foregoing reasons, I would reverse the judgment of the Court of Appeals.

VAN ORDEN V. PERRY
Supreme Court of the United States, 2005
455 U.S. —, 125 S.Ct. 2796, — L.Ed.2d —

BACKGROUND & FACTS Among the 21 historical markers and monuments surrounding the state capitol building in Austin, Texas, is a six-foot by three-and-a-half-foot monolith inscribed with the Ten Commandments. The monument was donated by the Fraternal Order of Eagles. Thomas Van Orden, regularly encountered the monument on his trips to and from the state law library located nearby. Van Orden sued Governor Rick Perry, seeking both a declaration that display of the monument on state grounds violated the Establishment Clause and an order requiring its removal. A federal district court ruled for the state and held that the state had a legitimate secular purpose in recognizing the Eagles for their work in reducing juvenile delinquency and that, given the history, purpose, and context of the monument, a reasonable observer would not conclude it endorsed religion. After a federal appellate court affirmed the judgment, Van Orden successfully sought certiorari from the Supreme Court.

Chief Justice REHNQUIST announced the judgment of the Court and delivered an opinion, in which Justice SCALIA, Justice KENNEDY, and Justice THOMAS join.

The question here is whether the Establishment Clause of the First Amendment allows the display of a monument inscribed with the Ten Commandments on the Texas State Capitol grounds. * * *

* * *

[We must] neither abdicate our responsibility to maintain a division between church and state nor evince a hostility to religion by disabling the government from in some ways recognizing our religious heritage * * *.

* * *

Whatever may be the fate of the *Lemon* test in the larger scheme of Establishment Clause jurisprudence, we think it not useful in dealing with the sort of passive monument that Texas has erected on its Capitol grounds. Instead, our analysis is driven both by the nature of the monument and by our Nation's history.

* * *

In this case we are faced with a display of the Ten Commandments on government property outside the Texas State Capitol. Such acknowledgments of the role played by the Ten Commandments in our Nation's heritage are common throughout America. We need only look within our own Courtroom. Since 1935, Moses has stood, holding two tablets that reveal portions of the Ten Commandments written in Hebrew, among other lawgivers in the south frieze. Representations of the Ten Commandments adorn the metal gates lining the north and south sides of the Courtroom as well as the doors leading into the Courtroom. Moses also sits on the exterior east facade of the building holding the Ten Commandments tablets.

Similar acknowledgments can be seen throughout a visitor's tour of our Nation's Capital. * * *

Of course, the Ten Commandments are religious—they were so viewed at their inception and so remain. * * * [But] [s]imply having religious content or promoting a message consistent with a religious doctrine does not run afoul of the Establishment Clause. * * *

There are, of course, limits to the display of religious messages or symbols. For example, we held unconstitutional a Kentucky statute requiring the posting of the Ten Commandments in every public schoolroom. Stone v. Graham, 449 U.S. 39, 101 S.Ct. 192(1980). In the classroom context, we found that the Kentucky statute had an improper and plainly religious purpose. * * * As evidenced by *Stone*'s almost exclusive reliance upon two of our school prayer cases, * * * (citing School Dist. of Abington Township v. Schempp, 374 U.S. 203, 83 S.Ct. 1560 (1963), and Engel v. Vitale, 370 U.S. 421, 82 S.Ct. 1261 (1962)), it stands as an example of the fact that we have "been particularly vigilant in monitoring compliance with the Establishment Clause in elementary and secondary schools," Edwards v. Aguillard, 482 U.S. 578, 583-584, 107 S.Ct. 2573 (1987). * * * Indeed, *Edwards* v. *Aguillard* recognized that Stone—along with *Schempp* and *Engel*—was a consequence of the "particular concerns that arise in the context of public elementary and secondary schools." * * * Neither *Stone* itself nor subsequent opinions have indicated that *Stone* 's holding would extend to a legislative chamber * * * or to capitol grounds.

The placement of the Ten Commandments monument on the Texas State Capitol grounds is a far more passive use of those texts than was the case in *Stone*, where the text confronted elementary school students every day. Indeed, Van Orden * * * apparently walked by the monument for a number of years before bringing this lawsuit. The monument is therefore also quite different from the prayers involved in *Schempp* and Lee v. Weisman [505 U.S. 577, 112 S.Ct. 2649 (1992]. Texas has treated her Capitol grounds monuments as representing the several strands in the State's political and legal history. The inclusion of the Ten Commandments monument in this group has a dual significance, partaking of both religion and government. We cannot say that Texas' display of this monument violates the Establishment Clause of the First Amendment.

The judgment of the Court of Appeals is affirmed.

* * *

Justice THOMAS, concurring.

* * *

There is no question that, based on the original meaning of the Establishment Clause, the Ten Commandments display at issue here is constitutional. In no sense does Texas compel petitioner Van Orden to do anything. The only injury to him is that he takes offense at seeing the monument as he passes it on his way to the Texas Supreme Court Library. He need not stop to read it or even to look at it, let alone to express support for it or adopt the Commandments as guides for his life. The mere presence of the monument along his path involves no coercion and thus does not violate the Establishment Clause.

Returning to the original meaning [of the Establishment Clause] would do more than simplify our task. It also would avoid the pitfalls present in the Court's current approach to such challenges. * * *

* * *

First, this Court's precedent permits even the slightest public recognition of religion to constitute an establishment of religion. * * *

Second, in a seeming attempt to balance out its willingness to consider almost any acknowledgment of religion an establishment, in other cases Members of this Court have concluded that the term or symbol at issue has no religious meaning by virtue of its ubiquity or rote ceremonial invocation. * * *

* * *

This analysis is not fully satisfying to either nonadherents or adherents. For the nonadherent, who may well be more sensitive than the hypothetical "reasonable observer," or who may not know all the facts, this test fails to capture completely the honest and deeply felt offense he takes from the government conduct. For the adherent, this analysis takes no account of the message sent by removal of the sign or display, which may well appear to him to be an act hostile to his religious faith. The Court's foray into religious meaning either gives insufficient weight to the views of nonadherents and adherents alike, or it provides no principled way to choose between those views. In sum, this Court's effort to assess religious meaning is fraught with futility.

Finally, the very "flexibility" of this Court's Establishment Clause precedent leaves it incapable of consistent application. * * *

The unintelligibility of this Court's precedent raises the further concern that, either in appearance or in fact, adjudication of Establishment Clause challenges turns on judicial predilections. * * * The outcome of constitutional cases ought to rest on firmer grounds than the personal preferences of judges.

Much, if not all, of this would be avoided if the Court would return to the views of the Framers and adopt coercion as the touchstone for our Establishment Clause inquiry. Every acknowledgment of religion would not give rise to an Establishment Clause claim. Courts would not act as theological commissions, judging the meaning of religious matters. Most important, our precedent would be capable of consistent and coherent application. While the Court correctly rejects the challenge to the Ten Commandments monument on the Texas Capitol grounds, a more fundamental rethinking of our Establishment Clause jurisprudence remains in order.

Justice BREYER, concurring in the judgment.

* * *

* * * The government must avoid excessive interference with, or promotion of, religion. * * * But the Establishment Clause does not compel the government to purge from the public sphere all that in any way partakes of the religious. * * * Such absolutism is not only inconsistent with our national traditions * * * but would also tend

to promote the kind of social conflict the Establishment Clause seeks to avoid.

* * *

If the relation between government and religion is one of separation, but not of mutual hostility and suspicion, one will inevitably find difficult borderline cases. And in such cases, I see no test-related substitute for the exercise of legal judgment. * * * That judgment is not a personal judgment. Rather, as in all constitutional cases, it must reflect and remain faithful to the underlying purposes of the Clauses, and it must take account of context and consequences measured in light of those purposes. While the Court's prior tests provide useful guideposts—and might well lead to the same result the Court reaches today * * *—no exact formula can dictate a resolution to such fact-intensive cases.

The case before us is a borderline case. * * * On the one hand, the Commandments' text undeniably has a religious message, invoking, indeed emphasizing, the Diety. On the other hand, focusing on the text of the Commandments alone cannot conclusively resolve this case. Rather, to determine the message that the text here conveys, we must examine how the text is *used*. And that inquiry requires us to consider the context of the display.

In certain contexts, a display of the tablets of the Ten Commandments can convey not simply a religious message but also a secular moral message (about proper standards of social conduct). And in certain contexts, a display of the tablets can also convey a historical message (about a historic relation between those standards and the law)—a fact that helps to explain the display of those tablets in dozens of courthouses throughout the Nation, including the Supreme Court of the United States. * * *

Here the tablets have been used as part of a display that communicates not simply a religious message, but a secular message as well. The circumstances surrounding the display's placement on the capitol grounds and its physical setting suggest that the State itself intended the latter, nonreligious aspects of the tablets' message to predominate. And the monument's 40-year history on the Texas state grounds indicates that that has been its effect.

The group that donated the monument, the Fraternal Order of Eagles, a private civic (and primarily secular) organization * * * sought to highlight the Commandments' role in shaping civic morality as part of that organization's efforts to combat juvenile delinquency. * * * The Eagles' consultation with a committee composed of members of several faiths in order to find a nonsectarian text underscores the group's ethics-based motives. * * * The tablets, as displayed on the monument, prominently acknowledge that the Eagles donated the display, a factor which, though not sufficient, thereby further distances the State itself from the religious aspect of the Commandments' message.

The physical setting of the monument, moreover, suggests little or nothing of the sacred. * * * The monument sits in a large park containing 17 monuments and 21 historical markers, all designed to illustrate the "ideals" of those who settled in Texas and of those who have lived there since that time. * * * The setting does not readily lend itself to meditation or any other religious activity. But it does provide a context of history and moral ideals. * * *

*** As far as I can tell, 40 years passed in which the presence of this monument, legally speaking, went unchallenged ***. And I am not aware of any evidence suggesting that this was due to a climate of intimidation. *** Those 40 years suggest that the public visiting the capitol grounds has considered the religious aspect of the tablets' message as part of what is a broader moral and historical message reflective of a cultural heritage.

*** The display is not on the grounds of a public school, where, given the impressionability of the young, government must exercise particular care in separating church and state. This case also differs from *McCreary County,* where the short (and stormy) history of the courthouse Commandments' displays demonstrates the substantially religious objectives of those who mounted them, and the effect of this readily apparent objective upon those who view them. *** [I]n today's world, in a Nation of so many different religious and comparable nonreligious fundamental beliefs, a more contemporary state effort to focus attention upon a religious text is certainly likely to prove divisive in a way that this longstanding, pre-existing monument has not.

***

Justice STEVENS, with whom Justice GINSBURG joins, dissenting.

The sole function of the monument on the grounds of Texas' State Capitol is to display the full text of one version of the Ten Commandments. The monument is not a work of art and does not refer to any event in the history of the State. It is significant because, and only because, it communicates *** [a religious] message ***.

Viewed on its face, Texas' display has no purported connection to God's role in the formation of Texas or the founding of our Nation; nor does it provide the reasonable observer with any basis to guess that it was erected to honor any individual or organization. The message transmitted by Texas' chosen display is quite plain: This State endorses the divine code of the "Judeo-Christian" God.

***

This case *** is not about historic preservation or the mere recognition of religion. The issue is obfuscated rather than clarified by simplistic commentary on the various ways in which religion has played a role in American life *** and by the recitation of the many extant governmental "acknowledgments" of the role the Ten Commandments played in our Nation's heritage. *** [T]he mere compilation of religious symbols, none of which includes the full text of the Commandments and all of which are exhibited in different settings, has only marginal relevance to the question presented in this case.

The monolith displayed on Texas Capitol grounds cannot be discounted as a passive acknowledgment of religion, nor can the State's refusal to remove it upon objection be explained as a simple desire to preserve a historic relic. This Nation's resolute commitment to neutrality with respect to religion is flatly inconsistent with the plurality's wholehearted validation of an official state endorsement of the message that there is one, and only one, God.

***

Though the State of Texas may genuinely wish to combat juvenile delinquency, and may rightly want to honor the Eagles for their efforts, it cannot effectuate these admirable purposes through an explicitly religious medium. * * *

* * *

The principle that guides my analysis is neutrality. * * * I recognize that the requirement that government must remain neutral between religion and irreligion would have seemed foreign to some of the Framers; so too would a requirement of neutrality between Jews and Christians. * * * The evil of discriminating today against atheists, "polytheists[,] and believers in unconcerned deities," * * * is in my view a direct descendent of the evil of discriminating among Christian sects. The Establishment Clause thus forbids it and, in turn, forbids Texas from displaying the Ten Commandments monument the plurality so casually affirms.

* * *

Justice O'CONNOR, dissenting.

For essentially the reasons given * * * [in Justice SOUTER's dissenting opinion], as well as the reasons given in my concurrence in *McCreary County v. American Civil Liberties Union of Ky.* I respectfully dissent.

Justice SOUTER, with whom Justice STEVENS and Justice GINSBURG join, dissenting.

* * *

[As we said about the posting of the Ten Commandments in] Stone v. Graham, 449 U.S. 39, 41-42, 101 S.Ct. 192 (1980)[:] "The pre-eminent purpose for posting the Ten Commandments on schoolroom walls is plainly religious in nature. The Ten Commandments are undeniably a sacred text in the Jewish and Christian faiths, and no legislative recitation of a supposed secular purpose can blind us to that fact. The Commandments do not confine themselves to arguably secular matters, such as honoring one's parents, killing or murder, adultery, stealing, false witness, and covetousness. Rather, the first part of the Commandments concerns the religious duties of believers: worshipping the Lord God alone, avoiding idolatry, not using the Lord's name in vain, and observing the Sabbath Day." * * *

[A] pedestrian happening upon the monument at issue here needs no training in religious doctrine to realize that the statement of the Commandments, quoting God himself, proclaims that the will of the divine being is the source of obligation to obey the rules, including the facially secular ones. In this case, moreover, the text is presented to give particular prominence to the Commandments' first sectarian reference, "I am the Lord thy God." That proclamation is centered on the stone and written in slightly larger letters than the subsequent recitation. To ensure that the religious nature of the monument is clear to even the most casual passerby, the word "Lord" appears in all capital letters (as does the word "am"), so that the most eye-catching segment of the quotation is the declaration "I AM the LORD thy God." * * * What follows, of course, are the rules against other gods, graven images, vain swearing, and Sabbath breaking. * * *

To drive the religious point home, and identify the message as religious to any viewer who failed to read the text, the engraved quotation is framed by religious symbols: two tablets with what appears to be ancient script on them, two Stars of David, and the superimposed Greek letters Chi and Rho as the familiar monogram of Christ. Nothing on the monument, in fact, detracts from its religious nature * * *. It would therefore be difficult to miss the point that the government of Texas is telling everyone who sees the monument to live up to a moral code because God requires it, with both code and conception of God being rightly understood as the inheritances specifically of Jews and Christians. * * *

* * *

* * * Texas * * * says that the Capitol grounds are like a museum for a collection of exhibits, the kind of setting that several Members of the Court have said can render the exhibition of religious artifacts permissible, even though in other circumstances their display would be seen as meant to convey a religious message forbidden to the State. * * *

But 17 monuments with no common appearance, history, or esthetic role scattered over 22 acres is not a museum, and anyone strolling around the lawn would surely take each memorial on its own terms without any dawning sense that some purpose held the miscellany together more coherently than fortuity and the edge of the grass. One monument expresses admiration for pioneer women. One pays respect to the fighters of World War II. And one quotes the God of Abraham whose command is the sanction for moral law. The themes are individual grit, patriotic courage, and God as the source of Jewish and Christian morality; there is no common denominator. * * *

When the plurality * * * confront[s] *Stone*, it tries to avoid the case's obvious applicability by limiting its holding to the classroom setting. * * * But *Stone* * * * [did nothing of the sort]. [T]he schoolroom was beside the point * * * and that is presumably why the *Stone* Court failed to discuss the educational setting, as other opinions had done when school was significant. * * * *Stone* did not, for example, speak of children's impressionability or their captivity as an audience in a school class. * * * Accordingly, our numerous prior discussions of *Stone* have never treated its holding as restricted to the classroom.

Nor can the plurality deflect *Stone* by calling the Texas monument "a far more passive use of [the Decalogue] than was the case in *Stone*, where the text confronted elementary school students every day." * * * Placing a monument on the ground is not more "passive" than hanging a sheet of paper on a wall when both contain the same text to be read by anyone who looks at it. The problem in *Stone* was simply that the State was putting the Commandments there to be seen, just as the monument's inscription is there for those who walk by it.

* * *

[T]he State's argument * * * seems to be that 40 years without a challenge shows that as a factual matter the religious expression is too tepid to provoke a serious reaction and constitute a violation. Perhaps, but the writer of Exodus chapter 20 was not lukewarm, and other explanations may do better in accounting for the late resort to the courts. Suing a State over religion puts nothing in a plaintiff's pocket and can take a great deal out, and even with volunteer litigators to supply time and energy, the risk of social ostracism can be powerfully deterrent. I doubt that a slow walk to the courthouse, even one that took 40 years, is much evidentiary help in applying the Establishment Clause.

I would reverse the judgment of the Court of Appeals.

In another of a series of anti-court actions taken by the House of Representatives during the Spring of 2005, it approved an amendment to the 2006 appropriations bill for the Department of Justice that directed the withholding of any funds to enforce a ruling by the U.S. District Court for the Southern District of Indiana that a Ten Commandments monument be removed from the county courthouse. Congressional Quarterly Weekly Report, June 20, 2005, p. 1664. The case is *Russelburg v. Gibson County*. The vote to adopt the amendment was 242-182. As *Marbury v. Madison* makes clear, an amendment of this sort is patently unconstitutional since it directly interferes with "the province and duty of the judicial department, to say what the law is." See Text at pp. 10-11.

▶ Insert at p. 1060 following the first paragraph

Two years later, the Supreme Court reversed the judgment of the appeals court in Elk Grove Unified School District v. Newdow, 542 U.S. 1, 124 S.Ct. 2301 (2004). A majority of the Justices did not reach the merits of the Establishment Clause claim, but instead voted to overturn the decision below on grounds Newdow lacked standing to sue. Speaking for the Court, Justice Stevens pointed out that, under California law, although Newdow and his former wife shared custody of their daughter, the mother "'makes the final decisions if the two . . . disagree.'" The mother did not share Newdow's religious views and did not support his constitutional challenge. As Justice Stevens explained, Newdow may have the "right to instruct his daughter in his religious views," but that was a far cry from the "ambitious" claim made here: "He wishes to forestall his daughter's exposure to religious ideas that her mother, who wields a form of veto power, endorses, and to use his parental status to challenge the influences to which his daughter may be exposed in school when he and [his former wife] disagree." The interests implicated in this case were "not merely Newdow's interest in inculcating his child with his views on religion, but also the rights of the child's mother as a parent generally" and "specifically" because of her state-recognized veto power. Moreover, this case "implicates the interests of a young child who finds herself at the center of a highly public debate over her custody, the propriety of a widespread national ritual, and the meaning of our Constitution." In light of these other interests and the extensiveness of Newdow's claim, the Court held that he lacked "prudential standing to bring this suit in federal court." "Prudential standing," Justice Stevens explained, was different from "Article III standing, which enforces the Constitution's case and controversy requirement." Prudential standing "embodies 'judicially self-imposed limits on the exercise of federal jurisdiction'" and cited the principles articulated by Justice Brandeis in his *Ashwander* opinion (see Text, p. 58). "It is improper for the federal courts to entertain a claim by a plaintiff whose standing to sue is founded on family law rights that are in dispute when prosecution of the lawsuit may have an adverse effect on the person who is the source of the plaintiff's claimed standing. When hard questions of domestic relations are sure to affect the outcome, the prudent course is for the federal court to stay its hand rather than reach out to resolve a weighty question of federal constitutional law."

Chief Justice Rehnquist and Justices O'Connor and Thomas thought the majority's sidestepping of the constitutional issue by invoking prudential standing was "novel" and unconvincing. They concluded that the phrase "under God" in the Pledge did not violate the Establishment Clause. Many events "strongly suggest that our national culture allows public recognition of our Nation's religious history and character[,]" including "[o]ur Court Marshal's [daily] opening proclamation [that the Supreme Court is now in session] [which] concludes with the words, 'God Save the United States and this honorable Court.'" Speaking for the trio, the Chief Justice continued, "I do not believe that the phrase 'under God' in the Pledge converts its recital into a 'religious exercise' of the sort described in *Lee v. [Weisman*, see Text, p. 1050]." Instead, it is a declaration of belief in allegiance and loyalty to the United States flag and the Republic that it represents. The phrase 'under God' is in no sense a prayer, nor an endorsement of any religion * * *. Reciting the Pledge, or listening to others recite it, is a patriotic exercise, not a religious one; participants promise fidelity to our flag and our Nation, not to any particular God, faith, or church."

Also concurring only in the judgment and completely agreeing with the Chief Justice, Justice O'Connor added that she saw no coercion either. Terming the recitation of "under God" in the Pledge an act of "ceremonial deism," she found it "a minimal reference to religion." She explained: "Any coercion that persuades an onlooker to participate in an act of ceremonial deism is inconsequential, as an Establishment Clause matter, because such acts are simply not religious in character. As a result, symbolic references to religion that qualify as instances of ceremonial deism will pass the coercion test as well as the endorsement test. This is not to say, however, that government could *overtly* coerce a person to participate in an act of ceremonial deism. Our cardinal freedom is one of belief; leaders in this Nation cannot force us to proclaim our allegiance to *any* creed, whether it be religious, philosophic, or political. That principle found eloquent expression in a case involving the Pledge itself, even before it contained the words to which respondent now objects. See *West Virginia Bd. of Ed. v. Barnette* [see Text, p. 858] (Jackson, J.). The compulsion of which Justice Jackson was concerned [there], however, was of the direct sort—the Constitution does not guarantee citizens a right entirely to avoid ideas with which they disagree. It would betray its own principles if it did; no robust democracy insulates its citizens from views that they might find novel or even inflammatory." Justice Scalia did not participate in the hearing or decision of this case. See p. 1 of this Supplement.

The *Lemon* Test and Financial Aid to Religion

▶ Insert at p. 1088 following the first paragraph of text

In the wake of its ruling upholding the constitutionality of school vouchers in *Zelman v. Simmons-Harris*, the Court went on to decide the "next question" identified in the Text—whether a state constitutional provision that prohibited the spending of public funds to aid religious institutions, practices, or instruction violated the First Amendment. In relevant part, Washington's state constitution reads as follows: "No public money or property shall be appropriated or applied to any religious worship, exercise, or instruction, or the support of any religious establishment." At issue was the denial of benefits under the state's "Promise Scholars" program (a program of state aid helping talented and needy students) to Davey, who was a student pursuing a degree in theology and whose career goal was pastoral ministry. Although he met the academic and financial requirements for scholarship funding, the state denied benefits because the Washington constitution prohibited aiding religion. Davey argued that denial of benefits on grounds of religion amounted to viewpoint discrimination in violation of the First Amendment and abridged the free exercise of religious belief. In Locke v. Davey, 540 U.S. 712, 124 S.Ct. 1307 (2004), the Supreme Court upheld the state ban.

Speaking for seven Justices, Chief Justice Rehnquist observed that "there are some state actions permitted by the Establishment Clause but not required by the Free Exercise Clause." This degree of latitude he described as the "play in the joints" of the two Religion Clauses. He explained that, under *Simmons-Harris*, "the link between government funds and religious training is broken by the independent and private choice of recipients. * * * As such, there is no doubt that the State could, consistent with the Federal Constitution, *permit* Promise Scholars to pursue a degree in devotional theology * * *." [Emphasis supplied.] The question in this case, however, was whether Washington could *prohibit* public funding of religious instruction without violating the Free Exercise Clause.

Unlike the ordinance struck down in *Church of the Lukumi Babalu Aye, Inc. v. Hialeah* (see Text, p. 1120), which "made it a crime to engage in certain kinds of animal slaughter" with the aim of "suppress[ing] ritualistic animal sacrifices of the Santeria religion," Washington's "disfavor of religion (if it can be called that) is of a far milder kind. It imposes neither criminal nor civil sanctions on any type of religious service or rite. * * * And it does not require students to choose between their religious belief and securing a government benefit. * * * The State has chosen merely to fund a distinct category of instruction." Chief Justice Rehnquist continued: "Even though the * * * Washington Constitution draws a more stringent line than that drawn by the United States Constitution, the interest it seeks to protect is scarcely novel. In fact, we can think of few interests in which a State's antiestablishment interests come more into play. Since the founding of our country, there have been popular uprisings against procuring taxpayer funds to support church leaders, which was one of the hallmarks of an 'established religion.'" He concluded: "The State's interest in not funding the pursuit of devotional degrees is satisfied and the exclusion of such funding places a relatively minor burden on Promise Scholars. If any room exists between the two Religion Clauses, it must be here." Justices Scalia and Thomas dissented. They were of the view that the Court's decision "sustain[ed] a public benefits program that facially discriminate[d] against religion."

B. THE FREE EXERCISE OF RELIGIOUS BELIEF

▶ Insert at p. 1122 following the last paragraph

Although the Religious Freedom Restoration Act, which mandates strict scrutiny in free exercise cases, is inapplicable to the states (for the reasons set out in *City of Boerne v. Flores*, see Text,

p. 119), it still applies to limit legislation passed by Congress. The Supreme Court has granted cert. to consider again the issue raised in *Employment Division, Department of Human Resources of Oregon v. Smith* (see Text, p. 1115), namely whether laws that ban the use of drugs can survive strict scrutiny against a claim of religious freedom by someone who ingests them as part of an act of worship. In O Centro Espirita Beneficiente Uniao Do Vegetal v. Ashcroft, 342 F.3d 1170 (10th Cir. 2003, *affirmed*, 389 F.3d 1084 (10th Cir. en banc, 2004), *cert. granted sub. nom.*, Gonzales v. O Centro Espirita Beneficiente Uniao Do Vegetal, 544 U.S. —, 125 S.Ct. 1846 (2005), a divided federal appeals panel, and then the Tenth Circuit by a vote of 8-5 sitting en banc, held that enforcement of the federal Controlled Substances Act did not present a compelling interest that outweighed the religious claims of a small sect to use hoasca (a tea made from plants that grow in the Amazon jungle region of Brazil) which contains elements regulated by the law. The 130-member group sought an injunction against the U.S. attorney general to block the federal government's seizure and ban on the importation of the tea.

CHAPTER 14

EQUAL PROTECTION OF THE LAWS

A. RACIAL DISCRIMINATION

Proving Discriminatory Intent

▶ **Insert at p. 1165 following the first paragraph of text**

To trigger *Batson*'s requirement that the prosecution defend its use of peremptory challenges by race-neutral criteria, the defendant must first make out a *prima facie* case that would permit the judge to infer that the government removed black jurors because of their race. In Johnson v. California, 545 U.S. —, 125 S.Ct. 2410 (2005), the Court by a 8-1 vote rejected the state's requirement that the defendant could be required to show it was "more likely than not" that the prosecution had engaged in purposeful racial discrimination. The Court held the defendant need only present a plausible case of racial discrimination to force the state to justify its strategy in jury selection, not that it show the probabilities favored the conclusion there was bias.

In the second case decided during its October 2004 Term, Miller-El v. Dretke, 545 U.S. —, 125 S.Ct. 2317 (2005), the Court for the second time set aside the death penalty imposed on a black defendant who was convicted of the murder of a motel clerk in a robbery 20 years earlier. In a 6-3 decision, the Court held there was clear and convincing evidence that the prosecution had intentionally used its peremptories to produce a racially-stacked jury by striking 10 of 11 blacks who participated in the voir dire. African-Americans, the Court found, had been much more aggressively questioned about their views on the death penalty, and the jury pool had been shuffled at least twice by the prosecution to increase the probability that whites would be selected. That is, as black jurors moved to the very front of the pool of qualified jurors to be examined, the prosecution twice rearranged the order in which jurors would be seated and questioned. In a concurring opinion, Justice Breyer cited with approval Justice Marshall's view, voiced in *Batson* two decades earlier, that the only way to "end the racial discrimination that peremptories inject into the jury-selection process" is to "eliminat[e] peremptory challenges entirely." Justice Thomas dissented in both cases; he was joined by Chief Justice Rehnquist and Justice Scalia in *Miller-El*.

Affirmative Action or "Reverse Discrimination"

▸ Insert at p. 1168 following the footnote

At the conclusion of its October 2002 Term, the Court decided both University of Michigan cases described in the footnote. The issues before the Court were: (1) whether academic institutions could further the goal of student body diversity by taking race into account in making admissions decisions; and, if so (2) whether the admissions policies used by the law school and the College of Literature, Science, and Arts at the University of Michigan were constitutional means for achieving that objective. Although Justice Powell's opinion in *Regents of the University of California* v. *Bakke*, which had responded positively to the first of these questions, provided the basis on which many contemporary affirmative actions plans operated at colleges and universities, it had been joined by no other member of the Court; it spoke only for Justice Powell. At bottom, then, was the question whether Justice Powell's position was valid law. In the *Grutter* and *Gratz* cases, which follow, a majority of the current Justices adopted Justice Powell's view as their own but reached different conclusions about the constitutionality of the two Michigan programs.

GRUTTER V. BOLLINGER
Supreme Court of the United States, 2003
539 U.S. 306, 123 S.Ct. 2325, 156 L.Ed.2d 304

BACKGROUND & FACTS   Encouraged by Justice Powell's view in the *Bakke case* that race could regarded as a "plus" for a candidate in making admissions decisions, the University of Michigan Law School sought to achieve diversity in its student body by looking beyond students' grades and performance on the Law School Admissions Test (LSAT) and taking into an applicant's race and Hispanic or Native American background. In reviewing the files of applicants for admission, the law school considered other "soft variables" as well, such as recommenders' enthusiasm, the quality of the undergraduate institution, the applicant's essay, and the areas and difficulty of the applicant's undergraduate major. The factors of race and ethnicity, therefore, were not in themselves decisive, but were considered along with many other variables in making admissions decisions.

After Barbara Grutter, a white female applicant with a 3.8 grade point average and a 161 LSAT score, was denied admission, she sued Lee Bollinger, the president of the University of Michigan, challenging the law school's policy as a violation of the Equal Protection Clause because it considered race as a factor. A federal district court agreed and found the law school's use of race as a factor in admissions unconstitutional. A federal appellate court reversed, citing Justice Powell's *Bakke* opinion as binding precedent. In the appeals court's view, the law school's approach was consistent with Justice Powell's position because race was simply a "potential 'plus' factor" and because its use of race was narrowly-tailored to achieve the objective of diversity.

Justice O'CONNOR delivered the opinion of the Court.

This case requires us to decide whether the use of race as a factor in student admissions by the University of Michigan Law School is unlawful.

* * *

In the wake of our fractured decision in *Bakke,* courts have struggled to discern whether Justice Powell's diversity rationale, set forth in part of the opinion joined by no other Justice, is nonetheless binding * * *.

[T]oday we endorse Justice Powell's view that student body diversity is a compelling state interest that can justify the use of race in university admissions.

* * *

Context matters when reviewing race-based governmental action under the Equal Protection Clause. * * * Not every decision influenced by race is equally objectionable and strict scrutiny is designed to provide a framework for carefully examining the importance and the sincerity of the reasons advanced by the governmental decisionmaker for the use of race in that particular context.

* * *

[S]ome language in * * * [past] opinions might be read to suggest that remedying past discrimination is the only permissible justification for race-based governmental action. See, e.g., Richmond v. J.A. Croson Co., 488 U.S., at 493, 109 S.Ct. 706 (1989) * * *. But we have never held that the only governmental use of race that can survive strict scrutiny is remedying past discrimination. * * *

The Law School's educational judgment that such diversity is essential to its educational mission is one to which we defer. * * * Our scrutiny of the interest asserted by the Law School is no less strict for taking into account complex educational judgments in an area that lies primarily within the expertise of the university. Our holding today is in keeping with our tradition of giving a degree of deference to a university's academic decisions, within constitutionally prescribed limits. * * *

* * * Our conclusion that the Law School has a compelling interest in a diverse student body is informed by our view that attaining a diverse student body is at the heart of the Law School's proper institutional mission, and that "good faith" on the part of a university is "presumed" absent "a showing to the contrary." * * *

As part of its goal of "assembling a class that is both exceptionally academically qualified and broadly diverse," the Law School seeks to "enroll a 'critical mass' of minority students." Brief for Respondents Bollinger et al. 13. The Law School's interest is not simply "to assure within its student body some specified percentage of a particular group merely because of its race or ethnic origin." *Bakke,* 438 U.S., at 307, 98 S.Ct. 2733 (opinion of Powell, J.). That would amount to outright racial balancing, which is patently unconstitutional. * * * Rather, the Law School's concept of critical mass is defined by reference to the educational benefits that diversity is designed to produce.

* * * As the District Court emphasized, the Law School's admissions policy promotes "cross-racial understanding," helps to break down racial stereotypes, and "enables

[students] to better understand persons of different races." * * * These benefits are "important and laudable," because "classroom discussion is livelier, more spirited, and simply more enlightening and interesting" when the students have "the greatest possible variety of backgrounds." * * *

* * * In addition to the expert studies and reports entered into evidence at trial, numerous studies show that student body diversity promotes learning outcomes, and "better prepares students for an increasingly diverse workforce and society, and better prepares them as professionals." * * *

These benefits are not theoretical but real, as major American businesses have made clear that the skills needed in today's increasingly global marketplace can only be developed through exposure to widely diverse people, cultures, ideas, and viewpoints. * * *

We have repeatedly acknowledged the overriding importance of preparing students for work and citizenship, describing education as pivotal * * *. Effective participation by members of all racial and ethnic groups in the civic life of our Nation is essential if the dream of one Nation, indivisible, is to be realized.

Moreover, universities, and in particular, law schools, represent the training ground for a large number of our Nation's leaders. * * *

In order to cultivate a set of leaders with legitimacy in the eyes of the citizenry, it is necessary that the path to leadership be visibly open to talented and qualified individuals of every race and ethnicity. All members of our heterogeneous society must have confidence in the openness and integrity of the educational institutions that provide this training. * * * Access to legal education (and thus the legal profession) must be inclusive of talented and qualified individuals of every race and ethnicity, so that all members of our heterogeneous society may participate in the educational institutions that provide the training and education necessary to succeed in America.

The Law School does not premise its need for critical mass on "any belief that minority students always (or even consistently) express some characteristic minority viewpoint on any issue." * * * To the contrary, diminishing the force of such stereotypes is both a crucial part of the Law School's mission, and one that it cannot accomplish with only token numbers of minority students. Just as growing up in a particular region or having particular professional experiences is likely to affect an individual's views, so too is one's own, unique experience of being a racial minority in a society, like our own, in which race unfortunately still matters. The Law School has determined, based on its experience and expertise, that a "critical mass" of underrepresented minorities is necessary to further its compelling interest in securing the educational benefits of a diverse student body.

* * *

[U]niversities cannot establish quotas for members of certain racial groups or put members of those groups on separate admissions tracks. * * * Nor can universities insulate applicants who belong to certain racial or ethnic groups from the competition for admission. * * * Universities can, however, consider race or ethnicity more flexibly as a "plus" factor in the context of individualized consideration of each and every applicant. * * *

We are satisfied that the Law School's admissions program * * * does not operate as a quota. Properly understood, a "quota" is a program in which a certain fixed number or proportion of opportunities are "reserved exclusively for certain minority groups." * * * Quotas "'impose a fixed number or percentage which must be attained, or which cannot be exceeded,'" * * * and "insulate the individual from comparison with all other candidates for the available seats." * * * In contrast, "a permissible goal ... require[s] only a good-faith effort ... to come within a range demarcated by the goal itself" * * * and permits consideration of race as a "plus" factor in any given case while still ensuring that each candidate "compete[s] with all other qualified applicants" * * *.

* * *

That a race-conscious admissions program does not operate as a quota does not, by itself, satisfy the requirement of individualized consideration. When using race as a "plus" factor in university admissions, a university's admissions program must remain flexible enough to ensure that each applicant is evaluated as an individual and not in a way that makes an applicant's race or ethnicity the defining feature of his or her application. The importance of this individualized consideration in the context of a race-conscious admissions program is paramount. * * *

Here, the Law School engages in a highly individualized, holistic review of each applicant's file, giving serious consideration to all the ways an applicant might contribute to a diverse educational environment. The Law School affords this individualized consideration to applicants of all races. There is no policy, either *de jure* or *de facto*, of automatic acceptance or rejection based on any single "soft" variable. Unlike the program at issue in *Gratz* v. *Bollinger*, * * * the Law School awards no mechanical, predetermined diversity "bonuses" based on race or ethnicity. * * * [T]he Law School's admissions policy "is flexible enough to consider all pertinent elements of diversity in light of the particular qualifications of each applicant, and to place them on the same footing for consideration, although not necessarily according them the same weight." * * *

* * *

* * * The Law School frequently accepts nonminority applicants with grades and test scores lower than underrepresented minority applicants (and other nonminority applicants) who are rejected. * * * This shows that the Law School seriously weighs many other diversity factors besides race that can make a real and dispositive difference for nonminority applicants as well. By this flexible approach, the Law School sufficiently takes into account, in practice as well as in theory, a wide variety of characteristics besides race and ethnicity that contribute to a diverse student body. * * *

* * *

We are mindful, however, that "[a] core purpose of the Fourteenth Amendment was to do away with all governmentally imposed discrimination based on race." Palmore v. Sidoti, 466 U.S. 429, 432, 104 S.Ct. 1879 (1984). Accordingly, race-conscious admissions policies must be limited in time. This requirement reflects that racial classifications, however compelling their goals, are potentially so dangerous that they may be employed no more broadly than the interest demands. Enshrining a permanent justification for racial preferences would offend this fundamental equal protection principle. We see no reason to exempt race-conscious admissions programs from the requirement that all governmental use of race must have a logical end point. * * *

In the context of higher education, the durational requirement can be met by sunset provisions in race-conscious admissions policies and periodic reviews to determine whether racial preferences are still necessary to achieve student body diversity. * * *

* * *

We take the Law School at its word that it would "like nothing better than to find a race-neutral admissions formula" and will terminate its race-conscious admissions program as soon as practicable. * * * It has been 25 years since Justice Powell first approved the use of race to further an interest in student body diversity in the context of public higher education. Since that time, the number of minority applicants with high grades and test scores has indeed increased. * * * We expect that 25 years from now, the use of racial preferences will no longer be necessary to further the interest approved today.

[T]he Equal Protection Clause does not prohibit the Law School's narrowly tailored use of race in admissions decisions to further a compelling interest in obtaining the educational benefits that flow from a diverse student body. * * * The judgment of the Court of Appeals for the Sixth Circuit, accordingly, is affirmed.

* * *

Justice THOMAS, with whom Justice SCALIA joins[,] dissenting * * *.

* * *

* * * I believe what lies beneath the Court's decision today are the benighted notions that one can tell when racial discrimination benefits (rather than hurts) minority groups, * * * and that racial discrimination is necessary to remedy general societal ills. This Court's precedents supposedly settled both issues, but clearly the majority still cannot commit to the principle that racial classifications are *per se* harmful and that almost no amount of benefit in the eye of the beholder can justify such classifications.

Putting aside what I take to be the Court's implicit rejection of *Adarand*'s holding that beneficial and burdensome racial classifications are equally invalid, I must contest the notion that the Law School's discrimination benefits those admitted as a result of it. * * * [N]owhere in any of the filings in this Court is any evidence that the purported "beneficiaries" of this racial discrimination prove themselves by performing at (or even near) the same level as those students who receive no preferences. * * *

* * * The Law School is not looking for those students who, despite a lower LSAT score or undergraduate grade point average, will succeed in the study of law. The Law School seeks only a facade—it is sufficient that the class looks right, even if it does not perform right.

The Law School tantalizes unprepared

students with the promise of a University of Michigan degree and all of the opportunities that it offers. These overmatched students take the bait, only to find that they cannot succeed in the cauldron of competition. And this mismatch crisis is not restricted to elite institutions. * * * Indeed, to cover the tracks of the aestheticists, this cruel farce of racial discrimination must continue—in selection for the Michigan Law Review, * * * and in hiring at law firms and for judicial clerkships—until the "beneficiaries" are no longer tolerated. While these students may graduate with law degrees, there is no evidence that they have received a qualitatively better legal education (or become better lawyers) than if they had gone to a less "elite" law school for which they were better prepared. And the aestheticists will never address the real problems facing "underrepresented minorities," instead continuing their social experiments on other people's children.

Beyond the harm the Law School's racial discrimination visits upon its test subjects, no social science has disproved the notion that this discrimination "engender[s] attitudes of superiority or, alternatively, provoke[s] resentment among those who believe that they have been wronged by the government's use of race." *Adarand*, 515 U.S., at 241, 115 S.Ct. 2097 (THOMAS, J., concurring in part and concurring in judgment). "These programs stamp minorities with a badge of inferiority and may cause them to develop dependencies or to adopt an attitude that they are 'entitled' to preferences." * * *

It is uncontested that each year, the Law School admits a handful of blacks who would be admitted in the absence of racial discrimination. * * * Who can differentiate between those who belong and those who do not? The majority of blacks are admitted to the Law School because of discrimination, and because of this policy all are tarred as undeserving. This problem of stigma does not depend on * * * whether those stigmatized are actually the "beneficiaries" of racial discrimination. When blacks take positions in the highest places of government, industry, or academia, it is an open question today whether their skin color played a part in their advancement. The question itself is the stigma—because either racial discrimination did play a role, in which case the person may be deemed "otherwise unqualified," or it did not, in which case asking the question itself unfairly marks those blacks who would succeed without discrimination. * * *

* * *

Chief Justice REHNQUIST, with whom Justice SCALIA, Justice KENNEDY, and Justice THOMAS join, dissenting.

* * *

Although the Court recites the language of our strict scrutiny analysis, its application of that review is unprecedented in its deference.

Respondents' asserted justification for the Law School's use of race in the admissions process is "obtaining 'the educational benefits that flow from a diverse student body.'" * * *

In practice, the Law School's program bears little or no relation to its asserted goal of achieving "critical mass." Respondents explain that the Law School seeks to accumulate a "critical mass" of *each* underrepresented minority group. * * * But the record demonstrates that the Law School's admissions practices with respect to these groups differ dramatically and cannot be defended under any consistent use of the term "critical mass."

From 1995 through 2000, the Law School admitted between 1,130 and 1,310 students. Of those, between 13 and 19 were Native American, between 91 and 108 were African-Americans, and between 47 and 56 were Hispanic. If the Law School is admitting between 91 and 108 African-Americans in order to achieve "critical mass," thereby preventing African-American students from feeling "isolated or like spokespersons for their race," one would think that a number of the same order of magnitude would be necessary to accomplish the same purpose for Hispanics and Native Americans. Similarly, even if all of the Native American applicants admitted in a given year matriculate, which the record demonstrates is not at all the case, how can this possibly constitute a "critical mass" of Native Americans in a class of over 350 students? In order for this pattern of admission to be consistent with the Law School's explanation of "critical mass," one would have to believe that the objectives of "critical mass" offered by respondents are achieved with only half the number of Hispanics and one-sixth the number of Native Americans as compared to African-Americans. But respondents offer no race-specific reasons for such disparities. Instead, they simply emphasize the importance of achieving "critical mass," without any explanation of why that concept is applied differently among the three underrepresented minority groups.

These different numbers, moreover, come only as a result of substantially different treatment among the three underrepresented minority groups, as is apparent in an example offered by the Law School and highlighted by the Court: The school asserts that it "frequently accepts nonminority applicants with grades and test scores lower than underrepresented minority applicants (and other nonminority applicants) who are rejected." * * * Specifically, the Law School states that "[s]ixty-nine minority applicants were rejected between 1995 and 2000 with at least a 3.5 [Grade Point Average] and a [score of] 159 or higher on the [Law School Admissions Test]" while a number of Caucasian and Asian-American applicants with similar or lower scores were admitted. * * *

Review of the record reveals only 67 such individuals. Of these 67 individuals, 56 were Hispanic, while only 6 were African-American, and only 5 were Native American. This discrepancy reflects a consistent practice. For example, in 2000, 12 Hispanics who scored between a 159-160 on the LSAT and earned a GPA of 3.00 or higher applied for admission and only 2 were admitted. * * * Meanwhile, 12 African-Americans in the same range of qualifications applied for admission and all 12 were admitted. * * * Likewise, that same year, 16 Hispanics who scored between a 151-153 on the LSAT and earned a 3.00 or higher applied for admission and only 1 of those applicants was admitted. * * * Twenty-three similarly qualified African-Americans applied for admission and 14 were admitted. * * *

* * * Respondents have *never* offered any race-specific arguments explaining why significantly more individuals from one underrepresented minority group are needed in order to achieve "critical mass" or further student body diversity. They certainly have not explained why Hispanics, who they have said are among "the groups most isolated by racial barriers in our country," should have

their admission capped out in this manner. * * *

* * *

[T]he Law School has managed its admissions program, not to achieve a "critical mass," but to extend offers of admission to members of selected minority groups in proportion to their statistical representation in the applicant pool. But this is precisely the type of racial balancing that the Court itself calls "patently unconstitutional." * * *

Finally, I believe that the Law School's program fails strict scrutiny because it is devoid of any reasonably precise time limit on the Law School's use of race in admissions. * * * Our previous cases have required some limit on the duration of programs such as this because discrimination on the basis of race is invidious.

The Court suggests a possible 25-year limitation on the Law School's current program. * * * Respondents, on the other hand, remain more ambiguous, explaining that "the Law School of course recognizes that race-conscious programs must have reasonable durational limits, and the Sixth Circuit properly found such a limit in the Law School's resolve to cease considering race when genuine race-neutral alternatives become available." * * * These discussions of a time limit are the vaguest of assurances. In truth, they permit the Law School's use of racial preferences on a seemingly permanent basis. Thus, an important component of strict scrutiny—that a program be limited in time—is casually subverted.

* * *

Justice KENNEDY, dissenting.

* * *

* * * The majority [also] fails to confront the reality of how the Law School's admissions policy is implemented. * * *

About 80 to 85 percent of the places in the entering class are given to applicants in the upper range of Law School Admissions Test scores and grades. An applicant with these credentials likely will be admitted without consideration of race or ethnicity. With respect to the remaining 15 to 20 percent of the seats, race is likely outcome determinative for many members of minority groups. That is where the competition becomes tight and where any given applicant's chance of admission is far smaller if he or she lacks minority status. At this point the numerical concept of critical mass has the real potential to compromise individual review.

* * * There was little deviation among admitted minority students during the years from 1995 to 1998. The percentage of enrolled minorities fluctuated only by 0.3%, from 13.5% to 13.8%. The number of minority students to whom offers were extended varied by just a slightly greater magnitude of 2.2%, from the high of 15.6% in 1995 to the low of 13.4% in 1998.

* * *

The narrow fluctuation band raises an inference that the Law School subverted individual determination, and strict scrutiny requires the Law School to overcome the inference. Whether the objective of critical mass "is described as a quota or a goal, it is a line drawn on the basis of race and ethnic status," and so risks compromising individual assessment. * * *

* * *

* * * The admissions officers consulted * * * daily reports which indicated the composition of the incoming class along racial lines. * * * These reports would "track exactly where [the Law School] st[ood] at any given time in assembling the class," and so would tell the admissions personnel whether they were short of assembling a critical mass of minority students. * * *

The consultation of daily reports during the last stages in the admissions process suggests there was no further attempt at individual review save for race itself. The admissions officers could use the reports to recalibrate the plus factor given to race depending on how close they were to achieving the Law School's goal of critical mass. The bonus factor of race would then become divorced from individual review; it would be premised instead on the numerical objective set by the Law School.

The Law School made no effort to guard against this danger. It provided no guidelines to its admissions personnel on how to reconcile individual assessment with the directive to admit a critical mass of minority students. The admissions program could have been structured to eliminate at least some of the risk that the promise of individual evaluation was not being kept. * * *

To be constitutional, a university's compelling interest in a diverse student body must be achieved by a system where individual assessment is safeguarded through the entire process. There is no constitutional objection to the goal of considering race as one modest factor among many others to achieve diversity, but an educational institution must ensure, through sufficient procedures, that each applicant receives individual consideration and that race does not become a predominant factor in the admissions decisionmaking. The Law School failed to comply with this requirement, and by no means has it carried its burden to show otherwise by the test of strict scrutiny.

* * *

GRATZ V. BOLLINGER
Supreme Court of the United States, 2003
539 U.S. 244, 123 S.Ct. 2411, 156 L.Ed.2d 257

BACKGROUND & FACTS Jennifer Gratz and Patrick Hamicher, both white Michigan residents, applied for admission to the University of Michigan's College of Literature, Science, and Arts (LSA). Both were denied admission and challenged the constitutionality of the university's program which considers a number of factors in making such decisions: high school grades, scores on standardized tests, quality of high school, curriculum strength, geography, alumni relationships, leadership, and race. The LSA considered African-Americans, Hispanics, and Native Americans to be "underrepresented minorities" and admitted virtually every qualified applicant in these groups. Each applicant was rated on a 150-point scale. In order to guarantee admission, an applicant had to score at least 100 points. An applicant from one of the under-represented minorities was automatically awarded 20 points.

Gratz and Hamacher sued Lee Bollinger, the president of the University of Michigan, for damages resulting from the alleged unlawful use of race in making its decisions and to enjoin the university from using race or ethnicity in future admissions decisionmaking. Both Gratz and Hamicher accepted admission offers from other state educational institutions before their applications were rejected by the LSA. Although it concluded—consistent with Justice Powell's opinion in the *Bakke* case—that diversity of the student body constituted a compelling interest, the federal district court found that the university's practice in 1995-1998 of awarding 20 points solely on the basis of race or ethnicity amounted to the use of a racial quota, was not narrowly tailored to achieving that objective, and therefore violated the Equal Protection Clause of the Fourteenth Amendment; but that its less rigid and predetermined policy of taking race and ethnicity into account after that did not violate the Constitution. Although the U.S. Court of Appeals for the Sixth Circuit upheld the use of race and ethnicity as a factor in law school admissions in *Grutter v. Bollinger*, it had not rendered judgment before the United State Supreme Court granted certiorari in this case as well.

Chief Justice REHNQUIST delivered the opinion of the Court.

* * *

* * * Petitioners * * * argue that "diversity as a basis for employing racial preferences is simply too open-ended, ill-defined, and indefinite to constitute a compelling interest capable of supporting narrowly-tailored means." * * * But for the reasons set forth today in *Grutter v. Bollinger*, * * * the Court has rejected these arguments of petitioners.

Petitioners alternatively argue that even if the University's interest in diversity can constitute a compelling state interest, the District Court erroneously concluded that the University's use of race in its current freshman admissions policy is narrowly tailored to achieve such an interest. * * *

* * *

Justice Powell's opinion in *Bakke* emphasized the importance of considering each particular applicant as an individual, assessing all of the qualities that individual possesses, and in turn, evaluating that individual's ability to contribute to the unique setting of higher education. The admissions program Justice Powell described, however, did not contemplate that any single characteristic automatically ensured a specific and identifiable contribution to a university's diversity. * * *

The current LSA policy does not provide such individualized consideration. The LSA's policy automatically distributes 20 points to every single applicant from an "underrepresented minority" group, as defined by the University. The only consideration that accompanies this distribution of points is a factual review of an application to determine whether an individual is a member of one of these minority groups. Moreover, unlike Justice Powell's example, where the race of a "particular black applicant" could be considered without being decisive, * * * the LSA's automatic distribution of 20 points has the effect of making "the factor of race ... decisive" for virtually every minimally qualified underrepresented minority applicant. * * *

Also instructive in our consideration of the LSA's system is the example provided in the description of the Harvard College Admissions Program, which Justice Powell both discussed in, and attached to, his opinion in *Bakke*. * * * It provided as follows: "The Admissions Committee, with only a few places left to fill, might find itself forced to choose between A, the child of a successful black physician in an academic community with promise of superior academic performance, and B, a black who grew up in an inner-city ghetto of semi-literate parents whose academic achievement was lower but who had demonstrated energy and leadership as well as an apparently abiding interest in black power. If a good number of black students much like A but few like B had already been admitted, the Committee might prefer B; and vice versa. If C, a white student with extraordinary artistic talent, were also seeking one of the remaining places, his unique quality might give him an edge over both A and B. Thus, the critical criteria are often individual qualities or experience *not dependent upon race but sometimes associated with it.*" * * *

This example further demonstrates the problematic nature of the LSA's admissions system. Even if student C's "extraordinary artistic talent" rivaled that of Monet or Picasso, the applicant would receive, at most, five points under the LSA's system. * * * At the same time, every single underrepresented minority applicant, including students A and B, would automatically receive 20 points for submitting an application. Clearly, the LSA's system does not offer applicants the individualized selection process described in Harvard's example. Instead of considering how the differing backgrounds, experiences, and characteristics of students A, B, and C might benefit the University, admissions counselors reviewing LSA applications would simply award both A and B 20 points because their applications indicate that they are African-American, and student C would receive up to 5 points for his "extraordinary talent."

Respondents emphasize the fact that the LSA has created the possibility of an applicant's file being flagged for individualized consideration * * * [but this] only emphasizes the flaws of the University's system as a whole when compared to that described by Justice Powell. * * * First, student A would never be flagged. * * * [E]very applicant like student A would simply be admitted.

It is possible that students B and C would be flagged and considered as individuals * * * [but] only * * * *after* admissions counselors automatically distribute the University's version of a "plus" that makes race a decisive factor for virtually every minimally qualified underrepresented minority applicant.

* * *

We conclude * * * that because the University's use of race in its current freshman admissions policy is not narrowly tailored to achieve respondents' asserted compelling interest in diversity, the admissions policy violates the Equal Protection Clause of the Fourteenth Amendment. * * * Accordingly, we reverse that portion of the District Court's decision granting respondents summary judgment with respect to liability and remand the case for proceedings consistent with this opinion.

It is so ordered.

Justice O'CONNOR, concurring.

* * * The law school considers the various diversity qualifications of each applicant, including race, on a case-by-case basis. See *Grutter v. Bollinger*. By contrast, the Office of Undergraduate Admissions relies on the selection index to assign *every* underrepresented minority applicant the same, *automatic* 20-point bonus without consideration of the particular background, experiences, or qualities of each individual applicant. * * * And this mechanized selection index score, by and large, automatically determines the admissions decision for each applicant. * * *

* * * The University, of course, remains free to modify its system so that it * * * [becomes an individualized, nonmechanical] one. * * *

* * *

Justice BREYER, concurring in the judgment.

I concur in the judgment of the Court though I do not join its opinion. I join Justice O'CONNOR'S opinion except insofar as it joins that of the Court. I join Part I of Justice GINSBURG'S dissenting opinion, but I do not dissent from the Court's reversal of the District Court's decision. * * *

Justice STEVENS, with whom Justice SOUTER joins, dissenting.

Petitioners seek forward-looking relief enjoining the University of Michigan from continuing to use its current race-conscious freshman admissions policy. Yet unlike the plaintiff in *Grutter v. Bollinger*, * * * the petitioners in this case had already enrolled at other schools before they filed their class-action complaint in this case. Neither petitioner was in the process of reapplying to Michigan through the freshman admissions process at the time this suit was filed, and neither has done so since. There is a total absence of evidence that either petitioner would receive any benefit from the prospective relief sought by their lawyer. While some unidentified members of the class may very well have standing to seek prospective relief, it is clear that neither petitioner does. Our precedents therefore require dismissal of the action.

* * *

Both Hamacher and Gratz, of course, have standing to seek damages as compensation for the alleged wrongful denial of their respective applications under Michigan's old freshman admissions system. * * * [but] petitioners' past injuries do not give them standing to obtain injunctive relief to protect third parties from similar harms. * * *

* * *

Justice SOUTER, with whom Justice GINSBURG joins as to Part II, dissenting.

I agree with Justice STEVENS * * * [but]

because a majority of the Court has chosen to address the merits, * * * I would dissent from the Court's judgment.

* * *

II

* * *

The plan here * * * lets all applicants compete for all places and values an applicant's offering for any place not only on grounds of race, but on grades, test scores, strength of high school, quality of course of study, residence, alumni relationships, leadership, personal character, socio-economic disadvantage, athletic ability, and quality of a personal essay. * * * A nonminority applicant who scores highly in these other categories can readily garner a selection index exceeding that of a minority applicant who gets the 20-point bonus. * * *

* * *

* * * Nonminority students may receive 20 points for athletic ability, socioeconomic disadvantage, attendance at a socioeconomically disadvantaged or predominantly minority high school, or at the Provost's discretion; they may also receive 10 points for being residents of Michigan, 6 for residence in an underrepresented Michigan county, 5 for leadership and service, and so on.

* * *

The very nature of a college's permissible practice of awarding value to racial diversity means that race must be considered in a way that increases some applicants' chances for admission. Since college admission is not left entirely to inarticulate intuition, it is hard to see what is inappropriate in assigning some stated value to a relevant characteristic, whether it be reasoning ability, writing style, running speed, or minority race. Justice Powell's plus factors necessarily are assigned some values. The college simply does by a numbered scale what the law school accomplishes in its "holistic review"[;] * * * the distinction does not imply that applicants to the undergraduate college are denied individualized consideration or a fair chance to compete on the basis of all the various merits their applications may disclose.

* * * The present record obviously shows that nonminority applicants may achieve higher selection point totals than minority applicants owing to characteristics other than race, and the fact that the university admits "virtually every qualified under-represented minority applicant," * * * may reflect nothing more than the likelihood that very few qualified minority applicants apply, * * * as well as the possibility that self-selection results in a strong minority applicant pool. It suffices for me, as it did for the District Court, that there are no *Bakke*-like set-asides and that consideration of an applicant's whole spectrum of ability is no more ruled out by giving 20 points for race than by giving the same points for athletic ability or socioeconomic disadvantage.

Any argument that the "tailoring" amounts to a set-aside, then, boils down to the claim that a plus factor of 20 points makes some observers suspicious, where a factor of 10 points might not. But suspicion does not carry petitioners' ultimate burden of persuasion in this constitutional challenge, * * * and it surely does not warrant condemning the college's admissions scheme on this record. *

* *

* * *

[T]he United States contends that Michigan could get student diversity in satisfaction of its compelling interest by guaranteeing admission to a fixed percentage of the top students from each high school in Michigan. * * *

[But] "percentage plans" are just as race conscious as the point scheme (and fairly so), but they get their racially diverse results without saying directly what they are doing or why they are doing it. In contrast, Michigan states its purpose directly and, if this were a doubtful case for me, I would be tempted to give Michigan an extra point of its own for its frankness. Equal protection cannot become an exercise in which the winners are the ones who hide the ball.

* * *

Justice GINSBURG, with whom Justice SOUTER joins [as to Part I], dissenting.

I

Educational institutions, the Court acknowledges, are not barred from any and all consideration of race when making admissions decisions. * * * But the Court once again maintains that the same standard of review controls judicial inspection of all official race classifications. * * * This insistence on "consistency" * * * would be fitting were our Nation free of the vestiges of rank discrimination long reinforced by law * * *. But we are not far distant from an overtly discriminatory past, and the effects of centuries of law-sanctioned inequality remain painfully evident in our communities and schools.

* * *

The Constitution instructs all who act for the government that they may not "deny to any person ... the equal protection of the laws." * * * In implementing this equality instruction, * * * government decision-makers may properly distinguish between policies of exclusion and inclusion. * * * Actions designed to burden groups long denied full citizenship stature are not sensibly ranked with measures taken to hasten the day when entrenched discrimination and its after effects have been extirpated. * * *

Our jurisprudence ranks race a "suspect" category, "not because [race] is inevitably an impermissible classification, but because it is one which usually, to our national shame, has been drawn for the purpose of maintaining racial inequality." * * * But where race is considered "for the purpose of achieving equality," * * * no automatic proscription is in order. For * * * "[t]he Constitution is both color blind and color conscious. To avoid conflict with the equal protection clause, a classification that denies a benefit, causes harm, or imposes a burden must not be based on race. In that sense, the Constitution is color blind. But the Constitution is color conscious to prevent discrimination being perpetuated and to undo the effects of past discrimination." United States v. Jefferson County Bd. of Ed., 372 F.2d 836, 876 (C.A.5 1966) (Wisdom, J.) * * *.

* * *

II

Examining in this light the admissions policy employed by the University of Michigan's College of Literature, Science, and the Arts, and for the reasons well stated by Justice SOUTER, I see no constitutional infirmity. * * *

* * *

B. "PRIVATE" DISCRIMINATION AND THE CONCEPT OF "STATE ACTION"

Private Discrimination and First Amendment Issues

▶ **Insert at p. 1208 following *Boy Scouts of America* v. *Dale***

In a case that presents the flipside of the question posed in *Boy Scouts of America* v. *Dale*, the Supreme Court has voted to grant cert. to consider whether the so-called Solomon Amendment adopted by Congress in 1994, violates the First Amendment. The Solomon Amendment, 10 U.S.C.A. § 983, requires that federal funds be shut off to any institution of higher education that denies military representatives access for recruiting purposes. Law schools adopted an across-the-board policy of withholding placement services from employers who discriminate against job applicants on the basis of race, ethnicity, national origin, religion, gender disability, age, and sexual orientation. Since the military excludes openly gay and lesbian individuals, branches of the U.S. military fell within the scope of those employers affected by the law school anti-discrimination policy. The law schools argued that the Solomon Amendment violates the First Amendment by compelling law schools to express support for a policy of discrimination with which they disagree. A divided federal appeals court struck down the Solomon Amendment in Forum for Academic and Institutional Rights v. Rumsfeld, 390 F.3d 219 (3rd Cir. 2004), *cert. granted*, 544 U.S. —, 125 S.Ct. 1977 (2005). The case is docketed for argument at the Court's upcoming October 2005 Term. See also the lower court decision in Burt v. Rumsfeld, 354 F.Supp.2d 156 (D.Conn. 2005).

C. VOTING RIGHTS AND ELECTORAL DISCRIMINATION

Voting Rights and Constitutional Access to the Ballot

▶ **Insert at p. 1220 following the note on Closed and Blanket Primaries**

But, as a majority of the Justices later ruled in Clingman v. Beaver, 544 U.S. —, 125 S.Ct. 2029 (2005), state regulation of party primaries need not always trigger strict scrutiny, even though plaintiffs may argue that their associational rights have been curtailed by the legislation. Oklahoma has a semi-closed primary system which limits participation to voters registered as members of that political party and to voters registered as Independents. Voters who are registered members of other political parties are excluded. In this case, the plaintiffs were the Libertarian Party of Oklahoma and registered voters of two other political parties. Six Justices held that strict scrutiny applied only where First Amendment rights are "severely burdened." The Court concluded that Oklahoma's restriction on participating in party primaries was substantially less than that imposed by the Connecticut law challenged in the *Tashjian* case. The Justices found the minor burden on associational rights challenged in *Clingman* was justified by its advancement of the following interests: (1) preserving the integrity of political parties as viable and identifiable groups; (2) facilitating efforts at party-building and electioneering; and (3) guarding against "party raiding" ("the organized switching of blocs of voters from one party to another in order to manipulate the outcome of the other party's primary election") and "sore loser" candidacies by rejected primary contenders.

In dissent, Justices Stevens, Souter, and Ginsburg, argued that "[t]he Court's decision * * * diminishes the value of two important rights protected by the First Amendment: the individual citizen's right to vote for the candidate of her choice and a political party's right to define its own mission." He continued, "The importance of vindicating that individual right far outweighs any public interest in punishing registered Republicans or Democrats for acts of disloyalty." He concluded: "[T]he Court focuses on interests that are not legitimate. States do not have a valid interest in manipulating the outcome of elections, in protecting the major parties from competition, or in stunting the growth of new parties. While States do have a valid interest in conducting orderly elections and in encouraging the maximum participation of voters, neither of these interests overrides (or, indeed, even conflicts with) the valid interests of both the [Libertarian Party] and the voters who wish to participate in its primary."

D. MALAPPORTIONMENT

▶ Insert at p. 1244 following note on *Davis* v. *Bandemer*

In Vieth v. Jubelirer, 541 U.S. 267, 124 S.Ct. 1769 (2004), the Supreme Court came within one vote of overruling *Davis v. Bandemer*. After what it called "18 years of fruitless litigation" during which the Justices attempted to define unconstitutional political gerrymandering, a plurality (Chief Justice Rehnquist and Justices O'Connor, Scalia, and Thomas) concluded that such cases presented a "political question" and were inherently nonjusticiable. In their view, no manageable judicial standard could ever be identified that would distinguish political gerrymandering that overstepped the constitutional line from district line-drawing that did not. In *Vieth*, some Pennsylvania Democratic voters brought suit challenging the congressional redistricting plan passed by the Republican-controlled legislature that did a particularly effective job of advantaging Republican candidates for the state's seats in the U.S. House.

Previously, in *Bandemer*, the Court had splintered over the test to be applied if a political gerrymander was unconstitutional. Although it conceded such occasions would be rare, it nonetheless said that it was possible partisan line-drawing could be so egregious as to deprive a victimized political minority of equal protection of the laws. The four dissenters in *Vieth* (Justices Stevens, Souter, Ginsburg, and Breyer) said that was still so, gave some examples, and repeated that a tell-tale sign was the bizarre shape of any legislative district not plausibly justifiable on a basis (for example, recognizing jurisdictional lines of local government) other than that of political exploitation.

Justice Kennedy, who cast the deciding vote, found the issue as it was presented in *Vieth* nonjusticiable, but was unwilling to slam the door on all suits challenging political gerrymanders in the future. However, unlike the dissenters, he was unprepared to identify the conditions under which plaintiffs in such suits might prevail; he only wanted to leave the door open. Presenting a caricature of Justice Kennedy's position, Justice Scalia (speaking for the plurality) wrote: "Justice Kennedy's opinion boils down to this: 'As presently advised, I know of no discernible and manageable standard that can render this claim justiciable. I am unhappy about that, and hope I will be able to change my opinion in the future.' What are the lower courts to make of this pronouncement?"

Republican attempts to strengthen their control over the U.S. House of Representatives also took the form of mid-decade redistricting. Although Colorado and Texas had their congressional boundary lines drawn after the 2000 census, Republicans gaining control of the state legislatures there in 2002 enacted new laws gerrymandering the seats to their considerable advantage. The new Colorado scheme was struck down by the state supreme court on grounds the state constitution permitted redistricting only once a decade. The effort to get the U.S. Supreme Court to review the Colorado Supreme Court's decision failed. Colorado General Assembly v. Salazar, 79 P.3d 1221 (Colo. en banc, 2003), *cert. denied*, 542 U.S. 1093, 124 S.Ct. 2228 (2004). Chief Justices Rehnquist and Justices Scalia and Thomas voted to grant review. Review in the case challenging the redistricting of Texas's House seats is still pending. In Session v. Perry, 298 F.Supp.2d 451 (E.D.Tex. 2004), a three-judge federal district court upheld the constitutionality of the new reapportionment, concluding that it violated neither the Elections nor the Census Clauses of Art. I, § 4 nor the federal statute requiring the creation of congressional districts in every state entitled to more than one representative. The court also held that the gerrymander did not violate either the Equal Protection Clause nor provisions of the Voting Rights Act. The U.S. Supreme Court vacated judgment in the case and remanded for further consideration in light of *Vieth*. 543 U.S. —, 125 S.Ct. 351, 352 (2004)

The Court took a somewhat different posture in summarily affirming a federal district court decision throwing out a congressional redistricting plan in Georgia passed by the Democrat-controlled legislature that favored the election of that party's candidates and disfavored Republicans. See Larios v. Cox, 300 F.Supp.2d 1320 (N.D.Ga. 2004), *affirmed*, 542 U.S. —, 124 S.Ct. 2806 (2004). Although the variance among districts was within the 10% "safe harbor" the Court identified in its previous reapportionment cases, the Court nonetheless agreed with the lower court that the scheme disclosed two unconstitutional reasons for population variance: (1) "a deliberate and systematic policy of favoring rural and inner-city interests at the expense of suburban areas north, east, and west of Atlanta"; and (2) "an intentional effort to allow incumbent Democrats to maintain or increase their delegation, primarily by systematically underpopulating the districts held by incumbent Democrats, by overpopulating those of Republicans, and by deliberately pairing numerous

Republican incumbents against one another." Justice Scalia, dissenting alone, wrote: "It is not obvious to me that a legislature goes too far when it stays within the 10% disparity in population our cases allow. To say that it does is to invite allegations of political motivation whenever there is population disparity, and thus to destroy the 10% safe harbor our cases provide. Ferreting out political motives in minute population deviations seems to me more likely to encourage politically motivated litigation than to vindicate political rights."

E. ECONOMIC AND SOCIAL DISCRIMINATION

Gender

▶ **Insert at p. 1284 in the fourth paragraph following the third sentence**

Moreover, indirect—as well as direct—victims of sex discrimination are entitled to relief under the law. Title IX of the Education Amendments of 1972, of course, clearly authorizes legal actions by those who are direct targets of sex discrimination, but in Jackson v. Birmingham Board of Education, 544 U.S. —, 125 S.Ct. 1497 (2005), the Supreme Court held that a third party—a whistle-blower—may have a legitimate cause of action. Jackson was the girls' basketball coach at a public high school. He repeatedly complained to his superiors that the girls' team was not receiving equal funding or access to equipment and facilities. Retaliation by the school district against him, the Court held, was an intentional act furthering the very sort of discrimination the law was designed to prohibit.

Age

▶ **Insert at p. 1301 following *Massachusetts Board of Retirement* v. *Murgia***

The statute challenged in *Murgia* intended to discriminate on the basis of age and, the Court held, for a good enough reason. But what about a state policy that has the effect of treating people differently along age lines, but which did not plainly have that intent? Could this constitute prohibited age discrimination? The answer is "yes," according to the Supreme Court's recent decision in Smith v. City of Jackson, 544 U.S. —125 S.Ct. 1536 (2005). In this case, several police officers in Jackson, Mississippi, argued that salary increases they received from the city in 1999 violated the Age Discrimination in Employment Act of 1967 (ADEA) because officers over the age of 40 were treated much less generously than younger officers. A plurality of the Justices held that, like discrimination based on race, color, religion, sex, or national origin—all prohibited by Title VII of the 1964 Civiol Rights Act—claims of age discrimination based on a policy's differential impact alone can constitute a legitimate grounds for a suit under the ADEA. But the ADEA's coverage is narrower because it permits "otherwise prohibited" actions "if the adverse impact was attributable to a nonage factor that was 'reasonable.'" Here, it was reasonable for the city to give higher raises to employees with less seniority and position—younger officers—because it reasonably advanced the city's legitimate goal of retaining those officers by bringing their salaries into line with salaries paid by surrounding communities.

Sexual Preference

▶ **Insert at p. 1315 following the note on Same-Sex Marriage**

GOODRIDGE V. DEPARTMENT OF PUBLIC HEALTH
Supreme Judicial Court of Massachusetts, 2003
440 Mass. 309, 798 N.E.2d 941

BACKGROUND & FACTS Several gay and lesbian applicants sued the Massachusetts Department of Public Health challenging its policy and practice of denying marriage licenses to same-sex couples in accordance with the General Laws of Massachusetts, chapter 207. The plaintiffs argued that this violated the equal protection and due process guarantees of the state constitution. The trial judge found in the department's favor on the constitutional questions. Hillary Goodridge and others bringing the suit then appealed to the state's highest court.

Present: MARSHALL, C.J., GREANEY, IRELAND, SPINA, COWIN, SOSMAN, & CORDY, JJ.

MARSHALL, C.J.

* * *

Although the plaintiffs refer in passing to "the marriage statutes," they focus, quite properly, on G.L. c. 207, the marriage licensing statute, which controls entry into civil marriage. * * *

* * *

* * * The everyday meaning of "marriage" is "[t]he legal union of a man and woman as husband and wife," Black's Law Dictionary 986 (7th ed.1999), and the plaintiffs do not argue that the term "marriage" has ever had a different meaning under Massachusetts law. * * * [A]s used in G.L. c. 207, * * * [this definition captures the legislature's] intent to hew to the term's common-law * * * meaning concerning the genders of the marriage partners.

* * *

* * *Does [government action that bars same sex couples from civil marriage] offend the [Massachusetts'] Constitution's guarantees of equality before the law? Or do the liberty and due process provisions of the Massachusetts Constitution secure the plaintiffs' right to marry their chosen partner? In matters implicating marriage, family life, and the upbringing of children, the two constitutional concepts frequently overlap, as they do here. * * * [As was the case in] *Bolling v. Sharpe*, [see Text, p. 1136] * * *[,] [m]uch of what we say concerning one standard applies to the other.

* * *

In a real sense, there are three partners to every civil marriage: two willing spouses and an approving State. * * * While only the parties can mutually assent to marriage, the terms of the marriage—who may marry and what obligations, benefits, and liabilities attach to civil marriage—are set by the Commonwealth. Conversely, while only the parties can agree to end the marriage (absent the death of one of them or a marriage void ab initio), the Commonwealth defines the exit terms. * * *

* * *

* * * Civil marriage is at once a deeply personal commitment to another human being and a highly public celebration of the ideals of mutuality, companionship, intimacy, fidelity, and family. * * * Because it fulfils yearnings for security, safe haven, and connection that express our common humanity, civil marriage is an esteemed institution, and the decision whether and whom to marry is among life's momentous acts of self-definition.

Tangible as well as intangible benefits flow from marriage. The marriage license grants valuable property rights to those who meet the entry requirements, and who agree to what might otherwise be a burdensome degree of government regulation of their activities. * * *

* * *

Exclusive marital benefits that are not directly tied to property rights include the presumptions of legitimacy and parentage of children born to a married couple * * * and evidentiary rights, such as the prohibition against spouses testifying against one another about their private conversations, applicable in both civil and criminal cases * * *. Other statutory benefits of a personal nature available only to married individuals include qualification for bereavement or medical leave to care for individuals related by blood or marriage[,] * * * an automatic "family member" preference to make medical decisions for an incompetent or disabled spouse * * * [,] the application of predictable rules of child custody, visitation, support, and removal out-of-State when married parents divorce[,] * * * [and] priority rights to administer the estate of a deceased spouse who dies without a will * * *.

Where a married couple has children, their children are also * * * directly or indirectly * * * the recipients of the special legal and economic protections obtained by civil marriage. * * * [M]arital children reap a measure of family stability and economic security based on their parents' legally privileged status that is largely inaccessible, or not as readily accessible, to nonmarital children. Some of these benefits are social, such as the enhanced approval that still attends the status of being a marital child. Others are material, such as the greater ease of access to family-based State and Federal benefits that attend the presumptions of one's parentage.

It is undoubtedly for these concrete reasons, as well as for its intimately personal significance, that civil marriage has long been termed a "civil right." See, e.g., Loving v. Virginia, 388 U.S. 1, 12, 87 S.Ct. 1817 (1967) * * *.

Without the right to marry—or more properly, the right to choose to marry—one is excluded from the full range of human experience and denied full protection of the laws for one's "avowed commitment to an intimate and lasting human relationship." Baker v. State, 170 Vt. 194, 744 A.2d 864.

Because civil marriage is central to the lives of individuals and the welfare of the community, our laws assiduously protect the individual's right to marry against undue government incursion. * * *

* * * Individuals who have the choice to marry each other and nevertheless choose not to may properly be denied the legal benefits of marriage. * * * But that same logic cannot hold for a qualified individual who would marry if she or he only could.

For decades, indeed centuries, in much of this country (including Massachusetts) no lawful marriage was possible between white and black Americans. * * * *Loving* ma[de] [it] clear [that] the right to marry means little if it does not include the right to marry the person of one's choice, subject to appropriate government restrictions in the interests of public health, safety, and welfare. * * * [A]s in * * * *Loving*, a statute deprives individuals of access to an institution of fundamental legal, personal, and social significance—the institution of marriage—because of a single trait: skin color in *Loving*, sexual orientation here. As it did in * * * *Loving*, history must yield to a more fully developed understanding of the invidious quality of the discrimination.

The Massachusetts Constitution protects matters of personal liberty against government incursion as zealously, and often more so, than does the Federal Constitution, even where both Constitutions employ essentially the same language. * * * Fundamental to the vigor of our Federal system of government is that "state courts are absolutely free to interpret state constitutional provisions to accord greater protection to individual rights than do similar provisions of the United States Constitution." Arizona v. Evans, 514 U.S. 1, 8, 115 S.Ct. 1185 (1995).

The individual liberty and equality safeguards of the Massachusetts Constitution protect both "freedom from" unwarranted government intrusion into protected spheres of life and "freedom to" partake in benefits created by the State for the common good. * * * [C]hoosing whether and whom to marry would be hollow if the Commonwealth could, without sufficient justification, foreclose an individual from freely choosing the person with whom to share an exclusive commitment in the unique institution of civil marriage.

The Massachusetts Constitution requires, at a minimum, that the exercise of the State's regulatory authority not be "arbitrary or capricious." * * * [R]egulatory authority must, at very least, serve "a legitimate purpose in a rational way"; a statute must "bear a reasonable relation to a permissible legislative objective." * * * Any law failing to satisfy the basic standards of rationality is void.

* * *

The department argues that no fundamental right or "suspect" class is at issue here, and rational basis is the appropriate standard of review. * * * Because the statute does not survive rational basis review, we do not consider the plaintiffs' arguments that this case merits strict judicial scrutiny.

The department p[resents] three legislative rationales for prohibiting same-sex couples from marrying: (1) providing a "favorable setting for procreation"; (2) ensuring the optimal setting for child rearing, which the department defines as "a two-parent family with one parent of each sex"; and (3) preserving scarce State and private financial resources. * * *

The judge in the Superior Court endorsed the first rationale, holding that "the state's interest in regulating marriage is based on the traditional concept that marriage's primary purpose is procreation." This is incorrect. Our laws of civil marriage do not privilege procreative heterosexual intercourse between married people above every other form of adult intimacy and every other means of creating a family. General Laws c. 207 contains no requirement that the applicants for a marriage license attest to their ability or intention to conceive children by coitus. Fertility is not a condition of marriage, nor is it grounds for divorce. People who have never consummated their marriage, and never plan to, may be and stay married. * * * People who cannot stir from their deathbed may marry. * * *

Moreover, the Commonwealth affirmatively facilitates bringing children into a family regardless of whether the intended parent is married or unmarried, whether the child is adopted or born into a family, whether assistive technology was used to conceive the child, and whether the parent or her partner is heterosexual, homosexual, or bisexual. * * * The attempt to isolate procreation as "the source of a fundamental right to marry" * * * overlooks the integrated way in which courts have examined the complex and overlapping realms of personal autonomy, marriage, family life, and child rearing. * * *

The "marriage is procreation" argument singles out the one unbridgeable difference between same-sex and opposite-sex couples, and transforms that difference into the essence of legal marriage. Like "Amendment 2" to the Constitution of Colorado, which effectively denied homosexual persons equality under the law and full access to the political process, the marriage restriction impermissibly "identifies persons by a single trait and then denies them protection across the board." Romer v. Evans, 517 U.S. 620, 116 S.Ct. 1620 (1996). In so doing, the State's action confers an official stamp of approval on the destructive stereotype that same-sex relationships are inherently unstable and inferior to opposite-sex relationships and are not worthy of respect.

The department's * * * [second] rationale * * * [is] that confining marriage to opposite-sex couples ensures that children are raised in the "optimal" setting. Protecting the welfare of children is a paramount State policy. Restricting marriage to opposite-sex couples, however, cannot plausibly further this policy. "The demographic changes of the past century make it difficult to speak of an average American family. The composition of families varies greatly from household to household." Troxel v. Granville, 530 U.S. 57, 120 S.Ct. 2054 (2000). Massachusetts has responded supportively to "the changing realities of the American family," * * * and has moved vigorously to strengthen the modern family in its many variations. * * * Moreover, we have repudiated the common-law power of the State to provide varying levels of protection to children based on the circumstances of birth. * * *

The department has offered no evidence that forbidding marriage to people of the same sex will increase the number of couples choosing to enter into opposite-sex marriages in order to have and raise children. There is thus no rational relationship between the marriage statute and the Commonwealth's proffered goal of protecting the "optimal" child rearing unit. Moreover, the department readily concedes that people in same-sex couples may be "excellent" parents. These couples (including four of the plaintiff couples) have children for the reasons others do—to love them, to care for them, to nurture them. But the task of child rearing for same-sex couples is made infinitely harder by their status as outliers to the marriage laws. While establishing the parentage of children as soon as possible is crucial to the safety and welfare of children, * * * same-sex couples must undergo the sometimes lengthy and intrusive process of second-parent adoption to establish their joint parentage. While the enhanced income provided by marital benefits is an important source of security and stability for married couples and their children, those benefits are denied to families headed by same-sex couples. * * * While the laws of divorce provide clear and reasonably predictable guidelines for child support, child custody, and property division on dissolution of a marriage, same-sex couples who dissolve their relationships find themselves and their children in * * * highly unpredictable terrain * * *. Given the wide range of public benefits reserved only for married couples, we do not credit the department's contention that the absence of access to civil marriage amounts to little more than an inconvenience to same-sex couples and their children. * * *

* * *

In this case, we are confronted with an entire, sizeable class of parents raising children who have absolutely no access to civil marriage and its protections because they are forbidden from procuring a marriage license. It cannot be rational under our laws, and indeed it is not permitted, to penalize children by depriving them of State benefits because the State disapproves of their parents' sexual orientation.

The third rationale advanced by the department is that limiting marriage to opposite-sex couples furthers the Legislature's interest in conserving scarce State and private financial resources. The marriage restriction is rational, it argues, because the [legislature] logically could assume that same-sex couples are more financially independent than married couples and thus less needy of public marital benefits, such as tax advantages, or private marital benefits, such as employer-financed health plans that include spouses in their coverage.

An absolute statutory ban on same-sex marriage bears no rational relationship to the goal of economy. First, the department's conclusory generalization—that same-sex couples are less financially dependent on each other than opposite-sex couples—ignores that many same-sex couples, such as many of the plaintiffs in this case, have children and other dependents (here, aged parents) in their care. The department does not contend, nor could it, that these dependents are less needy or deserving than the dependents of married couples. Second, Massachusetts marriage laws do not condition receipt of public and private financial benefits to married individuals on a demonstration of financial dependence on each other; the benefits are available to married couples regardless of whether they mingle their finances or actually depend on each other for support.

* * *

* * * Recognizing the right of an individual to marry a person of the same sex will not diminish the validity or dignity of

opposite-sex marriage, any more than recognizing the right of an individual to marry a person of a different race devalues the marriage of a person who marries someone of her own race. If anything, extending civil marriage to same-sex couples reinforces the importance of marriage to individuals and communities. * * *

* * * The Massachusetts Constitution requires that legislation meet certain criteria and not extend beyond certain limits. It is the function of courts to determine whether these criteria are met and whether these limits are exceeded. In most instances, these limits are defined by whether a rational basis exists to conclude that legislation will bring about a rational result. The Legislature in the first instance, and the courts in the last instance, must ascertain whether such a rational basis exists. To label the court's role as usurping that of the Legislature * * * is to misunderstand the nature and purpose of judicial review. We owe great deference to the Legislature to decide social and policy issues, but it is the traditional and settled role of courts to decide constitutional issues.

* * * Alarms about the imminent erosion of the "natural" order of marriage were sounded over the demise of antimiscegenation laws, the expansion of the rights of married women, and the introduction of "no-fault" divorce. Marriage has survived all of these transformations, and we have no doubt that marriage will continue to be a vibrant and revered institution.

* * *

We construe civil marriage to mean the voluntary union of two persons as spouses, to the exclusion of all others. This reformulation redresses the plaintiffs' constitutional injury and furthers the aim of marriage to promote stable, exclusive relationships. It advances the two legitimate State interests the department has identified: providing a stable setting for child rearing and conserving State resources. It leaves intact the Legislature's broad discretion to regulate marriage. * * *

* * * [B]arring an individual from the protections, benefits, and obligations of civil marriage solely because that person would marry a person of the same sex violates the Massachusetts Constitution. We vacate the summary judgment for the department. We remand this case to the Superior Court for entry of judgment consistent with this opinion. * * * [I]t shall be stayed for 180 days to permit the Legislature to take such action as it may deem appropriate in light of this opinion. * * *

So ordered.

GREANEY, J. (concurring).

* * *

Because our marriage statutes intend, and state, the ordinary understanding that marriage under our law consists only of a union between a man and a woman, they create a statutory classification based on the sex of the two people who wish to marry. * * * That the classification is sex based is self-evident. The marriage statutes prohibit some applicants, such as the plaintiffs, from obtaining a marriage license, and that prohibition is based solely on the applicants' gender. * * * Hillary Goodridge cannot marry Julie Goodridge because she (Hillary) is a woman. Likewise, Gary Chalmers cannot marry Richard Linnell because he (Gary) is a man. Only their gender prevents Hillary and Gary from marrying their chosen partners under the present law.

[C]onstitutional protections extend to individuals and not to categories of people. Thus, when an individual desires to marry, but cannot marry his or her chosen partner because of the traditional opposite-sex restriction, a [constitutional] violation * * * has occurred. * * * I find it disingenuous * * * to suggest that such an individual's right to marry has not been burdened at all, because he or she remains free to chose another partner, who is of the opposite sex.

* * *

* * * To define the institution of marriage by the characteristics of those to whom it always has been accessible, in order to justify the exclusion of those to whom it never has been accessible * * * [evades] the core question we are asked to decide. * * * [T]he case requires that we confront ingrained assumptions with respect to historically accepted roles of men and women within the institution of marriage and requires that we reexamine these assumptions * * * in order to ensure that the governmental conduct challenged here conforms to the supreme charter of our Commonwealth. * * * [A]s [a] matter of constitutional law, neither the mantra of tradition, nor individual conviction, can justify the perpetuation of a hierarchy in which couples of the same sex and their families are deemed less worthy of social and legal recognition than couples of the opposite sex and their families. * * *

SPINA, J. (dissenting, with whom SOSMAN and CORDY, JJ., join).

What is at stake in this case is not the unequal treatment of individuals or whether individual rights have been impermissibly burdened, but the power of the Legislature to effectuate social change without interference from the courts * * *. The power to regulate marriage lies with the Legislature, not with the judiciary. * * * Today, the court has transformed its role as protector of individual rights into the role of creator of rights, and I respectfully dissent.

1. *Equal protection.* * * * G.L. c. 207 does not unconstitutionally discriminate on the basis of gender. A claim of gender discrimination will lie where it is shown that differential treatment disadvantages one sex over the other. * * * [The statute] creates no distinction between the sexes, but applies to men and women in precisely the same way. It does not create any disadvantage identified with gender, as both men and women are similarly limited to marrying a person of the opposite sex. * * *

Similarly, the marriage statutes do not discriminate on the basis of sexual orientation. * * * The marriage statutes do not disqualify individuals on the basis of sexual orientation from entering into marriage. All individuals, with certain exceptions not relevant here, are free to marry. Whether an individual chooses not to marry because of sexual orientation or any other reason should be of no concern to the court.

* * *

[T]he court relies on Loving v. Virginia, 388 U.S. 1, 87 S.Ct. 1817 (1967), * * * [in which] the Supreme Court struck down as unconstitutional a statute that prohibited Caucasians from marrying non-Caucasians. It concluded that the statute was intended to preserve white supremacy and invidiously discriminated against non-Caucasians because of their race. * * * [I]t concluded that * * * the State had no compelling interest in limiting the choice to marry along racial lines. * * *

Unlike the *Loving* * * * cas[e], the Massachusetts Legislature has erected no barrier to marriage that intentionally discriminates against anyone. Within the institution of marriage, anyone is free to marry * * *. In the absence of any discriminatory purpose, the State's marriage statutes do not violate principles of equal protection. * * * This court should not have invoked even the most deferential standard of review * * * because no individual was denied access to the institution of marriage.

2. *Due process.* The marriage statutes do not impermissibly burden a right protected by our constitutional guarantee of due process * * *. There is no restriction on the right of any plaintiff to enter into marriage. Each is free to marry a willing person of the opposite sex. * * *

[T]oday the court does not fashion a remedy that affords greater protection of a right. Instead, using the rubric of due process, it has redefined marriage.

* * *

* * * Same-sex marriage, or the "right to marry the person of one's choice" as the court today defines that right, does not fall within the fundamental right to marry. Same-sex marriage is not "deeply rooted in this Nation's history" * * *. Except for the occasional isolated decision in recent years, see * * * Baker v. State, 170 Vt. 194, 744 A.2d 864 (1999), same-sex marriage is not a right, fundamental or otherwise, recognized in this country. * * *

3. *Remedy.* The remedy that the court has fashioned * * * amounts to a statutory revision that replaces the intent of the Legislature with that of the court. * * * [T]he alteration of the gender-specific language alters precisely what the Legislature unambiguously intended to preserve, the marital rights of single men and women. Such a dramatic change in social institutions must remain at the behest of the people through the democratic process.

* * *

SOSMAN, J. (dissenting, with whom SPINA and CORDY, JJ., join).

In applying the rational basis test to any challenged statutory scheme, the issue is not whether the Legislature's rationale behind that scheme is persuasive to us, but only whether it satisfies a minimal threshold of rationality. Today, rather than apply that test, the court announces that, because it is persuaded that there are no differences between same-sex and opposite-sex couples, the Legislature has no rational basis for treating them differently with respect to the granting of marriage licenses. Reduced to its essence, the court's opinion concludes that, because same-sex couples are now raising children, and withholding the benefits of civil marriage from their union makes it harder for them to raise those children, the State must therefore provide the benefits of civil marriage to same-sex couples just as it does to opposite-sex couples. Of course, many people are raising children outside the confines of traditional marriage, and, by definition, those children are being deprived of the various benefits that would flow if they were being raised in a household with married parents. That does not mean that the Legislature must accord the full benefits of marital status on every household raising children. Rather, the Legislature need only have some rational basis for concluding that, at present, those alternate family structures have not yet been conclusively shown to be the equivalent of the marital family structure that has established itself as a successful one over a period of centuries. * * *

* * * Same-sex couples can provide their children with the requisite nurturing, stable, safe, consistent, and supportive environment in which to mature, just as opposite-sex couples do. It is therefore understandable that the court might view the traditional definition of marriage as an unnecessary anachronism, rooted in historical prejudices that modern society has in large measure rejected and biological limitations that modern science has overcome.

It is not, however, our assessment that matters. Conspicuously absent from the court's opinion today is any acknowledgment that the attempts at scientific study of the ramifications of raising children in same-sex couple households are themselves in their infancy and have so far produced inconclusive and conflicting results. * * * The Legislature can rationally view the state of the scientific evidence as unsettled on the critical question it now faces: are families headed by same-sex parents equally successful in rearing children from infancy to adulthood as families headed by parents of opposite sexes? Our belief that children raised by same-sex couples *should* fare the same as children raised in traditional families is just that: a passionately held but utterly untested belief. The Legislature is not required to share that belief but may, as the creator of the institution of civil marriage, wish to see the proof before making a fundamental alteration to that institution.

* * *

* * * The issue is whether it is rational to reserve judgment on whether this change can be made at this time without damaging the institution of marriage or adversely affecting the critical role it has played in our society. Absent consensus on the issue (which obviously does not exist), or unanimity amongst scientists studying the issue (which also does not exist), or a more prolonged period of observation of this new family structure (which has not yet been possible), it is rational for the Legislature to postpone any redefinition of marriage that would include same-sex couples until such time as it is certain that that redefinition will not have unintended and undesirable social consequences. Through the political process, the people may decide when the benefits of extending civil marriage to same-sex couples have been shown to outweigh whatever risks * * * are involved. However minimal the risks of that redefinition of marriage may seem to us from our vantage point, it is not up to us to decide what risks society must run, and it is inappropriate for us to arrogate that power to ourselves merely because we are confident that "it is the right thing to do." * * *

* * *

CORDY, J. (dissenting, with whom SPINA and SOSMAN, JJ., join).

* * *

Although some of the [Supreme Court's]

privacy cases also speak in terms of personal autonomy, no court has ever recognized such an open-ended right. "That many of the rights and liberties protected by the Due Process Clause sound in personal autonomy does not warrant the sweeping conclusion that any and all important, intimate, and personal decisions are so protected...." Washington v. Glucksberg, 521 U.S. 702, 117 S.Ct. 2258 (1997). Such decisions are protected not because they are important, intimate, and personal, but because the right or liberty at stake is "so deeply rooted in our history and traditions, or so fundamental to our concept of constitutionally ordered liberty" that it is protected by due process. * * * Accordingly, the Supreme Court has concluded that while the decision to refuse unwanted medical treatment is fundamental, * * * because it is deeply rooted in our nation's history and tradition, the equally personal and profound decision to commit suicide is not because of the absence of such roots. * * *

While the institution of marriage is deeply rooted in the history and traditions of our country and our State, the right to marry someone of the same sex is not. No matter how personal or intimate a decision to marry someone of the same sex might be, the right to make it is not guaranteed by the right of personal autonomy.

* * *

* * * The consequences of deeming a right to be "fundamental" are profound, and this court, as well as the Supreme Court, has been very cautious in recognizing them. Such caution is required by separation of powers principles. If a right is found to be "fundamental," it is, to a great extent, removed from "the arena of public debate and legislative action"; utmost care must be taken when breaking new ground in this field "lest the liberty protected by the Due Process Clause be subtly transformed into the policy preferences of [judges]." *Washington* v. *Glucksberg* * * *.

* * *

On March 29, 2004, the Massachusetts legislature approved an amendment to the state constitution that would reverse the state supreme court's gay-marriage decision but also would legalize civil unions, thus duplicating Vermont's experience. Same-sex couples would then have the same rights and benefits enjoyed by heterosexual couples under state law but not be entitled to *federal* marriage benefits and privileges. The Massachusetts constitution requires that constitutional amendments proposed by the legislature receive majority support (101 votes) from a joint sitting of both houses of the legislature at two successive legislative sessions and then approval by the voters. In order to appear on the ballot in the November 2006 election, the measure would have to clear the legislature again in 2005. But this is increasingly unlikely. The proposed amendment cleared the legislature by only four votes last year and supporters of gay marriage opposed to the compromise picked up four seats in the November 2004 election. Moreover, some supporters of the amendment are rethinking their initial vote to approve it. Poll results for March 2005 suggest that a solid majority of the public now approve of gay marriage, whereas in March 2004 a majority opposed it. (The recent results show 56% in favor, 37% opposed.) See Boston Globe, May 16, 2005. Despite these figures, opponents of gay marriage are attempting to put before the voters a constitutional amendment that would end gay marriage and not recognize civil unions. A petition supporting that ballot initiative signed by some 65,000 voters would get the ball rolling. State law then requires at least 50 votes in support of it cast by legislators in each of two successive joint sessions of the state legislature and, finally, approval by the voters. The earliest such a measure could face Massachusetts voters would be November 2008. New York Times, June 17, 2005, p. A11.

In what looked like a desperate attempt (since the U.S. Supreme Court has repeatedly held that Guarantee Clause cases invariably present "political questions," see Text, p. 59-68; pp. 1226-1233), some members of the legislature and several Massachusetts voters challenged the decision in *Goodridge* as a violation of that clause of the U.S. Constitution, Art. IV, § 4, guaranteeing to each state a republican form of government (see Text, p. 69). Their suit was speedily rebuffed by the federal courts, see Largess, v. Supreme Judicial Court of Massachusetts, 317 F.Supp.2d 77 (D. Mass. 2004), *affirmed*, 373 F.3d 219 (1st Cir. 2004), *cert. denied*, 543 U.S. —, 125 S.Ct. 618 (2004). In an advisory opinion requested by the legislature, the Massachusetts court explained why a law recognizing civil unions would not provide the same rights as marriage, see Opinions of the Justices to the Senate, 440 Mass. 1201, 802 N.E.2d 565 (2004).

Meanwhile, opponents of gay marriage proposed to amend the U.S. Constitution as a pre-emptive strike against further rulings like that in Massachusetts. The proposed Marriage Amendment (H.J. Res. 56) read as follows: "Marriage in the United States shall consist only of the union of a man and a woman. Neither the Constitution or the constitution of any State, nor state or federal law, shall be construed to require the legal status or the legal incidents thereof to be conferred upon unmarried couples or groups." Although election-year politics led President George W. Bush to endorse the proposed amendment and the scheduling of debate two weeks before the Democratic presidential nominating convention, preliminary headcounts showed there was nowhere near the two-thirds majority in each chamber needed to pass the amendment and send it to the states for ratification. In the Senate, a falling-out between Republican conservatives and moderates—the latter mostly opposed to the second sentence (on grounds it violated the reserved power of the states to regulate marriage and would have prohibited civil unions)—sealed the measure's fate. As it turned out, the amendment's supporters failed to muster even a majority of the Senate—let alone the three-fifths majority necessary to impose cloture and bring the measure to a vote. The vote to cut off debate was 48-50. Proponents of the proposed amendment had better luck—but still fell shy of the mark—in the House. There the vote was 227-186, well short of the constitutional requirement of two-thirds of those present and voting (276 in this instance). Congressional Quarterly Weekly Report, Dec. 4, 2004, p. 2865.

Thus far, Massachusetts is the only American jurisdiction to recognize same-sex marriage. Eighteen states have a state constitutional ban on gay marriage, 22 others have a law prohibiting it. Eight states have neither a constitutional nor a statutory prohibition on gay marriage (Connecticut, Maryland, New Jersey, New Mexico, New York, Rhode Island, Wisconsin, and Wyoming). Connecticut and Vermont (as discussed in the Text at p. 1314) have legalized civil unions. While Delaware, Hawaii, Maine, and New Jersey recognize certain legal rights inhering in same-sex relationships, California's domestic partner law grants same-sex couples every spousal right shared by heterosexual couples, except the right to file joint state income tax returns. See www.cnn.com/2005/LAW/04/05/domestic.partner.law.ap/index.html. New York Times, Nov. 12, 2004, p. A16; Mar. 7, 2005, p. A16. In four cases, appeals are currently pending after courts have declared state bans unconstitutional. See Coordination Proceeding ... Marriage Cases, 2005 WL 583129 (Cal. Superior, 2005); Andersen v. King County, 2004 WL 1738447 (Wash. Superior 2004); Hernandez v. Robles, 794 N.Y.S.2d 579 (N.Y.Sup. 2005); Citizens for Equal Protection, Inc. v. Bruning, 368 F.Supp.2d 980 (D.Neb. 2005). The Nebraska ban, said to be "the most extreme anti-gay family law in the entire nation," because it not only banned gay marriage and civil unions but its "broad proscriptions could also interfere with or prevent arrangements between potential adoptive or foster parents and children, related persons living together, and people sharing custody of children as well as gay individuals." New York Times, May 13, 2005, p. A10.

On June 29, 2005, the Canadian House of Commons voted 158-133 to pass Bill C-38, legislation redefining marriage as "the voluntary union for life of two persons to the exclusion of all others." Approval by the Canadian Senate and assent by the Governor General then followed, which completed the legislative process. Parliamentary action followed rulings by the courts in eight prvinces and one Canadian territory striking down the common law definition of marriage eight ("the voluntary union for life of one man and one woman to the exclusion of all others") as a violation of § 15(1) of the Charter of Rights and Freedoms (Canada's Bill of Rights), see, for example, Halpern v. City of Toronto, 2003 CarswellOnt 2159, 225 D.L.R. (4th) 529, 65 O.R. (3rd) 201. Two and a half months earlier, the Spanish Congress of Deputies voted 187-147 to likewise legalize same-sex marriage. Canada and Spain join Belgium and the Netherlands as the only countries in the world in which same-sex marriage is recognized. Britain and New Zealand recognize civil unions.

APPENDIX C

BIOGRAPHIES OF THE CURRENT JUSTICES

▶ **Insert at p. C2 at the end of Justice O'Connor's biography**

Announced her decision to retire. Her letter of July 1, 2005 to President Bush indicated her retirement was "effective upon the nomination and confirmation of my successor."*

---

* Article II, section 2, paragraph 2 of the Constitution provides that the President "shall nominate, and by and with the Advice and Consent of the Senate, shall appoint . . . Judges of the supreme Court . . . ." Paragraph 3 then gives the President the "Power to fill up all vacancies that may happen during the Recess of the Senate, by granting Commissions which shall expire at the End of their next Session."

Taken together, the clear intent of these provisions would appear to be that the President is empowered to nominate individuals to fill *vacancies*. Justice O'Connor's letter announces something like a "conditional vacancy." Under the terms of her letter, the vacancy will occur only after someone has been confirmed to fill it.

This was tried 37 years ago when, in the spring of 1968, Chief Justice Earl Warren wrote to President Lyndon Johnson, saying "I hereby advise you of my intention to retire as Chief Justice of the United States effective at your pleasure." He continued, "There is a lot of administrative work . . . and if I selected a particular day and the vacancy was not filled it would be a vacuum." Warren's letter was widely thought motivated by a desire to allow Johnson to name a successor and keep the decision out of the hands of Richard Nixon, then substantially ahead in the polls before the 1968 presidential election.

Some Republicans criticized Johnson's nomination of Justice Abe Fortas to be the new Chief Justice on the grounds that there was no vacancy to fill. True, Warren's letter made it seem that a Supreme Court Justice serves at the pleasure of the President, but what really bothered them was the fact that no date had been specified. Johnson subsequently responded, "I will accept your decision to retire effective at such time as a successor is qualified."

But there is no vacancy until there has been a resignation. Interestingly enough, the author of this criticism was not a Republican—although many Republicans later agreed with it—but Senator Sam Ervin (D-N.C.), later of Watergate investigating fame. Indeed, in the Senate Judiciary Committee hearings on the purported Fortas nomination, the whole first day was devoted to precisely the question of whether there was, in fact, a vacancy to fill. Ervin's point was simply that making the vacancy contingent on the approval of a successor was putting the cart before the horse; the existence of a vacancy under such circumstances is a logical impossibility. See Robert Shogan, A Question of Judgment: The Fortas Case and the Struggle for the Supreme Court (1972), pp. 148, 152, 161-162.

Justice O'Connor's letter vacating her position upon the confirmation of a successor also would appear to deny the President the constitutional power to make a recess appointment. But how can there simultaneously be a vacancy under paragraph 2 but not a vacancy under paragraph 3? See the discussion of recess appointments at p. 12 of this Supplement.

The motivations attributed to Justice O'Connor are both compassionate and admirable (she would like to spend her time caring for the love of her life who is afflicted with advanced Alzheimer's, and she would stay on long enough to spare her colleagues, the country, and the litigants a deadlocked Court). But the Constitution, it would seem, provides for the filling of vacancies, not some other arrangement, no matter how well intended.

INDEX

References are to pages.

ABORTION
"Fetal protection" law, 125
"Partial-birth" ban, 126
Protesting, not "extortion," 126-127
Subpoenaing medical records, 126

AFFIRMATIVE ACTION, 190-204

AGE DISCRIMINATION IN EMPLOYMENT ACT, 207

AL QAEDA, 16, 25

ALIENS
Deportation, 14
Detention, 14, 25-28

AMENDMENT-ENFORCING POWER, 13-14, 57-62

AMERICANS WITH DISABILITIES ACT, 62-63, 109

ANTI-BALLISTIC MISSILE TREATY, 8

AUTHORIZATION FOR USE OF MILITARY FORCE, 16-18, 22, 33, 38

AUTOMOBILE SEARCHES, 121

BASEBALL AND USE OF STEROIDS, 15

BEEF ADVERTISEMENT, 145-147

BEGGING, 144

BIBLE IN THE JURY ROOM, 101

BIPARTISAN CAMPAIGN REFORM ACT, 150-151

BLOCKING
See Internet Blocking.

"BOOKER FIX" LEGISLATION, 94

BORDER SEARCH, 122

BRIBERY, 63-64

BRITAIN
See Great Britain.

BUSH, GEORGE W.
See President.

CAMPAIGN FINANCE REFORM, 150-151

CAPITAL PUNISHMENT
See Death Penalty.

CENSORSHIP, 154-155

CHENEY, DICK, 1-2, 39, 156

CHILD ON-LINE PROTECTION ACT, 164-165

CHILD PORNOGRAPHY, 158

CHILD SEXUAL ABUSE, 114-118

CHILDREN'S INTERNET PROTECTION ACT, 159

CIA OPERATIVE, 156

CIVIL UNIONS, 218

CLASS ACTIONS, 4

COCHRAN, JOHNNIE, 154-155

COMBATANT STATUS REVIEW TRIBUNALS, 31-37

COMMERCE CLAUSE
HMOs, 65-66
Nuclear waste, 69-70
Out-of-state wine purchases, 70-75
Trucking license, 67-69
See also Marijuana.

"COMPELLED SUBSIDY," 144-147

COMPETENCY TO STAND TRIAL, 96-97

CONFESSIONS
Taping in homicide cases, 101
See also Interrogations; *Miranda* Rights.

CONFIDENTIALITY OF SOURCES, 155-157

CONFRONTATION AND CROSS-EXAMINATION (Right to), 34-36, 99

CONSENT TO SEARCH, 119-120

CONTROLLED SUBSTANCES ACT, 46-55

COOPER, MATTHEW, 156

COUNSEL (Right to)
Effective assistance of, 95-96
See also Detention.

CROSS BURNING, 149-150

CUSTOMS SEARCH, 122

CYBER-LIBEL, 166-167

DEATH PENALTY
Aggravating and mitigating circumstances are even, 101
Bible in the jury room, 101
DNA testing, 101-102
Jury's role, 93
Young offenders, 100

DEPORTATION, 14

DETENTION
Aliens, 14, 25-28
Citizens, 16-25, 28
See also Enemy Combatants.

DISQUALIFICATION
See Recusal.

DIVIDED GOVERNMENT, 10

DNA TESTING, 101-102

DO-NOT-CALL REGISTRY, 152-153

DOGS SNIFFING FOR DRUGS, 121

DORMANT COMMERCE CLAUSE, 67-69

DRUGS
Banning drug users from neighborhoods, 144
Medication to stand trial, 96-97
Random testing, 123
Religious use of, 187-188
See also Marijuana.

DUAL FEDERALISM, 46, 63-64

DUE PROCESS
See Detention.
Dangerousness of sex offender registrants, 114
Medication of defendants, 96-97
See also Property Interests.

EFFECTIVE ASSISTANCE OF COUNSEL, 95-96

EIGHTH AMENDMENT
"Three strikes" laws, 102-108
See also Death Penalty; Prisoners' Rights.

ELECTRONIC SURVEILLANCE, 123-124

ELEVENTH AMENDMENT, 57-63

EMERGENCY DETENTION ACT of 1950, 21

INDEX

EMINENT DOMAIN, 76-84

ENEMY COMBATANTS, 16, 19, 24, 28, 31, 37

ENERGY TASK FORCE, 1, 39-40

ESTABLISHMENT CLAUSE
Subsidizing theology training, 186-187
Ten Commandments, 168-185
See also Pledge of Allegiance; Ten Commandments.

EX POST FACTO LAWS
Retroactive repeal of statute of limitations, 114-118
Sex offender registration, 109-114

EXECUTIVE AGREEMENTS, 41-44

EXTRA-TERRITORIAL JURISDICTION, 25-28

FAMILY MEDICAL LEAVE ACT, 14, 57-62

FEDERAL ADVISORY COMMITTEE ACT, 39-40

FEDERAL INTELLIGENCE SURVEILLANCE COURT, 124

FEDERAL MARRIAGE AMENDMENT
See Marriage Amendment.

FEDERAL SENTENCING GUIDELINES, 93-94

FETAL PROTECTION LAW
See Unborn Victims of Violence Act.

FILIBUSTER, 10-12

FITZGERALD, PATRICK, 156

FLAG DESECRATION AMENDMENT, 149

FOREIGN SOVEREIGN IMMUNITIES ACT, 45

FORTAS, ABE, 10, 221-222

FOSTER, VINCENT, 157

FREE EXERCISE CLAUSE, 187-188

FREEDOM OF INFORMATION ACT, 157-158

FRUIT OF THE POISONOUS TREE, 98-99

FUNDRAISING
See Telemarketing.

"GANGBUSTERS" LEGISLATION, 94

GAY RIGHTS
See Same-Sex Marriage; Sodomy Laws.

GENDER
See Sex Discrimination.

GERRYMANDERING, 205-207

GREAT BRITAIN
Anti-terrorism legislation, 29-31
Citizens detained at Guantanamo Bay, 29-30

GUANTANAMO BAY DETAINEES, 25-38

HANDICAPPED, 62-63, 109

"HATE SPEECH," 149-150

HEALTH MAINTENANCE ORGANIZATIONS (HMOs), 65-66

HOBBS ACT, 127

HOLOCAUST VICTIMS INSURANCE RELIEF ACT, 41-44

HOMOSEXUALITY
See Same-Sex Marriage; Sodomy Laws.

INDECENCY, 166
See also Child Pornography.

INTELLIGENCE IDENTITIES PROTECTION ACT, 156

INTERNET, 159-167

INTERROGATION
Breaking chain of police illegality, 98-99, 119
Civil damages, 97
During emergency treatment, 98
Taping required, 101
Two-step tactic, 97
Youthfulness of suspect, 98

IRAQ WAR, 4-8

JURY TRIAL
Peremptory challenges, 189
Proof of all elements of crime, 93-94

JUSTICES
See Supreme Court.

KNOCK-AND-ANNOUNCE, 120

LAW LORDS, 29-30

LIBEL
Cyber-libel, 166-167
Restraining order as response to, 154-155

LIMITATIONS
See Statute of Limitations.

MALAPPORTIONMENT, 205-207

MANDATORY MINIMUM (SENTENCES), 94

MARIJUANA, 46-55, 137-138

MARRIAGE AMENDMENT, 218

McCAIN–FEINGOLD LAW, 150-151

MEDIA OWNERSHIP RULES, 154

MEDICAL RECORDS, 126

MEDICATION TO STAND TRIAL, 96-97

MEGAN'S LAW, 109-114

MILLER, JUDITH, 156

MILITARY RECRUITERS, 148

MILITARY TRIALS OF SUSPECTED TERRORISTS, 31-38

MIRANDA RIGHTS
See Interrogation.

MOUSSAOUI, ZACARIAS, 38

NATIONAL ENERGY DEVELOPMENT GROUP
See Energy Task Force.

"NATIONAL SECURITY LETTER," 124

NEGATIVE COMMERCE CLAUSE, 67-69

"NEW PROPERTY," 85

9/11 ATTACK, 16, 29, 38

NINTH CIRCUIT, 2

"NO CHILD LEFT BEHIND" LAW, 66-67

NON-DETENTION ACT, 17, 21, 28

NOVAK, ROBERT, 156

"NUCLEAR OPTION," 11

NUCLEAR WASTE, 69-70

O'CONNOR, SANDRA DAY
Retirement, 11, 221-222
Swing vote, 55-56

"OPERATION RESCUE," 127

OUT-OF-STATE WINE SALES, 70-75

PANHANDLING, 144

PARENTAL NOTIFICATION
Abortion, 125
Pledge of Allegiance, 148

"PARTIAL-BIRTH" ABORTION BAN ACT, 126

PATRIOT ACT
See USA PATRIOT Act.

PHYSICIAN-ASSISTED SUICIDE, 143

PLAME, VALERIE, 156

PLEDGE OF ALLEGIANCE, 1, 8, 148, 185-186

PORNOGRAPHY, 158-165

PREEMPTION, 65-66

PRESIDENT
Detention of suspected terrorists, 16-29
Executive privilege, 39-40
Military trials, 31-38
Termination of treaty, 8
War power, 4-8

PRIMARIES, 204-205

PRISONERS' RIGHTS, 13, 108-109

PROPERTY INTERESTS, 76-92, 119-120

"PROTECT" ACT, 158

"PUBLIC USE"
See Takings Clause.

RANDOM DRUG TESTING, 123

REAPPORTIONMENT, 205-207

RECESS APPOINTMENTS, 12, 221-222

RECUSAL, 1-2

RELIGIOUS FREEDOM RESTORATION ACT, 187-188

RELIGIOUS LAND USE AND INSTITUTIONALIZED PERSONS ACT, 13

RESTRAINING ORDERS
Libel, 154-155
Property interest in, 85-92

RICO LAW, 126-127

RIPENESS, 4-8

ROADBLOCKS, 123

SAME-SEX MARRIAGE, 208-219

SCHIAVO, TERRY, 15, 139-142

SCHOOL VOUCHERS, 186-187

SEARCHES
Arrest, incident to, 120
Automobile, 121
Border searches, 122
Consent, 119-120
Detention during execution of search warrant, 120
Dogs, 121
Informational roadblocks, 123
Knock-and-announce, 120
Random drug testing, 123

SECRECY
See Freedom of Information Act.

SENTENCING REFORM ACT, 93-94

SEX DISCRIMINATION, 14, 207

SEX OFFENDERS
Registration, 109-114
Retroactive repeal of statute of limitations, 114-118

SHACKLING OF DEFENDANTS, 100

"SNEAK AND PEEK" LAW, 124

SODOMY LAWS, 128-137

SOLOMON AMENDMENT, 148, 204

SPEECH
Cross burning, 149-150
Nonresident at city housing project, 148
See also Campaign Finance Reform; "Compelled Subsidy"; "Hate Speech."

SPENDING POWER, 63-64

STANDING, 8-9, 185-186

STATES
Prohibiting out-of-state distributors, 70-75
Sovereign immunity, 57-63
Trucking licenses, 67-69
See also Marijuana; Preemption.

STATUTE OF LIMITATIONS, 114-118

STEROIDS, 15

SUICIDE
See Physician-Assisted Suicide.

SUPREME COURT
Constitutional and statutory cases, 3
Dissent rate, 3
Justices' voting, 56
Number of cases decided, 3

SUSPENSION CLAUSE, 18, 22, 32

TAKINGS CLAUSE, 76-84

TALIBAN, 25

TAXING AND SPENDING POWER, 63-64

TELEMARKETING, 151-153

TEN COMMANDMENTS, 168-185

"TERRORIST TIPOFF AMENDMENT," 124

"THREE STRIKES" LAW, 102-108

TREATY TERMINATION, 8-9

TWENTY-FIRST AMENDMENT, 70, 72, 74-75

UNBORN VICTIMS OF VIOLENCE ACT, 125

USA PATRIOT ACT, 45, 158

VICTIMS' RIGHTS, 101

VOUCHERS, 186-187

WAR POWER, 4-8
See Detentions.

WELFARE BENEFITS SEARCHES, 123

WILSON, JOSEPH, 156

WINE, 70-75

WIRETAPPING, 123-124

YOUNG OFFENDERS
Death penalty, 58
Interrogations, 56-57